AF654982

Globalization, Agrarian Economy and Environmental Challenges in India

About the Editors

Professor Pranab Kumar Chattopadhyay is the Chair Professor, A.K. Dasgupta Centre for Planning and Development, (A Centre sponsored by the Planning Commission, Government of India) Visva-Bharati, Santiniketan. Professor Chattopadhyay is Professor and former Head of the Department of Economics & Politics, Visva-Bharati. Prior to that he was in the West Bengal Educational Service [WBES] and served at various Government Colleges including Goenka College of Commerce and Business Administration, Kolkata. He obtained his M.A. from Jadavpur University and Ph.D. from the University of Calcutta. He also taught at the University of Burdwan. Professor Chattopadhyay in his credit has many research papers in journals and books with repute. He is the Co-ordinator of the UGC-SAP (DRS-I) of the Department.

Dr. Sudipta Bhattacharyya, Professor and Head, Department of Economics and Politics and Ex-officio Director, Agro-Economic Research Centre, Visva-Bharati, Santiniketan, West Bengal (India), graduated from Calcutta University and obtained M.Phil and Ph.D. from Jawaharlal Nehru University, New Delhi. He served as Visiting Professor at the Asia Research Centre, Copenhagen Business School, Denmark (2009-10), Commonwealth Fellow at the Department of Economics and International Development, University of Bath, UK (2003-04) and Visiting Scholar at the Queen Elizabeth House, Oxford (1997-98). He has in his credit four books and many papers in peer reviewed journals like Cambridge Journal of Economics, Journal of Agrarian Change, Journal of Peasant Studies, etc.

Mr. Biswajit Haldar graduated from Narendrapur Ramkrishna Mission, Calcutta University and completed M.A. and M.Phil. at Centre for Economic Studies and Planning, Jawaharlal Nehru University, New Delhi. His area of research is Poverty and the Indian Economy, Caste and Class Relations in India.

Globalization, Agrarian Economy and Environmental Challenges in India

Edited by
Pranab Kumar Chattopadhyay
Sudipta Bhattacharyya
Biswajit Haldar

CONCEPT PUBLISHING COMPANY PVT. LTD.
NEW DELHI-110059

© Editors

All rights reserved. No part of this work may be reproduced, stored, adapted, or transmitted in any form or by any means, electronic, mechanical, photocopying, micro-filming recording or otherwise, or translated in any language, without the prior written permission of the copyright owner and the publisher. The book is sold subject to the condition that it shall not, by way of trade or otherwise, be lent, resold, hired out, or otherwise circulated without the prior publisher's written consent in any form of binding or cover other than that in which it is published.

The views and opinions expressed in this book are author(s) own and the facts reported by him/her have been verified to the extent possible, and the publishers are not in any way liable for the same.

ISBN-13: 978-93-5125-185-9

First Published 2015

Published and Printed by

Concept
Since 1974

Concept Publisning Company Pvt. Ltd.
Regd. Office:
A/15-16, Commercial Block, Mohan Garden,
New Delhi-110059 (INDIA)
Phones : 25351460, 25351794, *Fax* : 091-11-25357109
Email : publishing@conceptpub.com
Website: www.conceptpub.com

Editorial Office:
H-13, Bali Nagar, New Delhi-110 015, India.

Cataloging in Publication Data–Courtesy: D.K. Agencies (P) Ltd. <docinfo@dkagencies.com>

Seminar on 'Globalization, Agrarian Economy and Environmental Challenges in India' (2012 : Santiniketan, India)
Globalization, agrarian economy and environmental challenges in India / edited by Pranab Kumar Chattopadhyay, Sudipta Bhattacharyya, Biswajit Haldar.
pages cm
Papers presented at the Seminar on 'Globalization, Agrarian Economy and Environmental Challenges in India' organized by the Department of Economics and Politics, Visva-Bharati, Santiniketan during 15-16 March 2012.
Includes bibliographical references and index.
ISBN 9789351251859

1. Agriculture—Economic aspects—India—Congresses. 2. Agriculture—Environmental aspects—India—Congresses. 3. India—Economic policy—1991- —Congresses. 4. Rural development—India—Congresses. 5. Globalization—Economic aspects—India—Congresses. I. Chattopadhyay, Pranab Kumar (Professor), editor. II. Bhattacharyya, Sudipta, editor. III. Haldar, Biswajit, editor. IV. Visva-Bharati. Department of Economics & Politics.organizer. V. Title.

HD2072.S46 2012 DDC 338.10954 23

Acknowledgements

This volume has been prepared on the basis of a UGC-SAP (DRS-I) seminar on 'Globalization, Agrarian Economy and Environmental Challenges in India' organized by the Department of Economics and Politics, Visva-Bharati, Santiniketan held during 15-16 March, 2012. We are grateful to Visva-Bharati Vice-Chancellor Professor Sushanta Dattagupta for providing the space for conducting meaningful research. We are particularly grateful to the external members of the Advisory Committee of UGC-SAP (DRS-I) namely Professors Biswajit Chatterjee and Nirankar Srivastava without the active support of them the volume would have remained incomplete. Articles contained in the volume are selected on the basis of peer reviewed doubly blinded review process. We are grateful to the reviewers of this volume who thoroughly went through all the papers and gave meaningful insight. We are also grateful to the chapter contributors who took the pain to revise their originally submitted paper after receiving comments from the reviewer of this volume. The editors are grateful to the participants of the seminar, the resource persons chaired the session and departmental teachers, students and research scholars who made this seminar a grand success. Particularly SAP-Project Fellow Tanmay Majumdar took great pain in assisting the editor during the process of editing. The editors are also grateful to Visva-Bharati administration to extend support at various stages.

Place: Santiniketan
Date: 21.10.2013

Pranab Kumar Chattopadhyay
Sudipta Bhattacharyya
Biswajit Haldar

Contents

1
Introduction

May like it or not, globalization has become a universal context of academic research in every field of social science (be it the supporters or the critics). Globalization, as a context of economic analysis, has become even more important for the underdeveloped countries like India. The choice of the seminar title, **"Globalization, agrarian economy and environmental challenges in India"** is an ample reflection of that fact. So a brief interpretation of the term "Globalization" is necessary to set the discussion on course.

Globalization in its wider sense means removal of barriers created by race, caste, colour, religion, politics, and economic power leading to increasing cross-cultural, political and economic exchange. In the inception, the proponents of it promised these mutual benefits. But since the late seventies, "globalization" is being used in a somewhat narrow sense referring to integration of the domestic markets to the global markets through a process guided by an active intervention on the part of developed nations. In doing so they have used the global institutions—IMF, World Bank and WTO. Right from the beginning of this process, people are divided in their opinion. Some viewed globalization as a means of subjugating the poor economies while others felt optimistic as it would somehow break the inertia and would take the poor nations to a kind of solvency. However, India has entered into the era of globalization under compulsion as the government had no other option left but to accept it to bail out the economy from severe BOP crisis in 1991. Actually, it has been showing the sign of arrival since the early 80s with trade liberalization. Since then India continued to take policies in line with the prescription suggested by the Trinity (IMF, World Bank and WTO). Researchers and academicians kept on evaluating the performance of Indian economy during the era of globalization and it was evident that India has seen an unbalanced growth path with rising disparities across States, regions, sectors, economic and social groups. Let us look at some aggregative statistics where we stand now.

During the first decade since 1991, Indian economy grew at a rate of 6 per cent yearly on an average compared to 5.7 per cent during the 80s. The economy grew at a faster pace (6.7%) during the first five years but slowed down at 5.4 per cent in the second half. Critics of liberalization blamed the trade policy while the policy makers have attributed this slowdown to the failures of implementing the reforms effectively not to the reforms itself. India's gross national income per capita had experienced high growth rates since 2002. India's Per Capita Income has tripled from Rs. 19,040 in 2002–03 to Rs.53,331 in 2010–11, averaging 13.7 per cent growth over these eight years peaking 15.6 per cent in 2010-11. However, growth in the inflation adjusted per capita income of the nation slowed down to 5.6 per cent in 2010-11, from 6.4 per cent in the previous year. As of 2010, according to World Bank statistics, about 400 million people in India, as compared to 1.29 billion people worldwide, live on less than $1.25 according to Purchasing Power Parity (PPP) per day.

The economy of India is the tenth largest in the world by nominal GDP and the third largest by (PPP). The country is one of the G-20 major economies and a member of BRICS. On a per capita income basis, India ranked 140th by nominal GDP and 129th by GDP (PPP) in 2011, according to the IMF. India recorded the highest growth rates in the mid-2000s, and is one of the fastest growing economies in the world. India has recorded a growth of over 200 times in per capita income in a period from 1947 (249.6) to 2011. The growth was primarily due to a huge increase in the size of the middle class consumer, a large labour force, and growth in the manufacturing sector due to rising education levels and engineering skills and considerable foreign investments. India is the nineteenth largest exporter and tenth largest importer in the world. Economic growth rate stood at around 6.5 per cent for the 2011–12 fiscal years.

The above information might make us believe in the nice and smooth going of Indian economy. One might dream that the miracles of growth would be changing the fate of poor India. Now incidentally poor India lives in the rural areas while liberalization and reform policies excessively focused on industry and service sector leaving the agricultural sector at bay. Moreover, public capital formation in agriculture kept on declining and phasing out of input subsidies continued. Let us look at the relative position of agriculture in Indian economy. India ranks second worldwide in farm output. Agriculture and allied sectors like forestry, logging and fishing accounted for 15.7 per cent of the GDP in 2009-10, employed 52.1 per cent of the total workforce, and despite a steady decline of its share in the GDP, is still the largest economic sector and a significant piece of the overall socio-economic development of India. But agricultural sector being the largest employment provider slowed down since the start of economic reforms in 1991. Critics argued that this slowdown is very much linked intrinsically to the reforms. Development Research Group (DRG), RBI made a study on "Agricultural Growth in India since 1991". It aimed to look for the proximate causes behind the observed slowdown in agricultural growth since 1991. DRG's study reveals:

> "Among the factors likely to be responsible for slow growth is stagnation of public investment for almost quarter of a century, a slowing of irrigation expansion since 1991 and a downscaling production due to farm fragmentation combined with evidence of gathering environmental stress. These amount to hardening of production condition in Indian agriculture."

This study recognizes a limited role of neo-liberal regime behind the observed slowdown and puts the primary blame on the structural factors. And the claim of agriculture benefiting from the shift of T-O-T in favour of it under neo-liberal policy is found to be a mere expectation.

Critics of the neoliberal turn to policymaking in India, and the world in general, since the mid-1980s have pointed out that the growth process under a neoliberal regime is inherently anti-poor. Most of the dividends of economic growth is cornered by the already well off. In parallel with an in-egalitarian growth process, neo-liberalism also whittles down whatever welfare State measures might have been in place before its adoption. In-egalitarian growth and erosion of State assisted welfare provisioning increases socio-economic inequality drastically. Let us have a look at the human development report and find how the poor people fare during the reform period in terms of employment, literacy, food consumption, calorie intake, nutrition status, life expectancy. Labour force participation rate are still very high in rural areas (mainly for SCs and STs) due to poor access to education. Worker population ratio declined only marginally. Unemployment rates (usual principal and subsidiary status) are increasing in rural India while marginally declining in urban India. Moreover, unemployment rates are higher for SCs in rural India and higher for STs in urban India. Now come to the food scene in India. Availability of cereals and calorie consumption has been declining and the poor are consuming calories way below the recommended norm and falling since 1972-73. Life Expectancy is increasing due to better health care and gradual improvements in literacy though, despite considerable improvement, India has the largest number of illiterate people in the world.

To understand the health of the agrarian economy in the context of globalization, there are so many areas of concern before the academicians and researchers that it is not difficult but impossible to touch upon every issue in a single seminar. This seminar volume could include the following few issues: rural health, infrastructure, migration, fiscal decentralization and Panchayati Raj, gender, rural credit, farm viability, food security, environment and informal sector.

The orthodox dual economic literature proposes a frictionless transition from traditional to modern economy. The main proponent of this orthodoxy was Arthur Lewis in "economic development with unlimited supplies of labour" (1954). Lewis put forward a smooth and self-sustaining process leading to modernization and economic development. Under the basic assumption of unlimited surplus labour in the subsistence sector, the modern capitalist sector would grow taking labour from the subsistence sector without raising the wages. Consequently this will lead to capital surplus and the assumption of reinvesting it leads to further capital accumulation. This process automatically continues till the **"Lewisian Turning Point"**. Now there had been critics of it from different schools (Jorgenson, 1966; Johnston and Mellor, 1961; Kaldor, 1979). During the last few decades, the discourse on development has been experiencing a shift away from the era of this **Lewisian Path.** In Chapter 2 entitled **"Myth of Frictionless Transition: A Structuralist Framework" by Saumya Chakrabarti** made a critical enquiry with a view to bringing to the fore certain fundamental contradictions of the mainstream development discourse. The author constructed a macro-framework along Structuralist-Kaleckian lines to capture the fundamentals of conflicts in the process of transition to capitalism. This work is an attempt to provide an appropriate theoretical set-up. Contrary to the usual belief of modern-traditional interlinkage, this formulation brings out the conflict between modern and traditional non-agricultural sectors. The author showed how the process of corporate-led modernization even though including some parts of agriculture into the global market could severely threaten the survival of larger sections of farm and non-farm population. He further showed that, with modernization there is increasing dichotomisation of the third world agriculture. While the diversified and technologically advanced segment of agriculture gets integrated with the rest of the modern economy, a large part of it still remains traditional. Secondly, modernisation and segmentation of agriculture even though feeds the process of accumulation and growth in modern industry and services, this very process induces a contraction of the traditional non-agriculture. This contraction, in its turn, creates the 'surplus population' as the mass of dispossessed cannot be accommodated in the modern segment; rather, 'surplus population' gets engaged in the 'informal economy'.

The presence of hunger on a substantial scale is arguably the most serious concern for policy makers in India while the economy is experiencing much talked about rapid economic growth. Declining per capita food availability and withdrawal of universal Public Distribution System (PDS) and the resultant galloping food prices in recent years has been adding to the miseries of the poor during the reform period. Universal PDS was withdrawn on account of the alleged inefficiency of the same. Till 1992, PDS used to include all households but after the inception of neoliberal reforms the government introduced Targeted Public Distribution System (TPDS) in 1997 which led to exclusion of deserving households. Since then the issue of food security has been at the centre of policy and academic debates. In chapter 3 entitled as **"Reaffirming Universal Food Provisioning –The Functioning of**

the PDS in Tamil Nadu (2005-2010)" Anita Dixit aims to analyze a structure of universal public distribution of food. This is done in the current context of discussions on a proposed Food Security Legislation, in the face of increasing state withdrawal from foodgrain subsidization. The author studied the UPDS in Tamil Nadu in the five years before the current government, viz., 2005-10. The study found that Tamil Nadu has the highest proportion of households accessing PDS foodgrain, as well as the largest per household foodgrain offtake. This negates the allegations of 'inefficiency' of a universal PDS. Moreover, demand for foodgrain is immediately responsive to reduction in prices for the AAY (Antyodaya Anna Yojana) section of households. However, the responsiveness of demand to increased availability of subsidized foodgrain (and increase in per unit subsidization) also extends to the rest of the (non-AAY) households. This indicates the importance of universal (or near universal) subsidization and makes a strong case for introduction of a universal Food Security Bill.

In chapter 4 entitled **"A Regional Analysis of Rural Infrastructural Development in Karnataka"**, the author Mr. Soumya Manjunath attempts to examine the nature of rural infrastructural development across the districts of Karnataka over a period of three decades. Based on secondary data, Indices of rural infrastructure development have been constructed using the methodology of Principal component analysis for both availability and utilization indicators. This chapter explains that a part of the reason for lop sided development of rural infrastructure in Karnataka is due to the lack of utilization of the available infrastructures. The study emphasises that realising the potential of infrastructures in rural areas would require joint provisions of different infrastructure types rather than isolated single provisioning. The results of the study reveal that there exists a large scale variation in the levels of infrastructures across districts and also in levels of individual components of infrastructures. Among other findings, the results show that North Karnataka continues to lag behind its southern counterpart in most categories of infrastructure.

The impact of globalisation on economic factors always draws immediate attention. But casually we overlook some very important and interesting changes brought about by globalisation in the individual choice making process. **Ritwika Mukherjee in chapter 5 entitled "Do Women have the Freedom to Decide the Sex of her Child? A Spatio-Temporal Analysis through Transition of Small Family Size in India"** has made an enquiry to how and to what extent the role of son preference has been intensified in the present context of two child family norm as an outcome of desired sex preference towards children. The regional patterns of son preference have been captured through Child Sex Ratio (girls/ 1000 males) (1991-2011) and Sex Ratio at Birth from Census of India data. Family size preferences brought about by the sex distribution of families and the desired as well as ideal number of children at the regional scales has been worked through the NFHS III unit level data (2005-06). Results depict a dilution of the traditional north-south divide of son preference supported by the converging trend of Child Sex Ratio and Sex Ratio at Birth, a proxy of sex selective abortions. States that have attained replacement level fertility like Maharashtra and Tamil Nadu seem to catch up with their Northern counterparts like Punjab and Haryana in terms of pre birth elimination of female foetus. The growths of the small family norms have thus become indistinguishable for planning for sons, and certainly not for only daughters. On the other extreme States with considerably large family size daughters predominate who are mostly unwanted with a desire of having sons. A strong instance of rural-urban convergence can also be seen due to the gradual diffusion of sex selection technologies across space. Therefore, as the study concludes, the continuity of the past with the present situations of girl child elimination through infanticide and neglect transmuted into a more focused pre-birth elimination.

We often read the news of farmers' suicide in newspapers, watch audio-visual stories of them in the Television. The problems before the farming community have been persisting for long. Now what is important is to seek an answer to a simple question 'Have the problems intensified under neo-liberal economic regime? **'Rajib Dey in chapter 6 entitled "Problem of Farm Viability and Agrarian Crisis: A Study of West Bengal"** has tried to explore the plausible answers in the context of West Bengal. This study used Patnaik's (1987) E-criterion and standard acreage groupings for classification of rural households. This study supports the Situation Assessment Survey (SAS), NSSO that over 40 per cent of farmers are willing to get out of farming because it had become non-viable.

The same report also indicated that farmers are fed up with crop cultivation as they could not recover even the cost of cultivation. Based on primary field survey over different crop regions in West Bengal, this study showed a significant degree of Farm-Labour-Deficit and Farm-Disposable-Deficit among all peasants and also among all acreage groups. They are unable to realize the surplus. A crisis in agriculture affects adversely all the classes and farm sizes. The most significant phenomenon is that it affects the rich farmers as well. This is in spite of the fact that there is a high level of differentiation within the peasantry in terms of concentration in land and non-land asset holding. The non-agricultural income of the peasants is unable to recuperate the situation of the deficit-ridden farmers.

The issue of rural credit has been gaining importance for the last two decades. Under Neo Liberal regime Micro-Finance Institutions (MFIs) and Self-Help Groups (SHGs) has been coming up to offer relief to the rural poor from the debt trap of the money lenders. These new institutions are supposed to work in coordination with the formal banking system. Despite these new institutions informal credit market continued to run. **Dr. Nikhil Kumar Mandal in chapter 7 "Sustainability Issues in Agriculture and Development, the Role of Rural Credit: A Study of West Bengal in Neo-liberalism"** has tried to answer the question of why the informal credit market continued to exist. Based on a primary field survey in rural West Bengal and secondary sources of information, this chapter would like to discourse on the informal credit market. There are two sources of credit, one is organised credit market controlled by banking system with some uniform interest rates and other is unorganised market, regulated by private lenders. There is no uniform interest rate in the latter market. Two criteria (E-criteria and Standard Acreage criteria) are used throughout this chapter. According to E-criteria developed by Utsa Patnaik, the six categories of economic classes can be reduced to three broad categories, namely, exploited classes (landless and poor peasant), self-employment classes (small peasant and middle peasant) and labour hiring or exploiting classes (rich peasant and landlord). Here we deal with the dominance of few people over the major markets of the rural economy. This includes markets of major means of production, viz., land and non-land assets, irrigation and credit. Here we analyse the distribution of the inflow of rural credit at the national level with special reference to West Bengal using secondary sources. It also enquires into the distribution of rural credit at a disaggregated level using ground level data. Here we deal with the crisis of sustainable development in agriculture. We know that the main objective of rural banking after bank nationalization was agricultural growth and alleviation of rural poverty. This chapter evaluates how far this objective has been achieved during the period of reforms.

Gender relations play an important role in the division of labour encompassing all countries and regions. As Ester Boserup puts in her book Women's Role in Economic Development,

> *"Even at the most primitive stages of family autarky there is some division of labour within the family, the main criteria for the division being that of age and sex. Both in primitive and in more developed communities, the traditional division of labour within the family is usually considered 'natural' in the sense of being obviously and originally imposed by the sex difference itself. "*

There is an obvious gender based difference in the distribution of work, both economic activities and non-economic ones, with some economic activities designated as unpaid family work in the official statistics, however, these tend to be largely specific to women. Out of the 3.0 billion people that were employed around the world in 2008, 1.2 billion were women amounting to about 40.4 per cent. (Global Employment Trends for Women, March 2009, ILO). But more than half of the female workers were vulnerable workers (unpaid family workers and own account workers) (GET March 2009, ILO); there are countries where the shares of women in 'vulnerable employment' were even above 65 per cent. About one-fourth of the women workers were unpaid contributing family workers, worldwide; twice the share of the men. In South Asia, more than 50 per cent of the female workers were family helpers in 2009, male counterparts comprising just 14.2 per cent (International Labour Office 2010). These family helpers are documented as self-employed workers; the concern, however, is to what extent they can be recognized as workers. In rural context, unpaid family work largely means assistance in the family farm without remuneration for their work. To what extent is the high prevalence of contributors to family work among women, though counted as workers, a reflection of choice? **Sharmishtha Sinha in chapter 8 entitled "Self-Employment among Rural Women in India: A Focus on Family Helpers"** attempts to explore this in the rural Indian context, which has a significant share of female self-employment. *Prima facie,* it looks encouraging that there has been an increase in female employment. However, the sudden spurt raises doubts as well and prods us to explore the plight of these women, what drives such large proportion of the women self-employed workers to contribute to family enterprises amidst the growing economy.

Expanding informal sector with increasing flexibility in the production process generally employs more women than men (Marilyn Carr, Martha Alter Chen, and Jane Tate 2000). Home-based work has a distinct characteristic that there is no account of persons who perform this work and who gets the actual remuneration. Largely female members of the family, wives, daughters, wives of married sons, help in the family farms and businesses, working full or part time but without any regular salary or wages. More than 80 per cent of the female workers are engaged in agriculture and allied activities. Among the rural women workers 56.3 per cent were self-employed in 2004-05. This chapter is an attempt to explore the extent and nature of female self-employed in rural India, focusing on the family helpers that comprise a significant proportion of the self-employed; the core factors behind taking up these activities and their implications.

The issue of environment in development discourse has been gaining in importance. The poor people time and again are found to be the worst victims of natural disasters and on top of that misplaced policies add more salt to their wounds. So study of the economies of the ecologically fragile regions is becoming important. One such region is "The Sundarbans" in West Bengal. **The author, Jyotirmoy Sircar, in chapter 9 entitled "Employment Diversification in Ecologically Fragile Regions: The Case of Sundarbans in West Bengal"** has drawn the trends and patterns in employment and employment diversification. He went on to analyse the differences in the observed trends and patterns, situating the differences within the context of the overall geographical location of the three villages under the study—Ramganga, Kumirmari and Herambagopalpur. Based on primary and secondary data, this chapter portrays the socio-economic, educational picture of these three villages and then setting that as a background tries to analyse the issues of unemployment and migration. The author attributed inter-State and intra-State migration as the main factors behind employment diversification in all these three villages. The rates of unemployment, migration and casualisation of labour vary across the three study villages with the locationally best off village (Ramganga) having the lowest rates. Moreover in all the villages those households which have diversified are found to be economically better off than those households which have not.

Much before the 73rd Constitutional Amendment in 1993 (providing decentralization of authority to local governments in respect of development of rural India), an initiative towards the same was witnessed in West Bengal since 1978 with the introduction of effective Panchayati Raj in a democratic set-up through three tier elections at five year interval. **Based on the secondary sources of information and primary data Manik Bhattacharya in chapter 10 entitled "Fiscal Decentralisation under Left Regime in West Bengal"** shows that the West Bengal rural local governance has raised per capita own source revenue to a significant extent, though the revenue autonomy is not very significant. There is also a positive association between development and effectiveness of fiscal decentralization. The author suggested that the Panchayats can generate own source revenue through proper implementation of the different schemes and in this context he thinks that NREGS scheme can play a vital role.

Governments throughout the world play a major role in providing better health facilities to its people. However, the degree of government and private intervention has varied. Public Spending on health in India, as a share of GDP, is among the lowest in the world. Consequently, private spending, of which out-of-pocket spending is the majority, as a share of total spending is among the highest in the world. One of the dichotomies in the delivery of health services in the country is that most of the hospitals and institutions of health service delivery are located in urban areas whereas most of the people live in rural parts of the country. During the decades of economic reforms urban-rural divide in the delivery of public health services have increased significantly. **In this context, Indranil Mukhopadhyay in chapter 11 entitled "Changing Patterns in Public Health Care Investments in Rural India: A Study of Kerala, Tamil Nadu and West Bengal"** analyses the pattern of public investment in health to show that squeeze in health spending has resulted in reduced investments in rural areas. Here we compare the pattern of spending before and after the introduction of the National Rural Health Mission (NRHM), which was instituted to bring in greater public investment in rural areas. It analyses public expenditure data from 1990-91 to 2008-09 obtained from detail demand for grants of the respective States and the Management Information System (MIS) of the NRHM. The study focused on Kerala, Tamil Nadu and West Bengal, which had history of stronger commitments to social sector spending, to show that considerable reprioritization has happened due to squeeze in overall spending in health.

2
Myth of Frictionless Transition
A Structuralist Framework

Saumya Chakrabarti[1]

I. INTRODUCTION

During the last few decades the discourse on development has been experiencing a shift away from the era of 'Lewisian path' (Lewis, 1954). It is increasingly being recognised that capital accumulation and growth mostly in the modern non-agricultural sectors based on labour-displacing technology is unable to provide livelihood for the vast majority of the third world population. Moreover, it is argued by the critics that the so called route of 'progress' based on accumulation and growth in modern industry and services not only excludes but also marginalises the indigenous population surviving on the petty subsistence/traditional economy by evicting them from the means of consumption and reproduction. The long run course of 'modernization' itself creates the mass of 'development refugee' the 'surplus population' (Davis, 2004; Sanyal, 2007) which, however, remains barred from capitalistic growth process. Thus, it is proposed that the modern-marginal dualism in the third world is not an exogenously given state, it is rather endogenously produced by the method of capitalistic expansion. As the modern sector expands, it drains out resources from the traditional subsistence economy and thus a vast section of indigenous population is dispossessed. Consequently, we have a continued phenomenon of accumulation with dispossession (Sanyal, 2007).

It is also opined by these critics that, faced with such an

endogenous process of creation of modern-marginal dualism the international agencies like UN, ILO and the World Bank are advocating for active government intervention to govern/contain and to rehabilitate the marginalized 'surplus humanity' (Davis, 2004).[2] It is indeed advocated by the current orthodoxy of 'development management' that the third world governments should undertake such policies which would entitle this dispossessed population to participate in the so called free market and thereby to interact with the globalized domain of capitalistic production and distribution. Furthermore, it is also opined that even the corporate capital cannot shed off its responsibility in promoting this 'surplus population'. Thus, 'corporate social responsibility' is also assuming significance.

Our task in this chapter is to formulate a macro-framework along Structuralist-Kaleckian lines to capture the fundamentals of the foregoing discussion. This critical enquiry brings to the fore certain fundamental contradictions of the mainstream development discourse. Contrary to the claim of 'frictionless model of transition to capitalism' we try to show that 'doing development' cannot be free from conflicts of interests (see also: Chakrabarti, 2009). However, to critically evaluate these orthodox positions we need to construct an appropriate theoretical set-up based on some empirical work. We construct our economy and follow the subsequent comparative static analyses incorporating the empirical results derived by using relevant Indian data. Even if we concentrate on Indian data, we claim that our project has a general appeal so far as development macroeconomics is concerned. We try to follow a Structuralist-Kaleckian framework given its contributions in the literature on development macroeconomics (Kalecki, 1934 and 1954; Taylor 1983; Kaldor, 1996; Bhaduri, 1986; Thirlwall, 1986; Bagchi, 1988; Bose, 1989; Chakrabarti, 2001, 2003, 2005, 2009, 2011; Bhaduri and Skarstein, 2003; Chakrabarti and Kundu, 2009b).

We construct an economy composed of modern/formal sector and the government and situate it within an (assumed) exogenously given subsistence/traditional economy consisting of petty farm and non-farm activities. We show, while on one hand formal sector–agriculture interaction is crucially dependent on an appropriate role of the government, there is a symbiotic relation between the petty farm and non-farm sectors where government becomes redundant. In this context we also delineate our crucial departures from the existing literature.

The dual phenomenon of accumulation and dispossession and creation of 'surplus population', as mentioned earlier, essentially indicates at a fundamental conflict between the modern and traditional sectors, which, however, was completely missed out in the traditional development economics proposing only a frictionless transformation of the 'dual economy' through capital accumulation. This constitutes our next departure. The orthodox discipline talks about transfer of resources including labour from traditional economy (Lewis, 1954; Ranis and Fei, 1961; and Harris and Todaro, 1970) but hides the destruction of petty non-farm sector as the very existence of such a sector was assumed away (Hymer and Resnick, 1969).

Next, following the prescriptions of the orthodox dual economy models, we assume, for growth of modern/formal sector a large part of traditional agriculture is 'modernised' (Ranis and Fei, 1961; World Bank, 2005, 2007). However, we claim, this implies a drain of resources from the traditional economy to feed the process of accumulation in the modern sector (we can refer: White and Dasgupta, 2010 for an insightful review). This resource-squeeze on the other hand, endangers the very existence of the petty non-farm economy (Chakrabarti, 2005; Chakrabarti and Kundu, 2009a; Kundu and Chakrabarti, 2010; Chakrabarti *et al.*, 2011). Thus accumulation in modern sector evicts a sizeable section of people from the means of consumption and reproduction, and this displaced population only exists in limbo. Consequently, a vast 'surplus population' is created endogenously, which remains outside the domain of capital. This 'surplus population' is not created by misguided choice (as in Harris-Todaro framework); it is rather a product of modernization. This critical policy analysis of effects on petty *non-farm* economy of 'agrarian modernisation' through 'green revolution' and 'crop diversification' constitutes another significant departure from the dominant doctrine (even incisive critique like White and Dasgupta, 2010 misses it).

However, to explicate all these departures we build up our model economy. We reiterate, in our theoretical analysis we have tried to use Indian data wherever relevant as a supportive building block.

II. A MODEL OF MODERN-TRADITIONAL CONFLICT[3]

Creation of 'Surplus Population'

First, we construct an economy composed of modern/formal sector (FS) and the government and situate it within an exogenously given subsistence/traditional sector consisting of petty farm and non-farm activities. These analyses of inter-linkages between agriculture, formal sector and the government on one hand and petty farm and non-farm economy on the other, in fact, help us in delineating our departures from the established literature.[4] We also explicate a conflict between the formal sector and the petty non-farm economy, which crucially depends on the generic agricultural supply-constraint. Furthermore, we propose that this fundamental conflict is found to be the basis of creation of 'surplus population' through the processes of 'modernization and dispossession'.

2.1 Agriculture—Formal Sector Interaction: Role of the Government

2.1.1. Review of Literature

(a) Demand-Side Linkage

There is a vast literature which argues that agriculture provides 'home market' for the formal/modern industrial sector (FS) and thereby mitigates its 'effective demand problem' through the following channels:

(i) Inter-sectoral redistribution of income away from net savers (mainly large farmers) in presence of differential propensities to consume FS output for different class of people. This redistribution is initiated either by policy-driven or by agricultural growth induced movement in the terms of trade (t-o-t) between agriculture and FS (Mitra, 1977; Rakshit, 1982; Taylor, 1983; Bagchi, 1988; Bose, 1989).

(ii) Mutual exchange of surpluses between FS and agriculture. As agricultural production rises, more of its output is sold to FS raising the agricultural income. Consequently, the demand for FS output rises (Kaldor, 1996).

On the other hand, it is also proposed that the development of capitalism in agriculture creates the home market for FS through the expansion of the scope for inter-sectoral exchange of commodities (Mundle, 1977).

(b) Supply-side Linkage

Agriculture providing supply-side support for FS, absence of which restricts accumulation:

(i) Supply of wage-goods and raw materials for FS are important contributions of agriculture. For the very existence of FS food-supply is extremely essential. These supplies are forwarded to FS through simple inter-sectoral exchange (Kalecki, 1954; Kaldor, 1976).

(ii) Food-constraint pushes up food-price in the face growing demand from FS, which leads to either wage-price upward spiral in FS (Kalecki, 1954) or deterioration of t-o-t for FS leading to 'profit squeeze' (Ricardo, 1815). This constricts the process of capital accumulation and growth in FS. Conversely, cheap and abundant food-supply to FS ensures transfer of surplus from agriculture to FS (Preobrazhensky, 1926; Ranis and Fei, 1961).

Thus we find that intra- and inter-sectoral redistributions and inter-sectoral exchange play crucial roles in agriculture-FS interactions, both on demand and supply sides. In this context we depart.

2.1.2 Our Departures

(a) We consider a situation where all the contending groups (capitalists and workers of FS and the farmers) form separate lobbies and all lobbies are equally strong. In such a situation these classes can collude, the political expression of which is a 'coalition government'. In a regime of 'coalition politics' each of the contending groups try to maintain its relative socio-economic position. Consequently, any process initiating redistribution is blocked through bargaining. Therefore, we assume rigidity of formal sector real-wage and product-wage and hence, rigidity of agriculture-formal sector t-o-t as well.[5] This assumption of rigidity of distributive factors will be found to play a significant role for our basic model economy and also for the subsequent critical analysis.

(b) We assume absence of any type of capital flow between agriculture and FS. Essentially, it means balanced trade between agriculture and FS. Implicitly, this assumption indicates that none of the sectors is growing at the cost of the other. We assume balanced trade to remove the possibility of extraction of (trade) surplus by any of the sectors from the other. However, it could be shown clearly that given our first departure this is only a simplifying one (Chakrabarti, 2001).

(c) Now we come to our third contention. Our claim is that equilibrium exchange with balanced trade between agriculture and FS cannot create any extra demand for FS. Accordingly agriculture cannot be a 'home market' for FS boosting its 'effective demand' (contrary to the claim by Raj, 1994; Chakravarty, 1994; Kaldor, 1996; Thirlwall, 1986; and Bhaduri and Skarstein, 2003). The argument is that a bumper crop facilitates industrial revival because it leads to increased income in agrarian sector raising demand for FS. The argument is based on an implicit assumption of constant t-o-t. The assumption is necessary because a bumper crop, *ceteris paribus*, will change the t-o-t against agriculture. This, in turn, will reduce the purchasing power of agricultural sector given an inelastic food-demand from FS. Even if we allow for the assumption of constant t-o-t, the increased agricultural output is translated into actual additional purchasing power only after it is sold to FS. Moreover, formal sector purchases of the additional agricultural output mean a leakage from the expenditure on FS incurred by that sector itself. This reduces demand for FS. On the other hand, when the additional income that accrues to agriculture through sale of additional amount of food to FS is, in turn, spent on FS, demand for FS rises. However, ultimately there is no impact on the demand for FS, as the two effects wash off. This result also follows from one of the fundamental propositions of macroeconomics: In a demand-constrained economy only an increase in the 'net exports' or 'export surplus' and not that in exports *per se* (with balanced trade) can lead to an expansion of output and employment.

2.1.3 *Agriculture and Formal Sector Fall-Apart*

If we put together all these departures and contentions, it implies complete absence of all the agriculture—FS demand-side interactions as discussed in the literature. Thus, agriculture cannot be the 'home market' for FS if channels of redistribution are blocked, because mutual exchange with balanced trade cannot raise the level of effective demand.

As agriculture experiences bumper harvest, though supply of marketable surplus of 'food' to FS increases, it fails to be absorbed in FS because of the lack of any consequent rise in demand for FS pushing up FS production. Lack of rise in the complementary demand for FS from any of the inside or outside sources restrict the increase in demand for food as well. Thus, agriculture suffers from the 'realization crisis' along with FS (see, Bhaduri and Skarstein, 2003). On the other hand, expansion of FS crucially depends on the (sufficient) exogenous supply of food, absence of which triggers off either profit squeeze or price-wage upward spiral in FS. Thus, even if agriculture cannot be the home market for FS, it provides the crucial supply-side support.

Essentially, the simultaneous expansions of both food-supply to and effective demand for FS are crucial for the expansion of FS, given our proposed departures. Stated otherwise, complementarities of both supply and demand-side supports for FS expansion is necessary. When food-supply rises we have to search for a complementary source of rising demand for FS. If, however, the internal demand of FS is not sufficient leading to the problem of effective demand, we have to look elsewhere.

2.1.4 *Kalecki : Concept of Domestic Exports*

We assume, for the time being that the primary problem for FS is the lack of 'internal effective demand' while agricultural supply to FS is sufficient. In such a situation, the only option left for the expansion of the demand-constrained FS, in a closed economy, is the path of government intervention given agriculture's inability to provide the 'external market' for FS under the conditions designed by our departures.

Kalecki quite correctly formulated the role of 'external market' and 'home market' in mitigating the demand problem of industry (Kalecki, 1934). Home market for industry is defined as any non-industrial sector within the national economy vis-à-vis which domestic industry can enjoy 'export-surplus'. The agrarian sector cannot be the home market since it suffers from the problem of financing its import-surplus (vis-à-vis industry). A well-known fact is that the agrarian sector lacks the power to issue any financial asset like shares and bonds.[6] Hence, the government sector is the proper candidate to play the role of home market. It can purchase goods from the industrial sector given its monopoly power over printing money. In its trade with government sector domestic industry 'exports' goods against the 'import' of money. This export which is, by definition, an export-surplus is what Kalecki terms as 'domestic exports'.

2.1.5 *Kalecki: Agricultural Supply-Constraint*

Kaleckian analysis rules out agriculture as a possible home market for industrial product. However, this does not mean that he considers agriculture as totally unimportant in the context of industry. There is clear recognition of agriculture as the source of supply of wage-good or 'food' to the industrial sector. If agricultural production fails to grow at the required rate, persistent excess demand for food will continually increase food-price which in turn, will lead to an upward wage-price spiral in the industrial sector. In other words, Kalecki recognizes the role of agriculture as a source of supply-constraint on industry (Kalecki, 1954).

Kalecki's concepts of domestic export and of agricultural supply-constraint constitute our point of departure. The two concepts are treated by Kalecki in an isolated manner. Our task is to unite the two in a single frame of analysis and to push it analytically to explicate the proposed contradictions of doing development.

2.2. Farm-Non-farm Inter-linkage : The Traditional Economy

Next, we discuss the interaction between petty agriculture and the traditional/petty non-farm sector (NFS). We assume that this traditional composite farm-non-farm economy exists exogenous and prior to the so-called phenomenon of modernization of the post-colonial era.[7] Thus, contrary to the orthodox 'dual economy' set-up where traditional sector consists of mainly agriculture our economy contains a sizeable section of population engaged in petty non-farm activities.[8] In this context we bring in the phenomenon of 'modernization'. Thus, given the explicit recognition of existence of both the petty farm and non-farm sectors we try to capture the impacts of capital accumulation and growth of modern sector on them. But before going into the analysis of impact of modernization/'progress' on this traditional economy we need to formulate the inter-sectoral interactions.

Agriculture-NFS relation is found to be distinctly different from agriculture-FS inter-linkage discussed above. While agriculture acts only as a supply-side support for FS, it helps NFS from both the demand and supply-sides. Furthermore, though in the former case there remains a possibility of 'realization crisis' for agriculture, the latter relation is free from any such problem. We will see below, this crucial difference between agriculture-FS and agriculture-NFS interactions is due to the fact that, while production is organized in capitalistic FS with the objective of accumulation, it is undertaken in NFS with the primary motive of consumption (like Marx's petty commodity producer). Furthermore, the farmers' purpose of production is also satisfaction of need irrespective of their asset size. Thus, the whole of non-capitalistic traditional economy consisting of petty farm and non-farm activities runs with the goal of appropriation of 'use value' and not for earning 'profit'. The petty farm and non-farm sectors exchange their products to satisfy mainly the consumption needs. But capitalistic FS produces to realize 'surplus value' in the form of profit.[9]

Afterwards, we discuss the relative positions of formal and non-farm sectors. As food-supply is allocated between these two divisions of the non-agricultural sector, output and employment of FS will be less in presence of NFS for a given level of food supply, generating a basic conflict between these two sub-sectors of non-agriculture. Next, we argue following the traditional 'dual economy' literature (e.g., Ranis and Fei, 1961) that, to support the process of accumulation and growth in FS a large part of agriculture is segregated from the traditional economy through rapid mechanization and use of modern technology embodied in strategic inputs produced in FS. Indeed, this has been the course of development of agriculture in LDCs during the post-colonial period. But, mainly the large farmers are able to take advantage of this process of integration of FS and modernized agriculture and the weaker groups are marginalized[10]. Against the cheap and abundant supply of agricultural produce to FS the rich farmers receive subsidized finance and inputs and also assured market. Thus, an alliance between rich farmers and formal industrial capital is forged which is also beneficial for the elite working population attached with FS.[11]

However, this whole process not only leaves out the largest section of the population engaged in petty production based NFS but also expropriates them from their means of production and consumption. Furthermore, modernization of traditional agriculture destroys the home market for NFS. Thus, the process of modernization of a part of the economy creates the mass of dispossessed and thereby we have intensification of the FS-NFS conflict.

Before going into these details of policy analysis, at first, we set the theoretical perspective and try to analyse the route of income and employment generation in FS and the role of agriculture and government in this specific context. Later on, we would juxtapose this FS – agriculture – government interaction with the NFS-agriculture inter-linkage. Next, our objective would be to comprehend the conflicting relationships between FS and NFS and the probable policy impacts.

2.3. Basic Features and Notations of our Economy

2.3.1 *The Features are as follows:*

(a) Four sectors: a capitalistic FS, a non-capitalistic agricultural sector producing 'food', a non-capitalistic NFS and the government sector.
(b) FS is characterised by excess capacity, unemployment and mark-up pricing. Price is cost-determined and output is demand-determined. Thus our model formal/modern (non-agricultural) economy's output is assumed to be

demand-determined and price is determined separately; quantity-determination and price-determination mechanisms are distinctly different. This is again a very crucial structural assumption for the construction of the present basic model. This should be especially true in the current period when the modern sectors across the world are still into a phase of recession! This is a contemporary relevance of the present work.

(c) All profits in FS are saved whereas all wages are consumed. A part of wage-income is spent on food so that there is the possibility of FS facing an agricultural supply-constraint.

(d) A fixed marketable surplus of foodgrain represents the agricultural supply-constraint for FS as well as for NFS. Consequently, we have demand-determined price for food. We consider food to be an important element as without appropriate supply of food the very existence of non-agricultural population is jeopardised. This food-constraint is in fact the 'classical' wage-good constraint.

(e) Contrary to FS with capital-labour dichotomy and accumulation-motive as the driving force for production, NFS is characterised by consumption-motive[12], self-employment and absence of fixed capital[13]. Moreover, there is surplus-labour in NFS. NFS is essentially consisted of 'petty commodity producers'. It is a subsistence sector where there is no net surplus over and above the requirements for food and non-food consumption at subsistence levels and for 'simple commodity reproduction' without expansion of scale.

(f) NFS is self-sufficient in terms of both implements and non-food consumption. However, like FS it has to depend on agriculture for food which is obtained with the proceeds received through sale of net-output (net of requirements for self-consumption and reproduction) to agriculture itself.

(g) Aggregate agricultural income is earned by selling marketable surplus in the (undifferentiated) food market, which is purchased by the agents of both FS and NFS at the single open market price. This income, in turn, is spent on the products of both FS and NFS. The division depends on the relevant terms of trade[14], cropping-pattern[15] and land-distribution pattern[16].

(h) We have balanced trade between agriculture and NFS, on one hand and between agriculture and FS on the other.[17]

(i) The government purchases FS products by money creation. It constitutes the 'domestic exports'[18] for FS and relaxes the 'effective-demand-constraint' by providing the 'home market'.

(j) The distribution of income among different classes is determined exogenously and there is social resistance to any change in this pattern.[19]

(k) We assume away any interaction between FS and NFS. As a very little part of NFS is able to interact with the sophisticated FS, this seems to be a plausible supposition. Though we have lack of direct interaction between FS and NFS, we try to show theoretically that there are serious indirect conflicts between the two. This is in fact a departure even from the radical political economy literature (e.g., Sanyal, 2007; Sanyal and Bhattacharya, 2009), which sees FS and NFS as mostly isolated.

(l) We restrict to a short-run static analysis and a closed economy set-up.

2.3.2 *Notations to be used are*

(i) Y: Level of FS output.
(ii) p_i: Price of FS output.
(iii) τ: Mark-up over prime (wage) cost in FS.
(iv) w_m: Money-wage rate in FS.
(v) L: Employment in FS.
(vi) l: Labour-output ratio in FS.
(vii) I: Real investment in FS in terms of FS output.
(viii) g: Real government expenditure on FS in terms of FS output.
(ix) G: Nominal government expenditure on FS.
(x) F: Aggregate supply of marketable surplus of food to FS and NFS.
(xi) a_f: Per capita food-demand in FS.
(xii) p_f: Food-price.
(xiii) D_f: Aggregate food-demand from FS.

(xiv) W: Total wage-bill of FS in terms of FS output.

(xv) α_u : Fraction of aggregate agricultural income or that of aggregate marketable surplus of food transacted with NFS.[20]

(xvi) Y_u: Level of NFS output.

(xvii) p_u : Price of NFS output.

(xviii) L_u : Employment in NFS.

(xix) l_u : Labour-output ratio in NFS.

(xx) β_u : Fraction of NFS output used for self-consumption and reproduction.

(xxi) S_u : Aggregate net-output of NFS used to purchase food.

(xxii) D_u : Aggregate demand for NFS output.

(xxiii) a_{fu} : Per capita food-demand in NFS.

2.4 Working of Our Model

The features (a) to (l) of section (2.3.1) imply the following formulations:

2.4.1 *Interaction between FS, Agriculture and the Government*

Excess capacity in FS implies a given *l*, and we take *l* = 1.

Hence, $$L = Y \qquad ...(1)$$

Using equation (1), mark-up pricing in FS is represented as:

$$p_i = (1+ \tau)\, w_m \qquad ......(2)$$

τ is a positive constant.

Workers' demand for a targeted real-wage is given by:

$$w_m/p_f = \beta \qquad ......(3)$$

β is a positive constant.

From equations (2) and (3), we write the following:
Product-wage in terms of FS output is,

$$(w_m/p_i) = 1/(1+\tau) = \alpha \qquad ...(3.1)$$

Terms of trade between agriculture and FS is,

$$(p_f/p_i) = b/(1 + \tau) = \theta \qquad ...(3.2)$$

α and θ are exogenously determined.

The basic income-expenditure equation for FS can be written as:

Total FS output =
(Total FS wage-bill in terms of FS output)[21]
+(Total FS investment in terms of FS output)
+(Total government expenditure on FS in terms of FS output) ...(4)

We take (autonomous) real investment in FS and nominal government expenditure on FS output (i.e., government budget) as exogenously given, i.e.,

$$I = I^0 \qquad ...(5)$$

$$G = G^0 \qquad ...(6)$$

Now, substituting equations (5) and (6) in equation (4) and using relevant notations we obtain:

$$Y = W + I^0 + G^0/p_i = (w_m/p_i).L + I^0 + (p_f/p_i).(G^0/p_f) \qquad ...(7)$$

Using equations (1), (3.1) and (3.2), equation (7) can be rewritten as:

$$Y = \alpha.Y + I^0 + \theta.(G^0/p_f) \qquad ...(7.1)$$

Given equation (1), equation (7.1) can be written as:

$$L = \alpha.L + I^0 + \theta.(G^0/p_f) \qquad ...(7.2)$$

Solution of (7.2) gives,

$$L^* = [I^0 + \theta.(G^0/p_f)]/(1 - \alpha) \qquad ...(8)$$

Now, food-demand per worker employed in FS depends on wage-share and t-o-t and it can be expressed as:

$$a_f = a_f(w_m/p_i, p_f/p_i) \quad ...(9)$$
$$a_{f1}>0, a_{f2}<0.$$

Using equations (3.1) and (3.2) we get,

$$a_f(w_m/p_i, p_f/p_i) = a_f^0 \quad ...(10)$$

a_f^0 is a positive constant.

Hence, aggregate food-demand from FS can be written as:

$$D_f = a_f^0.L \quad ...(10.1)$$

Substituting from equation (8):

$$D_f = a_f^0.[I^0 + \theta.(G^0/p_f)]/(1-\alpha) \quad ...(10.2)$$

There is an inverse relation between food-price and aggregate food-demand from FS, which gives us the negatively sloped D_f curve of figure 2.1. As p_f rises, given t-o-t, p_i rises as well. Now, for $G = G^0$, this rise in p_i reduces the size of real domestic exports. Consequently, the demand-determined FS employment contracts leading to a fall in food-demand.

Now, the assumption of a fixed marketable surplus of food[22] can be written as:

$$F = F^0 \quad ...(11)$$

Using equations (10.2) and (11), food-market equilibrium condition is:

$$F^0 = D_f = a_f^0.[I^0 + \theta.(G^0/p_f)]/(1-\alpha) \quad ...(12)$$

Equation (12) determines the equilibrium food-price p_f^*. It can be represented in a simple food-market demand-supply diagram (Figure 2.1). The equilibrium food-price, p_f^* determines the equilibrium money-wage in FS, i.e., w_m^* given equation (3). This w_m^*, in turn, determines equilibrium price of FS output, i.e., p_i^*

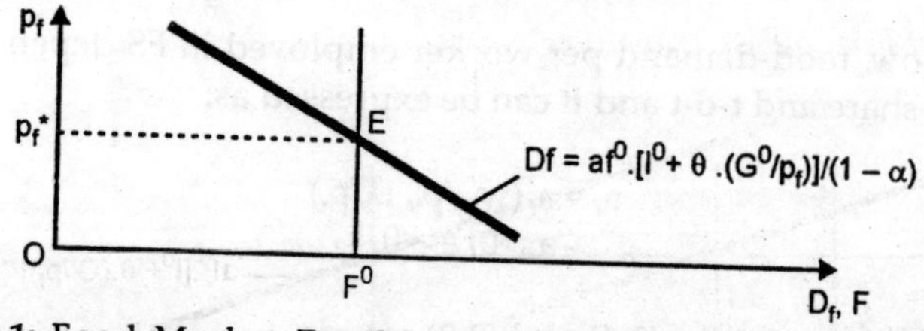

Fig. 2.1: Food-Market Equilibrium Representing Agriculture-FS Interaction

given equation (2). Consequently, the equilibrium size of the real government expenditure on FS output is endogenously determined as:

$$g^* = G^0/p_i^* \qquad ...(12A)$$

Proposition I: Given an exogenous food-supply-constraint and exogenously determined income distribution, the size of real domestic exports or that of the home market for FS is endogenously determined.

Furthermore, as an extension of this proposition-I we can also say that the government expenditure on FS output not only mitigates the problem of effective demand for FS but also that of agriculture.

Corollary

It clearly follows that given the amount of per capita food consumption in FS (i.e. a_f^0), bumper harvest creates a potential for FS expansion. However, realization of this potential requires an adequate increase in the value of real domestic exports. Such a case can be presented in terms of Figure 2.2.

Consider a case of downward flexibility of FS money-wage: Let us assume a bumper harvest raising the value of F to say, $F^{0/}$. As a result equilibrium food-price falls from p_f^* to $p_f^{*/}$. Given the distributive factors, this reduces w_m and subsequently, p_i also falls. This, in turn, expands the size of real domestic exports given $G = G^0$. Simultaneous increases in food-supply to and demand for FS induce its expansion (along with a process of general deflation). Thus we get the movement of equilibrium position from E_1 to E_2.

However, with downward rigidity of w_m, a fall in p_f due to bumper harvest does not automatically increase the real domestic

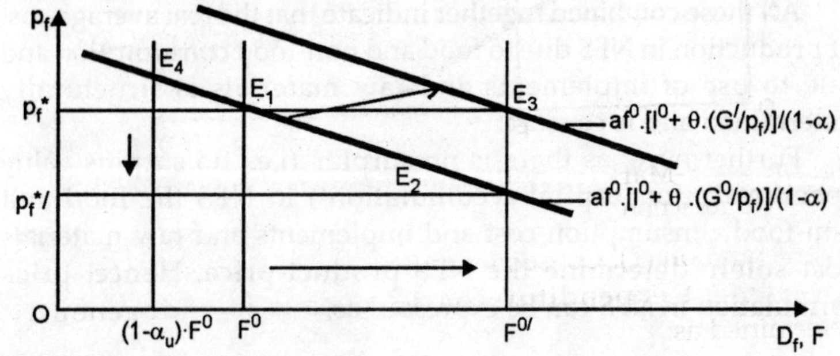

Fig. 2.2: Effects of Bumper Harvest on FS represented through Food-Market Equilibria

exports. In that case, adequate expansion of home market can only be achieved by a proper expansion of nominal government expenditure. The required expansion is such that the equilibrium position moves to E_3.

Proposition II: Bumper harvest creates the potential for *FS* expansion from the supply-side. However, on the demand-side, realization of this potential requires an adequate expansion of home market through increase in the value of real domestic exports. Such an expansion can be achieved by price-wage fall in case of downward flexibility of money-wage. A proper expansion of nominal government expenditure, on the other hand, is required in case of downward rigidity of money-wage.

2.4.2. *Interaction between Agriculture and NFS*

First, from the condition of labour-surplus NFS we can specify constancy of per capita food-demand at the minimum subsistence level[23]. Hence,

$$a_{fu} = a_{fu}^{0}$$

Moreover, the absence of (limiting) capital implies,

$$l_u = l_u^{0}, \text{ a constant.}$$

We also assume without loss of generality,

$$\beta_u = \beta_u^{0}, \text{ a constant.}^{24}$$

All these combined together indicate that the real average cost of production in NFS due to food and non-food consumption and due to use of implements and raw materials is structurally determined and is constant.

Furthermore, as there is no surplus (i.e., no surplus value specifically for 'capital-accumulation') in NFS the food and non-food consumption-cost and implements and raw materials cost solely determine the NFS product-price. Hence, price formulation in NFS can be expressed as,

$$p_u = p_f.a_{fu}^0.l_u^0+p_u.\beta_u^0$$

Rearranging,

$$(1-\beta_u^0).p_u = p_f.a_{fu}^0.l_u^0$$

Thus, the value of net-output in NFS is determined only by the subsistence cost or food-cost.

Now assuming, $l_u^0 = 1$ for simplicity,

$$p_u/p_f = a_{fu}^0/(1-\beta_u^0) \quad \text{...(i)}$$

Therefore, we have a given agriculture-NFS t-o-t. Moreover, at this given t-o-t the supply of net output, S_u will be perfectly elastic as there is no limiting factor within NFS. The S_u curve will be horizontal on the 'S_u–p_u/p_f' plane (Figure 2.3). Furthermore, the given t-o-t implies that a particular amount of food-supply to NFS always induces a definite volume of inter-sectoral trade. Hence, the level of production in NFS is set solely by the volume of food supplied to this sector. As the perfectly elastic S_u and hence Y_u and L_u are demand-determined, the equilibrium values of these variables are solely set by the portion of marketable surplus of food or more precisely, that of agricultural income transacted with NFS. As food-supply to NFS rises, output and employment in this sector are increased though the real income remains unchanged at the subsistence level. This happens as higher amount of employment can be maintained with higher amount of food given the real income. Conversely, this also raises the value of net output S_u in NFS. Hence, agriculture gets higher amount of NFS output with higher amount of food-supply. Thus, increased supply of food to NFS expands the volume of agriculture-NFS trade.

Stated otherwise, demand for food from NFS is perfectly elastic. There is no 'realization problem' for agriculture so far as its interaction with NFS is concerned.

Proposition III: Interaction between agriculture and NFS is found to be distinctly different from that between agriculture and FS. While in the latter case there remains a possibility of realization crisis for agriculture, the former relation is free from any such problem even if there is no government intervention and the t-o-t is given.

Mere supply of agricultural commodities does not automatically imply its sale in capitalistic formal economy, as production in this sector is organized by the capitalists with accumulation motive and not for consumption *per se*. Capitalistic economy would not invest and grow unless there is any (ex-ante) guarantee of absorption of its 'surplus'; mere (equivalent) exchange of its output with inputs like food and agro-raw materials cannot serve that purpose. Hence, just the supply of food cannot induce the demand-constrained capitalistic production. This very result has already been captured by our departures mentioned earlier.[25]

However, with food-supply to NFS agriculture simultaneously demands NFS output, as the farmers participate in production for satisfaction of need. On the other hand, this supply of food also induces production in NFS as the petty non-farm producers' sole objective is consumption of commodities, the most important item being food. Hence, marketable surplus of food gets easily absorbed in NFS. In our analysis the crucial characteristic of consumption motive for both the NFS producers and the farmers close the agriculture–NFS interaction. Marketable surpluses of both NFS and agriculture are mutually exchangeable as production in both these sectors is undertaken for consumption[26]. In fact, we have a symbiotic relation between agriculture and NFS and hence simple market exchange (without government) can close their interaction, which is not true for agriculture–FS interaction.[27]

Next, from our preceding analysis we know that the value of aggregate demand for NFS output is equal to the part of agricultural income spent on it or the value of marketable surplus of food transacted with NFS. Hence,

$$p_u.D_u = \alpha_u.p_f.F \qquad \text{...(ii)}$$

Now using feature (g) of section (2.3.1) and notation (xv) of section (2.3.2) we can formulate:

$$\alpha_u = \alpha_u (p_f/p_u, p_f/p_i, n_1, n_2) \quad \text{... (iii)}$$
$$\alpha_{u1}>0, \alpha_{u2}<0 \text{ and } \alpha_{u3}>0, \alpha_{u4}>0.$$

Here the exogenous factor 'n_1' is the land-distribution parameter, an improvement of which implies a more equitable pattern that helps NFS to grow[28]. However, we assume that n_1 is set say at n_1^0.

On the other hand, 'n_2' signifies cropping-pattern. Higher the extent of crop-diversification lower is the value of n_2 and hence, a squeeze on NFS (please see below for the relevant literature and for some empirical support on India). However, we assume that n_2 is set say at n_2^0.

Moreover, using equation (3.2) in equation (iii) we get:

$$\alpha_u = \alpha_u^0 (p_f/p_u, \alpha, n_1^0, n_2^0) = \alpha_u^0 (p_f/p_u) \quad \text{...(iv)}$$

Rearranging equation (ii) and using equation (iii) we get,

$$D_u = (p_f/p_u).\alpha_u (p_f/p_u, p_f/p_i, n_1, n_2).F \quad \text{...(v)}$$

Hence, generalizing we get,

$$D_u = D_u (p_u/p_f, \alpha_u, F) \quad \text{...(vi)}$$

Using equation (iv) and F = F^0 (equation 11) we have from equation (vi),

$$D_u = D_u^0 (p_u/p_f, a_u^0, F^0) = D_u^0 (p_u/p_f) \quad \text{...(vi)'}$$
$$Du^01 < 0.$$

This gives a downward sloping D_u^0 curve on the 'D_u–p_u/p_f' plane (Figure 2.3).

Now, we consider the determination of equilibrium values, i.e., $(p_u/p_f)^*$, α_u^{0*}, D_u^{0*}, S_u^*, Y_u^* and L_u^*. It is to be noted that $(p_u/p_f)^*$ is effectively determined by equation (i) as:

$$(p_u/p_f)^* = a_{fu}^0/(1 - \alpha_u^0) \quad \text{...(i)'}$$

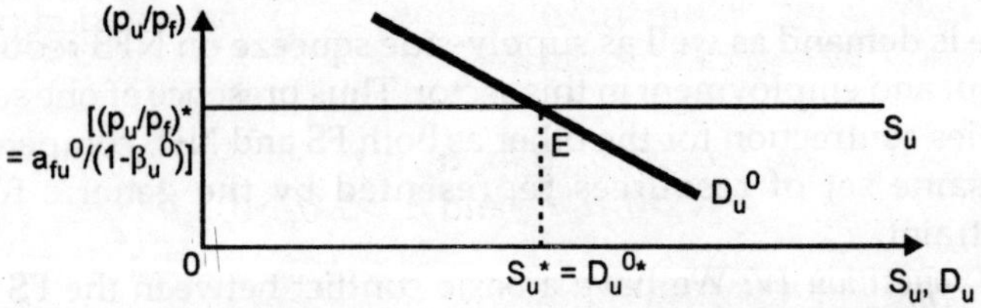

Fig. 2.3: NFS Equilibrium Representing Agriculture-NFS Interaction

Putting equation (i)′ in equation (iv) we get,

$$\alpha_u^{0*} = \alpha_u^{0*}[(p_f/p_u)^*] \qquad \text{...(vii)}$$

From our characterization of S_u (as demand-determined) and equation (vi)′ we can find out S_u^* by solving the following equation:

$$S_u = D_u^0 \qquad \text{...(viii)}$$

Putting equations (i)′, (vii) and $F = F^0$ in expression (v) and then using equation (viii) we get,

$$S_u^* = D_u^{0*} = [(1 - \alpha_u^0)/a_{fu}^0].\ \alpha_u^{0*}.F^0 \qquad \text{...(ix)}$$

This equilibrium is shown graphically by point E in Figure 2.3.

Furthermore, using $l_u^0 = 1$ equation (ix) gives:

$$Y_u^* = L_u^* = [S_u^*/(1 - \alpha_u^0)] = [(\alpha_u^{0*}.F^0)/a_{fu}^0] \qquad \text{...(x)}$$

This last equation clearly shows that equilibrium output in NFS is determined by the level of food-supply to this sector (i.e., $\alpha_u^{0*}.F^0$), given a_{fu}^0.

Now, in presence of NFS only $(1 - \alpha_u^{0*})$ fraction of the aggregate food-supply is directed to the FS. Thus, FS faces shrinkage of food-supply to $[(1 - \alpha_u^{0*}).F^0]$ from F^0 (which would have been the supply of food to FS in absence of NFS). This supply-side squeeze reduces potential employment and output in FS. The size of real domestic exports is reduced accordingly and hence, FS contracts which is reflected by the movement of equilibrium position from E_1 to E_4 in Figure 2.2. Conversely, in presence of FS there is demand as well as supply-side squeeze on NFS reducing output and employment in this sector. Thus presence of one sector implies contraction for the other as both FS and NFS compete for the same set of resources represented by the generic food-constraint.

Proposition IV: We have a basic conflict between the FS and NFS in terms of employment and output in presence of agricultural-supply-constraint.

This fundamental conflict marks a significant departure from the orthodox literature which hides the very existence of NFS in traditional economy and thereby conceals the FS-NFS conflict. Moreover, this contradiction is found to be intensified with the introduction of development strategies intended to 'modernize' the less-developed-economy, as discussed below.

With the help of our above framework let us now try to capture the effects of certain crucial 'modernizing' agricultural strategies on the NFS. We take up two such strategies in our subsequent analysis.

2.5 Green Revolution

There are several studies (Hazell and Haggblade, 1990; see also, Lanjouw and Lanjouw, 2001) which try to support Mellor's (1976) hypothesis that green revolution generates increased demand for locally produced labour-intensive non-farm goods and services. But, the assertion that even the big farmer class could be the driving force for non-farm growth has been questioned by several researches (Dunham, 1991; Saith, 1992).

According to Hazell and Roell (1983) small and middle peasants have much higher propensity to consume labour-intensive rurally produced goods compared to that of their larger counterparts. In this context, we can site the study by Bhalla and Chadha (1983) on Punjab (India), where they found that middle peasantry and not the big or very big farmers is the dominant source of demand for non-farm goods and services. Conversely, a survey (Harriss, 1991) on Arni, Tamil Nadu (India) has revealed that agricultural expansion has not encouraged local production of labour-intensive consumer goods; rather it has disproportionately expanded trade in 'big city' products. Based on this survey, Harriss asserts that it is the egalitarian growth process in agriculture that is essential for the progress of decentralised labour-intensive non-farm sector.[29] Given these, we take up the issue of impact of green revolution on NFS.

Green revolution implies rise in agricultural productivity. But in many cases it has caused land alienation for the small farmers leading to concentration of ownership.[30] On the other hand, green revolution because of its technological specificity invariably reduces the indigenous crop-diversity of traditional agriculture.[31] All these imply a rise in marketable surplus of food, F and an increase in n_2 representing change in cropping-pattern towards specialisation. But, green revolution also reduces n_1 as land-ownership concentration rises.

Thus, F^0 and n_2^0 rise to say, F' and n_2' respectively, while n_1^0 falls to say, n_1'. Hence, equation (iv) is modified as,

$$\alpha_u' = \alpha_u'(p_f/p_u, \alpha, n_1', n_2') = \alpha_u'(p_f/p_u) \quad \ldots\text{(iv)}'$$

Now, using equations (iv)′ and $F = F'$, we have from equation (vi),

$$D_u = D_u'(p_u/p_f, \alpha_u', F') = D_u'(p_u/p_f) \quad \ldots\text{(vi)}''$$

Comparing equations (iv) and (iv)′ we can summarise:

> even if, $n_2' > n_2^0$, $\alpha_u^0 >, =,$ or $< \alpha_u'$ as $n_1' < n_1^0$. Hence, in spite of $F' > F^0$, comparison between equations (vi)′ and (vi)″ generates ambiguous result. Thus, $D_u' >, =,$ or $< D_u^0$. Consequently, the direction and extent of shift of the D_u^0 curve (Figure 2.3) is ambiguous and it depends on the extent of variations of F, n_1 and n_2.

Given equation (vi)″, the equilibrium condition (viii) is modified as,

$$S_u = D_u' \quad \ldots\text{(viii)}'$$

Putting equations (i)′, (iv)′ and $F = F'$ in expression (v) and then using equation (viii)′ we get a modification of equation (ix) and accordingly the new S_u^* as,

$$S_u^{*\prime} = D_u'^* = [(1 - \alpha_u^0)/a_{fu}^0].\alpha_u'^*.F'$$

Consequently, modifying equation (x) with $F = F'$ we have,

$$Y_u^{*\prime} = L_u^{*\prime} = [(\alpha_u'^{*}.F')/a_{fu}^0]$$

As, $\alpha_u^0 >, =,$ or $< \alpha_u'$, the resultant impacts on S_u, Y_u and L_u are ambiguous. Only if the effects of rise in F and n_2 dominate the contractionary effect of fall in n_1, agricultural supply constraint gets relaxed. Consequently, demand for NFS products rises as well. This demand and supply side boosts help NFS to grow. However, contrarily, if the effects of rise in F and n_2 are dominated by the contractionary effect of fall in n_1, the NFS even contracts.

As the effect on α_u is ambiguous, the value of $(1 - \alpha_u)$ is also not certain. Hence, even if F rises with introduction of green revolution technology the level of supply of agricultural commodities to FS, i.e., $[(1 - \alpha_u).F]$ remains uncertain. Consequently, the effect of green revolution on FS is ambiguous.

Proposition V: Rise in agricultural productivity initiated through a policy of green revolution will have ambiguous effects on both FS and NFS.

If, however, green revolution occurs having distinct technological bias in favour of the rich farmers (as has happened in India), it is quite likely that the strong effect of fall in n_1 on α_u outweighs the effect of rise in n_2. Consequently, α_u falls raising the value of $(1 - \alpha_u)$. As a result, with rise in agricultural productivity $[(1 - \alpha_u).F]$ rises unambiguously relaxing the food-supply constraint on FS. Thus, the impact of green revolution on FS crucially depends on the extent of its technological bias favouring the large farmers triggering off an increase in land-ownership concentration. However, the impact on NFS depends on the relative strengths of fall in α_u and rise in F. If the former is stronger than the latter, green revolution in agriculture squeezes down the NFS.

2.6 Crop-diversification and Contract Farming

In several developing countries withdrawal of government subsidy, deregulations of agricultural commodity trade, dismantling of public distribution system and many such contractionary policy steps are discouraging basic food-crop producing agriculture. On the contrary, export possibilities for certain sophisticated food and non-food items (fruits, vegetables, flowers and agro-fuel feedstock) as well as shift of tastes and preferences of the richer sections of domestic population towards such products have induced high-value-crop (HVC) cultivation (World Bank, 2005, 2007; for comprehensive critique we can refer: Chakrabarti and Kundu, 2009a; Kundu and Chakrabarti, 2010; White and Dasgupta, 2010). We try to capture the impacts of such 'crop-diversification' in our following analysis. Crop-diversification could occur as an endogenous phenomenon of agriculture as a way out for distressed small farmer (Mukherjee and Chakrabarti, 2009). However, large scale HVC cultivation as proposed by the international agencies is something else!

HVC farming could serve well the course of capital-accumulation-driven 'modernization' by providing (fresh and processed) food to the relatively well-off population engaged in FS, through supply of raw material for sophisticated processing and of agro-fuel meant primarily for exports (Sidhu, 2005; Singh, 2004; White and Dasgupta, 2010). On the other hand, it is argued that through crop-diversification the third-world ('distressed') agriculture could be brought to the global market and thereby 'inclusive agricultural modernisation' could be ensured (World Bank, 2007). However, HVC cultivation could be a better option for farmers only if they have access to modern production-storage–processing–transportation inputs/facilities or have the ability to get attached with the big agro-business firms through corporate 'contract farming' (Dev and Rao, 2005; Kumar, 2006; World Bank, 2007; see also: White and Dasgupta, 2010 for a critique). Thus, the whole chain of contemporary crop-diversification: production–processing–packaging-transportation–retailing is argued to be organised in an efficient way through firm–farm contracts, as this requires large scale of operation (World Bank, 2005, 2007; Rao *et al.*, 2006; Sen and Raju, 2006; White and Dasgupta, 2010, 599). However, such contract farming ensures use of modern inputs and modern farm-services through the entry of corporate capital creating diversion of purchasing power in favour of 'big city' products and thereby initiating substantial leakage of potential demand away from the labour-intensive NFS.[32] On the other hand, there is drain of resources from NFS due to farm-firm contracts: not only that the basic raw materials needed for survival of petty NFS are replaced with HVC requiring sophisticated inputs/facilities and farm-services, these HVCs are siphoned out of local economy altogether for down-stream activities (White and Dasgupta, 2010, 603)[33]. This destruction of NFS due to global (HVC) capitalism (following White and Dasgupta's 'Agrofuel Capitalism') is not only missed out in contemporary orthodoxy but also in radical perspectives concentrating mainly on potential agrarian distress (White and Dasgupta, 2010; see also: Bhattacharya, 2010 for a review). These writings, in many cases, consider NFS as isolated from FS, which exists in limbo and hence overlooks (sometimes even negates) this destruction of NFS through resource drain by FS accumulation.

On the other hand, agricultural diversification may jeopardize local and household level food security creating significant supply-side squeeze on NFS. Hence, agriculture–NFS complementarities (symbiosis) are replaced with a tacit conflict and development of 'modern' agriculture displaces rural non-agricultural population. Though the huge population engaged in different types of NFS activities gets expropriated, only a minor fraction of it would be able to attach itself with the so called modernization process involving FS and HVC farming. Thus, through this project of corporate-led crop-diversification even though some parts of agriculture could get included into the global market, the survival of larger sections of farm and non-farm population would be severely threatened (we can refer: Chakrabarti and Kundu, 2009a and Kundu and Chakrabarti, 2010 for extensive analyses along this line of argument).

Let us assume that crop-diversification is not raising the level of agricultural productivity as such, it is rather occurring at the cost of crop-substitution.[34] Hence, F remains unchanged. However, with crop-diversification there is a clear fall in n_2. On the other hand, there is an induced decrease in n_1 due to the operation of two effects. First, with diversification there is land-alienation to some extent, especially for the small and marginal farmers who cannot independently practise diversified agriculture and transfer land rights to the bigger ones.[35] Secondly, as crop-diversification is practised by large agro-business firms under the institutional arrangement of contract farming, small and marginal farmers lose their independent decision-making power. This snaps the linkages between small farms based agriculture and NFS. The consequent effect on NFS is similar to that of increasing land-concentration.

As both n_1 and n_2 fall, from equation (iii) we can say that there is a clear decline in α_u from its initial value, α_u^0.

Now, with unchanged F and reduced value of α_u, from equation (vi) it is clear that D_u falls unambiguously from its initial value of D_u^0 as derived from equation (vi)′. Consequently, D_u^0 curve in Figure 2.3 should shift to the left.

Given the fall in the value of D_u, we can infer from our basic model that the equilibrium values of S_u, Y_u and L_u must also fall unambiguously. Thus NFS contracts.

However, such contractionary effects on NFS due to crop-diversification could be checked if an appropriate increase in F is ensured counter-balancing the effects of fall in both n_1 and n_2. This could be materialised only when crop-diversification takes place through extensive cultivation and/or increase in cropping intensity rather than crop-substitution.

On the other hand, as crop-diversification is practised with or without crop-substitution, α_u falls unambiguously. Hence, $(1-\alpha_u)$ rises, raising the value of $[(1-\alpha_u).F]$. Thus, the FS gets a crucial supply-side inducement for expansion. This sector is doubly benefited if diversification of agriculture occurs through extensive cultivation and/or increase in cropping intensity, which raise the value of F over and above the increase in $(1-\alpha_u)$.

Proposition VI: The effect of crop-diversification on NFS crucially depends on whether it takes place through extensive cultivation and/or increase in cropping intensity or through crop-substitution. Diversification with crop-substitution and contract-farming unambiguously reduces the size of NFS. However, the corresponding effect on the FS is definitely positive.

III. IN LIEU OF CONCLUSION

Thus, the two comparative static analyses capturing the effects of green revolution and crop-diversification could be summarised in the following way: First of all, with modernization there is increasing dichotomisation of the third world agriculture. While the modern and diversified segment of agriculture gets integrated with the modern FS having mutually beneficial effects, a large part of it still remains traditional. Secondly, modernisation and segmentation of agriculture even though feeds the process of

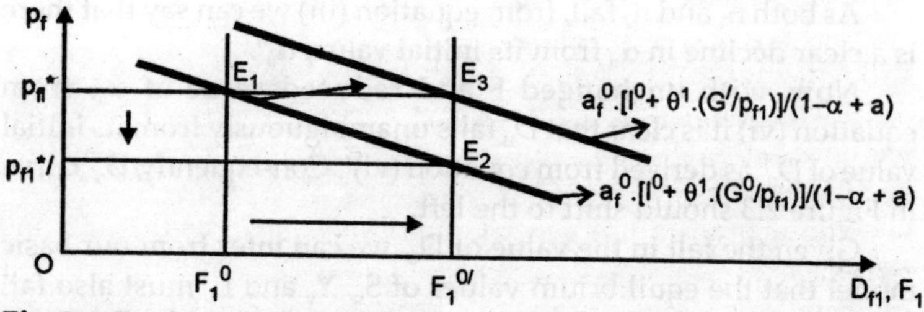

Fig. 2.4: Food-Market Equilibria for Modern Agriculture–FS Interaction

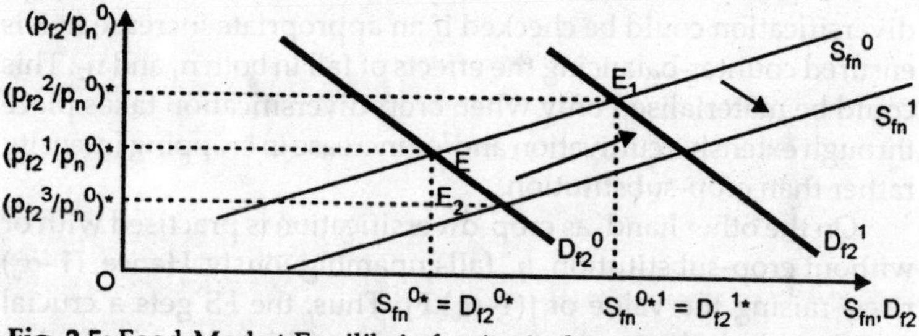

Fig. 2.5: Food-Market Equilibria for Agriculture-INFS Interaction

accumulation and growth in FS from the supply-side, this very process induces a contraction of NFS.

The contraction of NFS, in its turn, creates the 'surplus population' as the mass of dispossessed cannot be employed in FS even though this sector is experiencing growth.[36] We also argue that, this 'surplus population' gets engaged in the 'informal sector'.[37] However, in the contemporary literature this new born informal sector is being projected not as a 'residual' economy but as a dynamic sector capable of mitigating the problem of marginalization. Informal sector is allegedly the cushion which can productively employ the excluded mass of people in LDCs. Indeed, the third world governments and the international agencies are actively engaging into the rehabilitation of the 'development refugee' within this informal sector through variety of programmes.

Thus, a new form of dualism is produced endogenously through the process of growth of modern sectors and through modernization of parts of agriculture supporting this growth. In spite of such a process of expansion of the sphere of accumulation a large part of the economy still remains non-capitalistic. There still remains the traditional agriculture and NFS of significant size outside the domain of capital. However, what is new is that, now we have a third component beyond the modernizing economy, i.e., the 'informal sector'.

Though the traditional economy consisting of petty farm and non-farm activities exists as 'exogenous and prior' to the FS, this informal sector is essentially produced endogenously by the very expansion of FS inducing NFS contraction. Furthermore, unlike traditional agriculture and non-farm economy the informal sector exists in limbo estranged from all sorts of means of subsistence and production. Conceptualisation of this informal sector and analysis of its interactions with other sectors may constitute a very important extension of the this chapter (we can refer: Bhattacharya, 2010 for a comprehensive review).

The Lewisian framework proposes a frictionless transition of the traditional economy by hiding the destruction of NFS. However, we know that even in post-colonial third world there existed NFS of a significant size. With this context, we pose our idea of destruction of traditional non-farm activities by the process of modernization draining out the means of production and consumption (i.e., food and raw materials) from NFS. Furthermore, contrary to the Harris-Todaro framework of migration (Harris and Todaro, 1970) which rationalises the existence of informal sector (see for such an exposition Ranis and Stewart, 1994) using an expectation augmented choice-theoretic model following Sanyal (2007), we propose that the newly 'discovered' and valorized informal sector is in fact a product of accumulation driving dispossession. As the resources are drained out of traditional sector the NFS contracts even if inter-sectoral trade balances and the t-o-ts remain unchanged. And the expropriated population take refuge in the new born informal sector. In support of our analysis of creation of informal sector we can site the acknowledgement by the ILO that: "Contrary to earlier beliefs, the informal sector is not going to disappear spontaneously with economic growth. It is, on the contrary, likely to grow in the years to come, and with it the problems of urban poverty and congestion will also grow" (Bangasser, 2000, pp. 18).

NOTES

1. This chapter heavily draws from the author's earlier contributions (Chakrabarti, 2001, 2003, 2005, 2006, 2009, 2011, 2013; 2014; Chakrabarti and Kundu, 2009a,b; Chakrabarti *et al.*, 2011 and Kundu and Chakrabarti, 2010). The ideas of these contributions have been useful in developing this chapter.
2. UN-Habitat (2003) notes that "(w)ith respect to urban poverty and slums, greater state involvement is, in fact, necessary now more than ever, especially in developing countries, given increasing levels of urban poverty, decreasing levels of formal employment and growing levels of income inequality and vulnerability of the urban poor"(pp. xxvii). Similarly, in rural areas state support to poor and marginalised through micro-credit institutions, self-help groups and NGOs is assuming significant position. Furthermore, massive employment generation programmes like National Rural Employment Guarantee Scheme of India are undertaken.
3. In this context we refer: Chakrabarti, 2006, 2009, 2011; Chakrabarti and Kundu, 2009b. But these frameworks have been developed significantly, theoretically and more importantly, empirically.
4. Agricultural sector may also be dichotomized like the modern non-agriculture *versus* the petty non-farm. In fact, a relatively well off section of agricultural population is much more integrated with the modern non-agriculture through demand as well as supply side channels, while there are significant interactions between the petty farm and non-farm segments of the economy. However, at present, we do not discuss this dichotomy explicitly in our analysis, though this is implicitly present in the modelling exercise through the specific assumptions. We defer explicit recognition of agricultural dichotomization till the policy analysis part, because our target at present is to show theoretically the dual role of agriculture as a whole for modern non-agricultural sectors on one hand and petty non-farm sector on the other.
5. We can also refer for this distributional rigidity the works of Kaldor (1996), Thirlwall (1986), Bhaduri and Skarstein (2003), Chakrabarti (2001, 2003, 2009 and 2011) and of Chakrabarti and Kundu (2009b). First, the scope for redistribution is always limited. Secondly, with this assumption we concentrate only on the non-neoclassical discursive possibilities of real expansion of industry arising out of the changes in the level of agricultural production by blocking the redistributive channel. Thus, we are enquiring only about real expansions keeping the relative prices unchanged.
6. The only case under which purchase of industrial products by agriculture creates home market is when such purchases are financed

by loans from the industrial sector through the financial channel (using the instrument such as agricultural 'commodity derivatives'). However, in the context of our study, the focus is on the role of expansion of agricultural output in creating a home market for industry. This does not happen even in the case under consideration.

7. We are very much aware that this traditional/subsistence economy of farm–non-farm composite is a product of the prolonged process of colonial exploitation. However, for the sake of our particular analysis we assume away that historical past and take into account the (so called backward) economic structure of the developing countries in general as our starting point.
8. Ranis and Stewart (1993), contrary to Hymer and Resnick's (1969) claim of deindustrialisation, point at significant existence of such activities in post-colonial Taiwan and Philippines. Moreover, during the initial years of planning in post-colonial India the existing small and cottage industry was considered as a very important source of cheap consumer goods and also a provider of sizeable employment. In this context, we refer: Chakrabarti, 2005, 2006, 2009; Chakrabarti and Kundu 2009a, b; Chakrabarti *et al.*, 2011; Kundu and Chakrabarti, 2010.
9. Similar dichotomy is also found in the traditional 'dual economy' literature (even in Lewis, 1954).
10. While commenting on modernization of Indian agriculture in post-colonial period, Rao and Storm (1998) observes, "with growing commercialization, the poorer groups...have lost control over much of their resources through privatization of communal lands, including grazing lands, waste lands, forests and water resources" (pp. 212). Furthermore, there is increasing inequality within the farming community also as the "small farmers are handicapped by lack of resources for technological modernization" (*ibid.*, pp. 221) On the other hand, they also note that "employment opportunities within agriculture have shrunk relative to the growth of the workforce" (*ibid.*, pp. 213).
11. Such alliances have been noted by Rao and Storm (1998, pp. 217) in the context of New Agricultural Strategy of India. Recognition of existence of a "resilient mechanism for conflict management and transactional negotiations among the proprietary classes" of India can also be found in Bardhan (1998, pp. 77). He argues that such a "political equilibrium of subsidies and patronage distribution" persists also in post-reform India (*ibid.*, pp. 132-7).
12. Production takes place with the sole objective of consumption. This is the crucial characteristic of NFS. See, Sanyal (2007, pp. 211-3) in this regard.
13. Simple tools produced in NFS itself are used (for these characteristics we can refer: Bangasser, 2000).

14. Between agriculture and FS, on one hand and between the former and NFS, on the other.
15. As we will see empirically, 'basic-food-crop' producing agriculture is much more integrated with NFS, while the 'high-value-crop' segment is more linked with FS.
16. Small farm based agriculture is closely linked with NFS, though the big farmer class allies with the beneficiaries of FS (please see below for empirical support).
17. Unbalanced trade is financially unsustainable. Furthermore, it is only a simplifying assumption.
18. Kalecki (1934).
19. We consider a situation where we have rigidity of FS real-wage and product-wage and hence, rigidity of agriculture-FS t-o-t. On the other hand, agriculture-NFS distribution cannot be altered as NFS is a subsistence sector (please see below).
20. As we have assumed balanced trade between agriculture and NFS and a single (market) price for food, α_u represents fraction of both agricultural income and marketable surplus of food transacted with the non-farm sector.
21. A part of wage-bill though spent on food, it fully comes back to FS as agriculture-FS trade is balanced.
22. Since in our analysis we have assumed a fixed terms of trade, we can safely take food-supply as perfectly inelastic due to short-run natural, technical and institutional rigidities in agriculture. Furthermore, only a fraction of food-supply should go to FS in presence of NFS as we see below. However, for the time being we assume away such a presence of NFS. As we introduce NFS the relevant conditions will be modified.
23. This is a classical assumption.
24. Summary of fraction (%) of value added going for self-consumption and reproduction in unorganized manufacturing enterprises (India: 2005-6):

		No.of Enterprise	*Mean*	*Median*	*Standard Deviation*	*Maxi-mum*	*Mini-mum*	*First Quartile (Q_1)*	*Third Quartile (Q_3)*	*Inter quartile range (Q_3-Q_1)*
OAME	Rural	7543305	12.20	4.47	73.50	11515.15	0.03	1.62	11.17	9.55
	Urban	2106683	9.76	3.37	37.62	4545.45	0.02	1.37	8.94	7.57
NDME	Rural	447633	12.97	4.40	43.97	1697.13	0.04	1.66	12.57	10.91
	Urban	489255	11.92	3.05	107.06	6666.67	0.04	1.11	7.08	5.97
DME	Rural	153077	6.48	1.99	22.07	880.28	0.04	0.70	6.55	5.85
	Urban	149728	5.79	2.34	12.24	203.80	0.03	1.12	6.34	5.22

Source: Calculated from NSS 62nd Round: Unorganised Manufacturing Enterprise (2005-2006) Unit Level data (large macro disaggregated data).

From this above Table it is evident that: so far as the average/mean of value added in reproduction and self-consumption as a percentage of total annual value added is concerned we see across different enterprise types (especially OAME and NDME) both in rural and urban sectors there is no wide difference. It is much more prominent if we consider median value instead of mean. Similarly, standard deviation is not a resistant measure and hence it shows a wide variability across enterprises for each enterprise type (it is basically due to wide difference between maximum and minimum value). But inter quartile range, which is a resistant measure of dispersion and also depicts the middle 50% of the data set, shows the variability of this share ranges, for all types of enterprises, between 5.22 per cent and 10.91 per cent. It does not show any abrupt change. Hence median value along with IQR depicts the fact that the value of consumption and production to total gross value added is varying within a particular range, which partially indicates that this value is more or less constant across all enterprises.

25 Both agricultural sector and industry suffer simultaneously from surplus productions that remain unrealized in absence of appropriate government intervention. This 'problem of realization is how to find for each part of the (aggregate) product, in terms of value...............and in its material form (means of production, and articles of consumption.........), that other part of the product which replaces it on the market' (Lenin, 1899, pp. 46). In the present case where we have realization crises for both agriculture and industry it is rather this non-concurrence of 'material forms' originating in the two lines of production that is creating the problem for exchange. Even if there is concurrence in terms of value there is failure of exchange. This is because the industrial capitalists' motive of production is accumulation of surplus value through sale of their products at profitable prices and not the simple exchange of the whole of their real surplus with that of food. Food is nothing but one of the inputs that can only generate still higher amount of unsold stock of industrial output, if used in production.

26. This is perfectly plausible as petty NFS is linked mainly with that portion of agriculture which is run by small and marginal farmers. Please see the next section for the relevant literature and some empirical support.

27. The above mentioned dichotomy could be explained only if the specificity of the capitalistic production, i.e., the presence of 'capital', the profit motive of the capitalist class and the dependence of the working class on that, are accepted. This is different from the simplest form of production free from class-division with solely consumption motive and hence generating surplus for exchange of 'use values'. This occurs within the agriculture-NFS 'complex'. In such a case,

'the simple circulation of commodities – selling in order to buy – is a means of carrying out a purpose..........namely, the appropriation of use values, the satisfaction of wants' (K. Marx, *Capital*, Vol. I). On the contrary, 'the possession of other goods is not the immediate aim of capitalist production, but the appropriation of value, of money, of abstract wealth' (K. Marx, *Theories of Surplus Value*). Thus, while the rise in agricultural productivity raises output and employment in NFS through (mutual) exchange, it fails to do so for FS. This is because, while in formal production with capitalistic mode we have 'separation and opposition' of production and consumption, in case of NFS we have their 'unity' (this dichotomy is rigorously discussed in a different context by Karl Marx in his *Theories of Surplus Value*).

28. There is a vast literature supporting such a claim. See for example Saith (1992). Please see below for some empirical support in case of India.
29. It is observed that because of highly skewed distribution of land and farm income in Latin America the benefits of agricultural growth could not be appropriated by the NFS (Lanjouw and Lanjouw, 2001). Saith notes that "(a) widely cited feature of South Asian (and other poor agricultural) economies is a high degree of rural demand leakage through the pockets and spending patterns of the rural rich. The tastes and consumer preferences of this group are heavily biased in favour of items which are not produced by the rural non-farm sector" (1993, pp. 17).
30. We know Punjab (India) agriculture could reap the maximum benefits of green revolution in India. But at the same time it had experienced increasing concentration. The index of concentration of operational holding has risen sharply from 0.42 to 0.70 during 1970-1 to 1981-2, whereas for India as a whole this index has shown a marked decline during the same period (Mukherjee, 2007, pp. 50).
31. Here also, Punjab happens to be a classic case.
32. It is found that the regions practicing intensive HVC cultivation in India have concentrated in urban and semi-urban areas (Rao *et al.*, 2006). Production especially processing of HVC seems to be more capital-intensive even across Africa. Haggblade *et al.*, (1989) report that activities like oil extraction, sugar production, tea drying and packaging, etc., are often performed in rural areas by large scale enterprises. Such a situation could also be found in Punjab where non-farm activities are actually labour saving (Saith, 1991; Singh, 2004).
33. For severity of contract farming in general we can refer: White and Dasgupta, 2010, 603-4.
34. In India crop-substitution's contribution to diversification is 63.37 per cent, whereas for whole of South Asia it is 57.02 per cent (Joshi *et al.*, 2004). There is clear indication of such a phenomenon at a

global scale in White and Dasgupta, 2010. On the other hand, there is a serious phenomenon of public land grabbing to cultivate HVCs (*ibid.*, 600-2); this may have far reaching implications for petty NFS largely dependent on commons.

35. WBHDR (2004) reports that, land-alienation for the small owners is "highest in those areas where the alternative use of land, typically by larger scale operations (e.g., extension of tea estates, brackish water fish cultivation, etc.), has become more profitable" (p. 41).
36. FS already faces a surplus labour situation. Stated in Marxian language, there exists the 'reserve army' of labour for FS. Our dispossessed 'surplus population' is distinctly different from this reserve army (see also Sanyal, 2007).
37. *UN-Habitat* (2003) highlights the enormous growth of slums across all the third world countries. In fact, there is almost one-to-one correspondence between slum population and urban informal sector. In India during the period 1999-00 to 2004-05 the change in formal employment has been nil and the increase in total employment has been only of an informal kind (NCEUS, 2007, 4).

REFERENCES

Bagchi A.K. 1988. Problems of effective demand and contradictions of planning in India, in A.K. Bagchi (ed.) *Economy, Society and Polity*, New Delhi, Oxford University Press.

Bangasser, P.E. (2000). "The ILO and Informal Sector: An Institutional History", *Employment Paper, 2000/9, ILO, Geneva (www.ilo.org, Informal Economy Resource Database).*

Bardhan, P. 1998. *The Political Economy of Development in India*, New Delhi, Oxford University Press.

Bhaduri, A. 1986. *Macroeconomics: The Dynamics of Commodity Production*, India, Macmillan.

Bhaduri, A. and Skarstein, R. 2003. Effective demand and the terms of trade in a dual economy: A Kaldorian perspective, *Cambridge Journal of Economics*, Vol. 27, No. 4, 583-95.

Bhalla, G.S. and Chadha, G.K. 1983. *Green Revolution and the Small Peasant: A Study of Income Distribution among Punjabi Cultivators*, New Delhi, Concept Publishing.

Bhattacharya, S. 2010. *Non/Capital, Class, and Development: The Case of Informal Manufacturing in India*. Unpublished Ph.D. Thesis, USA: University of Notre Dame.

Bose, A. 1989. "Short period equilibrium in a less developed economy." Rakshit, M. (ed.) *Studies in the Macroeconomics of Developing Countries*. India: Oxford University Press.

Chakrabarti, S. 2001. "Agriculture-Industry relation: aggregate demand, supply constraint and the concept of 'domestic exports'". Acharyya, R. and B. Moitra (ed.) *Effects of Globalization on Industry and Environment*. New Delhi: Lancer's Books.

Chakrabarti, S. 2003. Agriculture-industry linkage: The problems of effective demand and supply constraint, *Review of Development and Change*, Vol. 8, No. 2, 145-170.

Chakrabarti, S. 2005. "The informal sector and the question of development: role of agriculture and the government". Karanth, G.K. (ed.) *Social and Economic Change Monograph, No. 8*. India: Institute for Social and Economic Change.

Chakrabarti, S. 2006. *Agriculture-Industry Relation, the Problems of Effective Demand and Supply Constraint: Towards A Theoretical Framework*. Unpublished Ph.D. Thesis, India: University of Calcutta.

Chakrabarti, S. 2009. Contradictions of 'doing development': A structuralist framework, *American Review of Political Economy*, Vol. 7, No. 1 & 2, June/December 1-36.

Chakrabarti, S. 2011. A macroeconomic structure of employment: rural-urban conflict in a Kaleckian framework, *Review of Radical Political Economics*, Vol. 43, No. 2. DOI: 10.1177/0486613410391404.

Chakrabarti, S. 2013. Interrogating inclusive growth, *Cambridge Journal of Economics*, Vol. 37, No. 6, 1349-1379.

Chakrabarti, S. 2014. Formal-informal dichotomy: revisiting the debate on agricutlure-industry linkage, *The Economic and Labour Relation Review*, Vol. 25, No. 1, 157-178.

Chakrabarti, S. and Kundu, A. 2009a. Rural non-farm economy: A note on the impact of crop diversification and land-conversion in India, *Economic and Political Weekly*, Vol. XLIV, No. 12, 69-75.

Chakrabarti, S. and Kundu, A. 2009b. Formal-Informal sectors' conflict: a structuralist framework for India, *Journal of Economic Development*, Vol. 34, No. 2, December, 27-67.

Chakrabarti, S.; Kundu, A.; and Nandi, A.K. 2011. Farm-Non-farm linkage in India: A structuralist perspective, *Indian Journal of Agricultural Economics*, Vol. 66, No. 2.

Chakravarty, S. 1994. On the question of home market and prospects for Indian growth, in D. Nayyar (ed) *Industrial Growth and Stagnation: The Debate in India*, India, Oxford University Press.

CMIE 2006. *EIS: Time-Series Database*, India: Centre For Monitoring Indian Economy.

Davis, M. 2004. Planet of slums: Urban involution and the informal proletariat, *New Left Review*, Vol. 26, No. March-April, 5-34.

Dev, S.M. and Rao, N.C. 2005. Food processing and contract farming in Andhra Pradesh: A small farmer perspective, *Economic and Political Weekly*, Vol. 40, No. 26, 2705-12.

Dunham, D. 1991. Agricultural growth and rural sector: Some reflections on the rural growth linkages debate, *Working Paper No. 114*, The Hague, Institute of Social Studies.

Haggblade, S., Hazell, P. and Brown, J. 1989. Farm-Non-farm linkages in rural Sub-Saharan Africa, *World Development*, Vol. 17, No. 8, 1173-1201.

Harris, J. and Todaro, M.P. 1970. Migration, unemployment and development: A two-sector analysis, *American Economic Review*, Vol. 60, No. 1, March, 126-42.

Harriss, J. 1991. Agriculture/non-agriculture linkages and the diversification of rural economic activity', in J. Breman and S. Mundle (eds) *Rural Transformation in Asia*, India, Oxford University Press.

Hazell, P. and Haggblade, S. 1990. Rural-urban growth linkages in India, *PR Working Paper No. 430*, World Bank.

Hazell, P. and Roell, A. 1983. Rural growth linkages: Household expenditure patterns in Malaysia and Nigeria. *Research Report, No. 41*, Washington DC, IFPRI.

Hymer, S. and Resnick, S. 1969. A model of an agrarian economy with non-agricultural activities, *American Economic Review*, Vol. 59, No. 4, 493-506.

Joshi, P.K.; Gulati, A.; Birthal, P.S. and Tewari, L. 2004. Agriculture diversification in South Asia: Patterns, determinants and policy implication, *Economic and Political Weekly*, Vol. 39, No. 24, 2457-2468.

Kaldor, N. 1976. Inflation and recession in the world economy, *Economic Journal*, Vol. 86, No. 344 December, 703-14.

Kaldor, N. 1996. The problem of intersectoral balance, in *Causes of Growth and Stagnation in the World Economy* (Mattioli Lectures, 1984), pp. 39-54, Cambridge, Cambridge University Press.

Kalecki, M. 1934. On foreign trade and 'domestic exports', in *Selected Essays on the Dynamics of the Capitalist Economy*, Cambridge, Cambridge University Press (1971).

Kalecki, M. 1954. The problem of financing economic development, in J. Osiatynski (ed) *Collected Works of Michal Kalecki*, Vol. 5, pp. 45-60, Oxford, Clarendon Press (1993).

Kumar, P. 2006. Contract farming through agribusiness firms and state corporation: A case study in Punjab, *Economic and Political Weekly*, Vol. 41, No. 52, 5367-75.

Kundu, A. and Chakrabarti, S. 2010. "Non-agricultural informal sector in India: Impacts of agrarian conditions", *Indian Journal of Labour Economics*, April-June, 53 (2).

Lanjouw, J.O. and Lanjouw, P. 2001. The rural non-farm sector: Issues and evidence from developing countries, *Agricultural Economics*, Vol. 26, No. 1, 1-23.

Lenin, V.I. 1899. "The Development of Capitalism in Russia", in *Collected Works*, Vol. 3, Moscow, Progress Publishers (1977).

Lewis, W.A. 1954. Economic development with unlimited supplies of labour, *Manchester School of Economic and Social Studies Journal*, May.

Marx, K. 1951. *Theories of Surplus Value*, K. Kautsky (ed.) and G.A. Bonner and E. Burns translated, London, Lawrence and Wishart.

Marx, K. 1958. *Capital*, Vol. I, Moscow, Foreign Languages Publishing House.

Mellor, J.W. 1976. *The New Economics of Growth – A Strategy for India and Developing World*; New York, Cornell University Press.

Mitra, A. 1977. *Terms of Trade and Class Relations*, London, Frank Cass.

Mukherjee, A. 2007. Bharatio krishir charitrayan (Characterization of Indian agriculture), in A. Mukherjee, R. Khasnobis and P. Sinharoy (eds) *Arthaniti, Samaj O Sanskriti*, Kolkata, People's Book Society.

Mukherjee, A. and Chakrabarti, S. 2009. "A Study on Transformation of Indian Agriculture in the Post Doha Scenario and its Macro Economic Impact", *Project Report submitted to SANEI.*

Mundle, S. 1977. Home market capitalism in agriculture and drain of agricultural surplus, *Economic and Political Weekly*, June, A49-A54.

NCEUS. 2007. *Report on Conditions of Work and Promotion of Livelihoods in the Unorganised Sector*, National Commission for Enterprises in the Unorganised Sector, Government of India, www.nceuis.nic.in.

NSSO: National Sample Survey Organization, Government of India, NSS 62nd Round: (Unorganised) Manufacturing Enterprise (2005-2006) Unit Level (Schedule 2.2).

NSSO: National Sample Survey Organization, Government of India, Reports: 424, 459, 474, 495, 497 and 512. http://mospi.nic.in/mospi_nsso_rept_pubn.htm.

Preobrazhensky, E. 1926. *The New Economics*, Oxford, Clarendon Press.

Raj, K.N. 1994. Growth and stagnation in Indian industrial development, in D. Nayyar (ed.) *Industrial Growth and Stagnation: The Debate in India*, India, Oxford University Press.

Rakshit, M. 1982. *The Labour Surplus Economy*, India, McMillan.

Ranis, G. and Fei, J. 1961. A theory of economic development, *American Economic Review*, Vol. 51, No. 4, 533-65.

Ranis, G. and Stewart, F. 1993. Rural non-agricultural activities in development: Theory and application, *Journal of Development Economics*, Vol. 40, No. 1, 75-101.

Ranis, G. and Stewart, F. 1994. V-goods and the role of the urban informal sector in development, *Centre Discussion Paper No. 724*, Economic Growth Centre, Yale University.

Rao, J. Mohan, and Storm, S. 1998. Distribution and growth in Indian agriculture, in T.J. Byres (ed.) *The Indian Economy: Major Debates since Independence*, India, Oxford University Press.

Rao, P.P.; Birthal, P.S.; and Joshi, P.K. 2006. Diversification towards high value agriculture: Role of urbanisation and infrastructure, *Economic and Political Weekly*, Vol. 41, No. 26, 2747-53.

Ricardo, D. 1815. An essay on the influence of low price of corn on the profits of stocks; in P. Sraffa (ed.) *Works and Correspondence of David Ricardo*, Vol. 1, UK, Cambridge University Press.

Saith, A. 1991. "Asian Rural Industrialization: Context, Features and Strategies", in: J. Breman and S. Mundle (eds). "Rural Transformation" *In Asia*, India: Oxford University Press.

Saith, A. 1992. *The Rural Non-Farm Economy: Processes and Policies*, Geneva, ILO.

Saith, A. 1993. *Chinese Rural Industrialisation: Some Lessons for Reforming and Developing Economies*, New Delhi, ILO-ARTEP.

Sanyal, K. 2007. *Rethinking Capitalist Development: Primitive Accumulation, Governmentality and Post Colonial Capitalism*, New Delhi, Routledge.

Sanyal, K and Bhattacharyya, R. 2009. Beyond the factory: Globalisation, informalisation of production and the new locations of labour, *Economic and Political Weekly*, Vol. 44, No. 22, pp. 35-44.

Sen, S. and Raju, S. 2006. Globalisation and expanding markets for cut-flower: who benefits?, *Economic and Political Weekly*, Vol. 41, No. 26, 2725-31.

Sidhu, M.S. 2005. Fruits and vegetables processing sector in India: An appraisal of the post-reform period, *Economic and Political Weekly*, Vol. 40, No. 28, 3056-61.

Singh, S. 2004. Crisis and diversification in Punjab agriculture: Role of state and agribusiness, *Economic and Political Weekly*, Vol. 39, No. 52, 5583-9.

Taylor, L. 1983. *Structuralist Macroeconomics*. New York: Basic Books.

Thirlwall, A.P. 1986. A general model of growth and development along Kaldorian lines, *Oxford Economic Papers*, Vol. 38, 199-219.

UN-Habitat. 2003. *The Challenge of Slums: Global Report on Human Settlements 2003*, United Nations Human Settlements Programme, London and Sterling, Earthscan Publications Ltd.

WBHDR. 2004. *West Bengal Human Development Report*, India, Development and Planning Department, Government of West Bengal.

White, B. and Dasgupta, A. 2010. Agrofuels capitalism: A view from political economy, *Journal of Peasant Studies*, Vol. 37, No. 4, pp. 593-607.

World Bank. 2005. *India–Re-energizing the Agricultural Sector*, India, Oxford University Press.

World Bank. 2007. *Agriculture for Development*, World Development Report 2008, Washington, DC.

3
Reaffirming Universal Food Provisioning

The Functioning of the PDS in Tamil Nadu (2005-2010)

*Anita K. Dixit**

1. Introduction

The issue of food security is a highly relevant one in the current economic context in India. Especially in the background of rising levels of calorific undernourishment in the face of declining levels of income (or expenditure) based poverty (highlighted in Nayyar 1991, Viswanathan and Meenakshi 2003, Patnaik 2007), it is important to understand the various means by which an adequate supply of food can be made available to poor households and those vulnerable to poverty. In this context, a study of public provisioning of food becomes highly relevant.

While the earlier Universal Public Distribution System (UPDS) of foodgrains served the essential purpose of ensuring food

* Anita K. Dixit (anidixit@gmail.com) is based in Kolkata, with the Azim Premji Foundation. The views expressed in this chapter are entirely those of the author and not of the organisation.
I thank Prof. Madhura Swaminathan for guidance and suggestions, and the Faculty of the Sociological Research Unit, Indian Statistical Institute for useful comments on an initial draft of this article. I also thank the officials of the Tamil Nadu Food and Civil Supplies Corporation for their cooperation and help in providing the data used in this article. The work for this article was done during my tenure with ISI Kolkata as a Visiting Scientist.

security to the needy population, the added burden to the State exchequer, and also the perceived 'inefficiency' of the system, came in for a lot of criticism. However, the new Targeted Public Distribution System (TPDS) instituted in 1997 in response to these criticisms has also been criticized, chiefly on the grounds that in its attempt to target the poor, it has actually excluded a large proportion of poor households.

At this crucial juncture in the controversy surrounding the PDS, this chapter aims to assess the universal public distribution system (UPDS), to throw some light on whether indeed it is inefficient and a burden on the exchequer, or whether the gains in terms of universal coverage outweigh the monetary costs. Today, all the States of the country barring Tamil Nadu and Chhattisgarh have adopted the TPDS instead of the earlier UPDS. This chapter studies the PDS in Tamil Nadu, and aims to answer the following questions:

(1) Does the UPDS answer the requirements for subsidized food?
(2) Does it answer the issues of equity in distribution?
(3) What is the real burden on the exchequer?
(4) How does it perform in terms of 'efficiency'?

The rest of this chapter is organized as follows. Section 2 deals with the controversies surrounding the PDS in India. The following section discusses the State of Tamil Nadu in terms of its demographics and poverty characteristics, and gives an overview of the PDS in the State. Section 4 analyses the functioning of the UPDS in Tamil Nadu during the period 2005 to 2010. Section 5 concludes and makes some policy recommendations.

2. The Public Distribution System in India—Functioning and Controversies

Public provisioning of foodgrain, first introduced in India by the British Government as a wartime measure, was accepted by the Government of India as a permanent and universal scheme in the 1960s. In the late 1980s and the early 1990s, after more than two decades of functioning of the PDS, there was increasing opposition to the universal system. The critique centred on the burden on the exchequer created in the process of procurement, storage and distribution, and on the lack of effectiveness of the Food Corporation of India and the Commission for Agricultural Costs and Prices.

Bhalla (1993) argued that the costs of maintaining buffer stocks were much higher than originally estimated, and that declining foodgrain prices in the international market meant that it would be less costly to depend to some extent on imports, rather than to maintain large buffer stocks. Similarly, Gulati *et al.* (1996) maintained that the FCI was inefficient and depended on government subsidies, due to the excessive costs of operation, which have been higher than those incurred by private traders. The argument of Radhakrishna and Subbarao (1997) was that the situation of agriculture had changed drastically from the scarcity ridden one of the 1960s during which the PDS was established. In the new, dynamic, agricultural scenario, public provisioning of foodgrain at heavily subsidized rates was neither efficient nor feasible. Thus there was pressure to target the scheme to the needy population alone, and in response, the government introduced the Targeted PDS (TPDS) in 1997.

However, the criticisms of the UPDS narrated above have also been contested. The 'high costs' of the FCI consist mainly of increases in statutory charges and procurement prices of foodgrains, which have really to do with external political decisions and can, therefore, not be attributed to the inefficiency of the FCI, as Swaminathan (1999) argues. Moreover, the highest estimate of the food subsidy is still not so high that the country's fiscal problems would be solved if it was eliminated. Additionally, both Swaminathan (*ibid.*) and Jha and Srinivasan (2001) argue that it is not appropriate to compare efficiency of the FCI and private traders merely through the difference between consumer and producer prices. Private traders and the FCI work with different objectives, and the PDS under the FCI has a number of 'indirect benefits' such as that of stabilizing prices, proved by the greater stability of domestic compared to international foodgrain prices, and of domestic prices as compared to domestic production (Pal, *et al.*, 1993; Nayyar and Sen, 1994).

Thus, the claims of inefficiency and unsustainably high subsidy costs of the original UPDS are far from being unquestionably proved. Moreover, the experience of the TPDS since 1997 has raised wide criticism regarding its coverage of the poor. The TPDS is based on the definition of poor—the so-called below poverty line (BPL) households. It is extremely difficult to identify the poor in terms of incomes, which are difficult to calculate in the agricultural and informal sectors. This was one of the reasons for inclusion of non-income criteria in BPL identification, which moreover have been changed over the different rounds of BPL surveys. These measures have come under heavy criticism for their arbitrariness (see Hirway, 2003; Sundaram, K. 2003; Shah and Yagnik, 2007). This becomes especially difficult since there is a lot of vertical movement in and out of poverty (Krishna *et al.*, 2003). A policy for food security must consider not only the chronically hungry but also those who are vulnerable to food poverty, and the only possible way to ensure this is through a universal PDS.

Swaminathan and Misra (2001) point out that TPDS runs a higher risk of 'exclusion errors' whereby the deserving poor are excluded from its purview, and this has social (welfare) consequences which outweights the costs (subsidy burden) of inclusion of undeserving households under the UPDS. A recent evaluation of the PDS by the Planning Commission (GoI 2005, hereafter referred to as the Evaluation Report) in fact recognizes the problems of targeting. The Evaluation Report states that only about 57 per cent of the BPL households are covered by the TPDS. There are large errors of both exclusion and inclusion.

Apart from the above, a more basic argument is provided by Swaminathan (2000), who challenges the entire rationale of targeting in the context of India. The United States has calculated poverty for its food stamps programme on the basis that about a third of the total expenditure of the poor was on food and, therefore, the poverty line should be thrice the food expenditure. In the case of India, even if a food share of 60 per cent of expenditure is assumed, it would put 80 per cent of the rural and 60 per cent of the urban population below the poverty line. With such high proportions of food insecure population, targeting makes little sense.

3. An Overview of the PDS in Tamil Nadu

With a per capita income about 20 per cent higher than the all India figure (2008-09), and poverty levels lower than the all-India levels, Tamil Nadu is one of the better performers among the Indian States[1].

The PDS in the State has been functioning on the basis of the understanding that 'poverty (is)... a dynamic and relative concept (and)... accurate estimation is not possible in the absence of acceptable criteria and methodology. The process of identifying BPL families is also fraught with errors and bias resulting in high levels of exclusion of deserving families. Further due to unforeseen natural calamities like droughts, floods and disaster, etc., a large number of vulnerable APL families may be forced into poverty trap again (*sic*)' (GoTN, 2010). This is the basis on which the State rejected the implementation of TPDS and decided to take upon itself the responsibility of providing subsidized foodgrain to the entire population. It is noteworthy that this logic is in line with the arguments of Krishna *et al.*, (*ibid.*), and of Hirway (*ibid.*) and others.

The GoTN has various sub-strata within the PDS, creating an entire set of PDS cards depending on the goods purchased. Most households are holders of the green rice PDS cards (an allotment of 12-20 kg. of rice depending on household size)[2]. Sugar (white) PDS card holders are allowed to get an additional 3 kg. of sugar per household (apart from the regular allotment ceiling of 2 kg.) in lieu of rice. Police personnel are issued special khaki cards with essential commodities sold at 50 per cent of PDS price. Within the universal scheme, GoTN follows limited targeting – the poorest among the poor (as identified by local bodies) are assigned AAY cards, whereby they get a higher allotment of rice – 35 kg. per household.

Since the Central Government provides subsidized foodgrain from the FCI godowns only to the extent of the BPL estimation, the rest of the purchase is made from open market sources and subsidized by the State government. In case of rice, GoI provides rice at three differential prices—the AAY price of Rs. 3, the BPL price of Rs. 5.65 and the APL price of Rs. 8.30 per kg. The GoTN provides rice at Rs. 1/kg. across the board, requiring a per kg. subsidy of Rs. 2 for AAY, Rs. 4.65 for BPL and Rs. 7.30 APL allocation. Moreover, the GoTN also procures rice from the open market (through the Central Government Open Market Sales Scheme OMSS and from the Government of Andhra Pradesh) to the extent of the shortfall, and again the difference between the open market rate and the price charged at the FPS level is borne by the GoTN as subsidy cost. Similarly, GoI provides wheat through the FCI at APL rates, with some *ad hoc* additional provision at economic cost. The GoTN provides wheat to the consumers at Rs. 7.50/kg., sugar at Rs. 13.50, kerosene at Rs. 8.40 to Rs. 9 and small amounts of other items (fortified wheat flour, various pulses, etc.) also at subsidized rates. The difference is provided as subsidy by the GoTN.

4. Functioning of the PDS during 2006-2010

Tamil Nadu PDS Compared to India

The GoTN had made it a policy not to implement targeting in the PDS. Accordingly, the percentage of population covered by the PDS is higher in Tamil Nadu compared to the all-India level. According to NSS data, 89 per cent of rural and 78 per cent urban households in the State had ration cards in 2004-05. At the all-India level, these figures stood at 81 per cent and 67 per cent respectively.

Table 3.1: State-wise Percentage ... Cereal-Consuming Households Purchasing Specific Cereals from PDS

States	*Households consuming rice*				*Households consuming wheat*			
	Rural	*Ranking*	*Urban*	*Ranking*	*Rural*	*Ranking*	*Urban*	*Ranking*
Andhra Pradesh	64.79	2	33.09	2	2.22	13	1.25	15
Assam	9.00	11	2.47	12	0.36	16	0.38	17
Bihar	1.00	14	0.71	14	1.77	14	1.55	13
Chhattisgarh	21.92	9	13.61	5	17.10	7	7.11	7
Gujarat	33.51	5	7.66	7	34.58	2	7.47	6
Haryana	0.12	16	0.00	17	4.04	12	5.31	8
Jharkhand	4.44	13	3.04	11	6.06	10	2.25	11
Karnataka	59.69	3	23.08	4	61.62	1	18.02	1
Kerala	35.31	4	25.05	3	20.33	6	16.81	3
Madhya Pradesh	22.38	7	9.35	6	21.60	5	10.51	4
Maharashtra	29.57	6	6.45	8	30.00	4	7.58	5
Orissa	21.94	8	6.24	9	0.56	15	1.47	14
Punjab	0.14	15	0.12	16	0.30	17	0.63	16
Rajasthan	0.00	17	0.29	15	14.60	9	2.00	12
Tamil Nadu	81.34	1	51.29	1	30.69	3	17.54	2
Uttar Pradesh	6.04	12	2.19	13	5.66	11	2.65	10
West Bengal	12.93	10	5.74	10	14.75	8	4.27	9
All-India	26.52		14.24	—	15.28	—	6.99	—

Source: ... Report No. 510: Public Distribution System and Other Sources of ...hold Consumption, 2004-05 Volume I (compiled from Table 12, ...

It is also undoubted that the PDS is a larger source of consumption in Tamil Nadu than it is at the all India level. For example, about 81 per cent of the rice-consuming rural households in the State purchased rice from the PDS; at the urban level it was 51 per cent. At the all-India level, however, only 27 per cent of the rice-consuming population purchased it from the PDS in the rural sector, and the corresponding figure for the urban sector was 14 per cent. While the proportion of households purchasing wheat from the PDS is somewhat lower, Tamil Nadu still ranks very high among the States in dependence on PDS for purchase of wheat.

Table 3.2: Proportion of Rice and Wheat purchased from PDS and Other Sources of Tamil Nadu and all-India

(kg. per household per month for 2004-05)

Rural cardholder households	*Tamil Nadu*				*India*			
	PDS	*Other sources*	*Total*	*PDS as % of total*	*PDS*	*Other sources*	*Total*	*PDS as % of total*
Rice	19.8	18.5	38.3	51.8	9.5	25.2	34.8	27.4
Wheat	0.3	0.2	[illegible]	[illegible]	[illegible]	[illegible]	[illegible]	[illegible]
	20.1	18.6	38.7	51.9	13.5	35.4	48.9	27.6
All Rural households	*Tamil Nadu*				*India*			
	PDS	*Other sources*	*Total*	*PDS as % of total*	*PDS*	*Other sources*	*Total*	*PDS as % of total*
Rice	15.4	22.8	38.2	40.4	4.1	27.0	31.1	13.2
Wheat	0.3	0.4	0.7	40.2	1.5	19.0	20.5	7.3
Total cereals	15.7	23.2	38.9	40.4	5.6	46.0	51.6	10.8
Urban Cardholder households	*Tamil Nadu*				*India*			
	PDS	*Other sources*	*Total*	*PDS as % of total*	*PDS*	*Other sources*	*Total*	*PDS as % of total*
Rice	18.0	18.8	36.8	48.9	10.7	19.8	30.5	35.0
Wheat	0.7	0.7	1.5	51.2	4.3	11.0	15.3	28.1
Total cereals	18.7	19.5	38.2	49.0	15.0	30.9	45.8	32.7
All Urban households	*Tamil Nadu*				*India*			
	PDS	*Other sources*	*Total*	*PDS as % of total*	*PDS*	*Other sources*	*Total*	*PDS as % of total*
Rice	8.8	22.5	31.3	28.0	2.3	18.2	20.6	11.2
Wheat	0.4	1.3	1.8	23.4	0.7	18.3	19.0	3.8

Source: NSS Report No. 510: Public Distribution System and Other Sources of Household Consumption, 2004-05 (compiled from Tables 1-R and 1-U)

The details of these differential purchases are set down in Table 3.1, where it becomes obvious that households in Tamil Nadu make the maximum use (among all the States) of the PDS for purchase of major cereals. Table 3.2 analyses the difference at the Tamil Nadu and all-India levels in the *proportion* of cereals purchased through the PDS and other sources (as against the proportion of households reported in Table 3.1). Here too, the dependence of Tamil Nadu households is seen to be greater than that at the all-India level, both in the rural and urban sectors, and even when non-cardholder households are also included.

This data from 2004-05 is corroborated in Venkatasubramanian (2006). The author has used NSS data from 1999-00 which indicate the same trend for the State, and quoted several studies to indicate that these positive trends have been present in the State even earlier. According to the author, the political commitment of Tamil Nadu governments towards the PDS emerged from food shortages resulting in the electoral defeat of the Congress in 1967. Since 1967, therefore, successive governments have considered the provision of subsidized food as a non-negotiable priority. This is also why Tamil Nadu did not adopt targeting when the TPDS was introduced at the Central level in 1997.

Our analysis of the period 2005-2010 also supports the above trends. Rice is the staple food of the State, and the single largest foodgrain allocation in the Tamil Nadu PDS, while other cereals have a minor share in the total PDS distribution. We have, therefore, studied the allotment and offtake of rice as indicative of the entire State foodgrain distribution system. As noted above, rice subsidy was increased and the Tamil Nadu government adopted a universal price of Rs. 2/kg. for rice in 2006 (which was further reduced to Re. 1/kg. in 2008). The allotment of rice per household was also increased—households covered under the AAY were allotted 35 kgs per month, while all other households qualified for 12-20 kg. per month, depending on household size.

Between 2005 and 2006, i.e., in the first year of the DMK government, total allotment of rice to non-AAY (Rice Card) holders increased by 12 per cent. During the five years period thereafter, total allotment remained stable (growth was only 3 per cent over 2006-2010). However, the response was not immediate. In the first year of the programme, offtake of rice by non-AAY (Rice Card) households increased less than proportionately, i.e., by only 2.72

per cent. Between 2005 and 2010, the percentage point increase in allotment and offtake in the universal scheme (Rice Cards) were similar, around 15-16 per cent.

On the other hand, allotment to AAY card holders increased by a hefty 31.6 per cent between 2005 and 2006, and remained steady thereafter, with a total growth of 3.4 per cent over the next five years. In a single year between 2005 and 2006, AAY households responded to the reduction in price with an increase in offtake of 31.4 per cent. Price reduction from Rs. 3.50 to Rs. 2 (in 2006), as well as the increase in allotment per household from 20 kg. to 35 kg., had an immediate impact on AAY households. During the five years period following, AAY offtake again increased by 13 per cent. Therefore, over the period 2005-2010, AAY offtake increased by more than 44 per cent as against a 35 per cent increase in total allotment to AAY cardholders. The maximum increase was between 2008 and 2009. It is to be noted that 2008 was the year when the price of rice was further reduced from Rs. 2 to Re. 1 per kg. However, there was no increase in the amount of allotment per AAY card. The entire increase in total allotment at this point was, therefore, attributable to the price reduction. Over the entire period, AAY offtake as a percentage of allotment increased from 83 per cent—already one of the highest among the States—to as much as 90 per cent.

It is, therefore, quite clear that the 'limited targeting' undertaken by the Tamil Nadu government for the poorest among the poor has achieved massive success through food subsidization. More importantly, however, the universal programme, covering the rest of the population of the State, has also been successful, as proved by the increased demand for non-AAY rice in proportion to the increased allotment. Offtake of rice by Rice Card holders remains as high as 81 per cent of allotment. Another indicator of the importance of PDS for non-AAY households is the proportion of Rice Cards. The GoTN gives households the option to register for a 'None Card'—that is to say, a card that merely acts as an identity document and does not provide any items. This scheme has introduced an element of 'self-targeting' in the system—a household which does not wish to purchase from the PDS outlet can opt out of the subsidy system. Households can also purchase extra sugar in lieu of rice—through the 'Sugar Card'. However, the 'Rice PDS Cards' form the largest proportion of cards in the

State. The fact that a miniscule 0.31-0.35 per cent households opt for the 'None Cards', and that the proportion of 'Sugar Cards' has actually declined from 6 per cent to 5 per cent—indicates the importance of subsidized rice—staple foodgrain—for the rest of the (non-AAY) population in the State. A targeted scheme would have overlooked this demand, focusing instead on the demand of an arbitrarily decided 'BPL' population.

Table 3.3: Allotment and Offtake of Rice under AAY and Rice Cards (metric tonnes)

Period	*Rice Cards*		*AAY Card*	
	Allotment	*Offtake*	*Allotment*	*Offtake*
2005	3291532	2655178	578776	482717
2006	3690908	2718714	755670	616425
2010	3801157	3088521	780975	699061
Growth 2005-2006 (%)	12.5	2.72	31.59	31.41
Growth 2006-2010 (%)	2.99	13.6	3.35	13.4

Source: Compiled from data provided by TNCSC.

Intra-State Distribution

The discussion so far has focused on the PDS in the State as a whole. We now come to the issue of intra-State distribution. Table 3.4 lists the original (in 2005) 30 districts classified and ordered according to HDI[3]. Chelliah and Shanmugam (http://www.mse.ac.in/pub/wp_shanmugam.pdf) have worked out their own set of HDIs for the districts[4], and find that HDI in the districts is related to, among other variables, GDDP per capita and the share of the non-primary sector in district income. In other words, the Chelliah and Shanmugam study indicates that human development levels in the state depend on the growth of secondary and tertiary sectors. Indeed, the map indicates this since Chennai and Coimbatore, districts with high levels of industrialization and urbanisation, have high HDI rankings. Moreover, the authors also find a strong correlation between per capita income and rice productivity. It could, therefore, be inferred, in line with general economic understanding, that districts with low agricultural productivity (in the case of Tamil Nadu, productivity of rice) and low levels of non-agricultural output are likely to have low per

Table 3.4: Classification of Districts by HDI

Sl. No	Districts	HDI	HDI Rank	Sl. No	Districts	HDI	HDI Rank
1.	Chennai	0.842	1	16.	Trichy	0.732	13
2.	Kancheepuram	0.778	3	17.	Thanjavur	0.714	19
3.	Thiruvallur	0.767	5	18.	Thiruvarur	0.719	16
4.	Vellore	0.71	20	19.	Nagapattinam	0.738	10
5.	Thiruvannamalai	0.678	27	20.	Pudukkotai	0.705	22
6.	Villupuram	0.667	28	21.	Dindigal	0.705	23
7.	Cuddalore	0.709	21	22.	Theni	0.726	14
8.	Dharmapuri	0.656	30	23.	Madurai	0.759	7
9.	Salem	0.717	17	24.	Sivaganga	0.701	25
10.	Namakkal	0.715	18	25.	Virudhunagar	0.737	11
11.	Erode	0.721	15	26.	Ramnad	0.703	24
12.	Coimbatore	0.775	4	27.	Toothukudi	0.791	2
13.	Nilgiri	0.745	8	28.	Tirunelveli	0.74	9
14.	Karur	0.737	12	29.	Kanyakumari	0.763	6
15.	Perambalur	0.697	26	30.	Krishnagiri	0.665	29

Source: Eleventh Five Year Plan Document Tamil Nadu (available at http://www.tn.gov.in/spc/english/default.htm), Chapter 1, Table 1.2.2.

capita incomes (and, therefore, high poverty levels), which also translate into low levels of HDI. HDI ranking and poverty are, therefore, found to be related in the State.

Within the State, in order to be truly redistributive, the focus of the PDS should be on poorer districts (with a lower HDI ranking). A higher share of AAY cards in those districts with a lower HDI ranking would indicate effectiveness of the PDS. Moreover, districts with lower HDI status would benefit from a larger allocation of foodgrain. To test the relationship between HDI status and the PDS, a set of correlations were worked out, presented in Table 3.5. We have used the HDI ranking (not the absolute HDI value) and, therefore, the Spearman's rank correlation coefficient was used.

The results indicate that growth in AAY cards between 2005 and 2006, when the new scheme started, was inversely related to HDI ranking, and statistically significant at 1 per cent. While the inverse relation continues into the period 2006-2010, it is no longer statistically significant. In terms of absolute numbers, AAY cards in the State increased from somewhat fewer than 15 lakhs to more

Table 3.5: Correlation between District HDI Rank and Number of Cards, Allocation and Offtake of Rice

	Growth in No. of Rice Cards		*Growth in No. of AAY Cards*	
	2005-2006	*2006-2010*	*2005-2006*	*2006-2010*
HDI Rank	– 0.537**	0.063	0.523**	0.188
	Growth for Rice Cardholders (2005-2010)		*Growth for AAY Cardholders (2005-10)*	
	Allotment	*Offtake*	*Allotment*	*Offtake*
	–0.305	–0.252	0.537**	0.576**

** Statistically significant at 0.01 level (2-tailed)
Source: Compiled from data provided by TNCSC.

than 18 lakhs in the single year 2005-06, raising the share of AAY cards from 7.21 per cent of all cards to 8.92 per cent. The data thus indicates the policy focus on reaching the most needy, with growth in AAY cards being correlated to the HDI status of the district.

The trend in ordinary Rice Cards reflects the converse of this situation—between 2005 and 2006, the growth in Rice Cards was *directly related* to HDI status. But actual numbers show that this growth was *negative,* i.e., between 2005 and 2006, there was a small *decline* in the number of Rice Cards. Clearly, some Rice Cards were replaced by AAY cards. The focus of the AAY has definitely been in the poorer districts, with ordinary Rice Cards being concentrated in the better-off districts. This is as expected, and indicates a redistribution process that is under way *within the PDS.*

Changes in allotment and offtake between districts over the period 2005-2010 also indicate positive redistribution. HDI rank is inversely (though not significantly) related with growth in allocation and offtake under the AAY scheme during the period 2006-10. Districts with a higher HDI rank register lower allotment as well as offtake on AAY cards, as expected. Taking the entire period 2005-10, moreover, the relation becomes highly significant (at 1%). The converse situation holds for Rice Cards: a positive (but not significant) relation between HDI rank and growth in rice allocation as well as offtake. Lower allocation as well as offtake is indicated on Rice Cards in the poorer districts, because there is higher allocation (and offtake) on AAY cards.

Subsidisation of the PDS

One of the most important critiques of the universal PDS, and an important reason for its withdrawal in most of the States, is the cost to the exchequer. In discussing the positives and negatives of subsidization, there has been much debate on the components of the subsidy. We have earlier referred to the work of Swaminathan (1999) in which the 'high costs' of the PDS were discovered to be mainly attributable to statutory charges and procurement prices of foodgrain. In the following discussion, however, we have taken the 'cost' of the PDS as defined in the State government budget, without venturing into the details of its components.

Table 3.6 gives a few details of the estimated expenditure on the public distribution system. We have taken into account the expenditure listed under the subhead 'Civil Supplies' under the 'General Economic Services' head of the current or revenue expenditure. Over the period 2005-06 to 2010-11, the size of the budget (total disbursements on the Revenue Account) has increased from about Rs. 32,000 crore to Rs, 75,000 crore. As a proportion of the budget, the size of food subsidy has increased from 3.75 per cent to 5.3 per cent over six years.

While total expenditure on the PDS, so defined, has increased from Rs. 1,200 crore in 2005-06 to Rs. 2,700 crore in 2008-09, and further to Rs. 4,005 crore in 2010-11, the increase in real terms has been from Rs. 1,141 crore in 2005-06 to Rs. 2,406 crore in 2008-09. Expenditure per household (per family card) has also increased from Rs. 550.4 in 2005-06 to Rs. 1083.1 in real terms, i.e., it nearly doubled in four years. The major increase, however, was in 2006, when expenditure per card rose from Rs. 550.4 to Rs. 839.6. As we have seen earlier, this was the year in which the new PDS scheme was initiated, and unit price of items was reduced, along with increase in magnitude of distribution per household (we have taken the example of rice, which forms the major proportion of PDS distribution). Clearly, the increase in per household subsidy in that single year reflects these changes.

As with other State governments, the size of the food subsidy has also been a cause of concern for the Tamil Nadu government. As Table 3.6 indicates, food subsidy is substantial, and its proportion in the total budget is also increasing. However, when the per household figure of Rs. 1,083 is perceived in terms of per

Table 3.6: Some Estimates of Subsidy on the Tamil Nadu PDS

Year	Expenditure on PDS[1]	No. of Family Cards[3]	Expenditure/ Card[2]	Budget[3]	Expenditure as % of budget	Inflation (per cent)[4]	Expenditure (real terms)	Expenditure/ card (real terms)
2005-06	1200	20723920	579.0	32009	3.75	5.2	1141	550.4
2006-07	1950	20905036	932.8	38265	5.10	11.1	1755	839.6
2007-08	1950	21790067	894.9	42975	4.54	11.0	1757	806.2
2008-09	2700	22217853	1215.2	55403	4.87	12.2	2406	1083.1
2009-10	2800	21957141	1275.2	59375	4.72	—	—	—
2010-11	4005	21663662	1848.7	75543	5.30	—	—	—

1. Revised estimates of current account expenditure on 'Civil Supplies' under 'General Economic Services' head, measured in Rs. crore.
2. For respective calendar years, e.g., 2005-06 refers to calendar year 2005.
3. Measured as total disbursements on the Revenue Account.
4. Based on point-to-point Wholesale Price Index, for primary articles (base year 1970-71 = 100).

Source: Budget and PDS expenditure—Tamil Nadu Budget documents (various years); Family Cards – TNCSC documents; WPI values – GoTN Department of Evaluation and Applied Research, available at http://www.tn.gov.in/dear/3.Prices.pdf

capita expenditure, assuming a household size of five members, we get a figure of Rs. 216 per capita annually, or Rs. 18 per month. The annual figure translates to an outlay of Rs. 2.97 *per household* per day, or Re. 0.59 per capita per day. NSS data from the Consumption Expenditure Report of 2009-10 indicates that the average MPCE of the State was Rs. 1,160 for rural areas and Rs. 1,948 for the urban sector in 2009-10. In other words, the PDS is subsidizing each rural household to the extent of 1.5 per cent, or each urban household to the extent of 0.9 per cent of their MPCE.

Leakages

Apart from the cost of PDS in terms of subsidy, another issue raised is that of leakages from the system. This study has not analysed the magnitude of leakages, which we believe can only be roughly estimated from the available secondary data. However, various estimates of leakages are available. The Planning Commission Performance Evaluation Report on the Targeted PDS (GoI 2005) has found that Tamil Nadu is a State with an extremely low level of leakages and diversion. The Report has classified leakages into those occurring at the FPS level, and those occurring through the existence of ghost cards. Tamil Nadu is the only State which has an extremely low level of leakage at both these levels.

Himanshu and Sen (2011) emphasize the fact that universalization of the PDS in Tamil Nadu itself helps reduce leakages in the following two ways—the BPL list does not have to be followed, and the single price at a PDS shop (for both the BPL and APL clients) reduces the possibility of the shop owner charging discretionary rates. Moreover, Tamil Nadu has put into place several safeguards which minimize leakages in the system. At a country-wide level, the authors use inter-State data to argue that there is a negative correlation between percentage of households accessing PDS and the extent of leakages.

Other studies, such as that by Dreze and Khera (2011), on the basis of an individual survey, have also found Tamil Nadu to have the lowest level of leakage. While NSS data found that Tamil Nadu recorded only 7 per cent leakages, the Dreze and Khera study found that people received 90 per cent of their entitlements. The authors have noted a recent improvement in the functioning of the PDS across States. They conclude that making the PDS more broad-based gives people a greater stake in it and increases public pressure for its efficient functioning.

Conclusion

The Universal Public Distribution System has been subject to a number of criticisms at the all-India level, resulting in the initiation of a Targeted PDS since 1997. As narrated above, however, the TPDS is also prone to a number of problems and weaknesses. We have in this chapter attempted an evaluation of a functioning system of universal public distribution to assess its impacts and costs and thus address the controversies surrounding the issue of subsidized foodgrain provision.

We have found that the PDS remains a large source of foodgrain (cereal) consumption in Tamil Nadu, one of the only two States with a UPDS in place. Tamil Nadu ranks the highest of all major States in the proportion of households purchasing rice and wheat from the PDS. Moreover, the average (per household) purchases from the PDS are also much higher in Tamil Nadu than at the all India level. At the very least, this indicates the extent to which the Tamil Nadu population depends on the PDS for foodgrain and, therefore, shows a level of reliability of the system that goes against the myth of 'inefficiency' of the PDS.

The increased allocation of cereals in the scheme in 2006, along with a reduction in prices, has had a clear impact on offtake. As expected, the AAY households—the poorest of the poor – responded promptly. In fact, with a reduction in prices, offtake in case of AAY households increased more than proportionately to allotment. This is also indicated by the fact that regionally, the poorer (lower HDI ranking) districts responded to a greater extent through an increase in offtake, especially by the AAY card holders. The redistributive nature of the scheme is seen in the fact that it is the poorer districts have seen a *reduction* (indicated by the negative sign of the correlation coefficient) in allocation and offtake under the Rice Cards, replaced by offtake (and allocation) under the AAY cards.

However, the positive response from the other households (not covered by the AAY) indicates that foodgrain subsidization is a need felt by a large proportion of the population. There has been a proportionate increase in offtake on the part of non-AAY households as well, with the increased allocation. A targeted PDS would have neglected the demand for subsidized foodgrain on the part of these households. Moreover, the fact that only a miniscule proportion of the population has chosen to opt out of the subsidized foodgrain system is an indication of the need for State subsidization to be on a large scale and not restricted to the income-poor. This indicates once more the stark divide between the merely income-(or expenditure-) poor and the proportion of population suffering from inadequacy of nutritional intake, for whom State subsidization is an imperative. There is a gap in foodgrain requirement that needs to be filled by subsidized provision to households not officially categorized as poor. Therefore, the additional expenditure (increase in subsidy as a proportion to the budget) cannot be classed as unproductive. Moreover, in view of the fact that 81 per cent of rural and 31 per cent of urban households purchase rice through the PDS, the size of the subsidy does not appear to be excessive.

Himanshu (2011) has made an inter-State study of the PDS, and argued in favour of a universal (or near-universal) PDS under the Food Security Act. We have further detailed that argument, detailing the system in Tamil Nadu as an example of a universal PDS that is functional and efficient. It negates the allegations of inefficiency and high unproductive costs that were routinely levelled against the UPDS. Tamil Nadu is also a State which has managed to effectively reduce leakages to controllable size, which other States following a targeted PDS have not succeeded in doing. This proves once more that a universal PDS does not promote leakages; stringent monitoring and universal distribution can and do coexist. It is, therefore, found that a universal provisioning of staple foodgrain is not only efficient, but also fulfils a fundamental requirement of most of the population. The demand for subsidised foodgrain in Tamil Nadu makes a strong case for a universal PDS under the Food Security Act in the country as a whole.

NOTES

1. The per capita income of Tamil Nadu was Rs. 30,652 in 2008-09, when the per capita income at the all-India level was Rs. 25,474. Moreover, the State has also performed well in human development

indicators. Its HDI ranking was third in all the Indian States according to the latest available HDI data (National Human Development Report 2001). The percentage of population officially poor (2004-05) was 22.7 per cent in the rural and 24.1 per cent in the urban sectors. In the same year, the all-India levels of poverty were 28.7 per cent and 25.9 per cent respectively (data drawn from Himanshu 2007).

2. The earlier PDS scheme (2001-2005) had initially provided up to 20 kg of rice depending on number of household members, at Rs. 3.50 per kg. This was later revised to the first 10 kg at Rs. 3.50 per kg., and the additional quantity above 10 kg. at Rs. 6 per kg. The new scheme from 2006 onwards reduced the unit price to Rs. 2 and then (in 2008) to Re. 1 across the board.
3. Of the 32 districts in the State, two districts (Aliyur and Tiruppur) were carved out during the study period (2006 and 2008 respectively) from the district of Perambulur in 2007 (in case of Aliyur) and Erode and Coimbatore districts (in case of Tiruppur) respectively. We have used the original 30 districts for the analysis, combining the data for the newly formed districts with the new boundaries of the source districts.
4. The HDI rankings calculated by Chelliah and Shanmugam (*ibid.*) are different from the official rankings presented in this chapter. Therefore, the arguments of the authors regarding the variables related to HDI are not entirely applicable to the data we have used. We have only used these arguments as broadly indicative possibilities.

REFERENCES

Bhalla, G.S. (1993), "Policy for Food Security in the Context of New Economic Policy Framework", Paper presented at *ISID-FAO Workshop*, New Delhi, September.

Dreze and Khera (2011). "PDS Leakages: The plot thickens", *The Hindu*, Opinion: Lead, August 12.

Government of India (2005). "Performance Evaluation of the Targeted Public Distribution System (TPDS)" *Programme Evaluation Organisation*, Planning Commission, New Delhi.

Government of Tamil Nadu (2010), "Policy Note 2010-2011", Food and Consumer Protection (Cooperation, Food and Consumer Protection Department).

Gulati, Ashok; Pradeep Sharma; and Satu Kähkönen (1996), "The Food Corporation of India: Successes and Failures in Indian Foodgrain Marketing", IRIS-India Working Paper No. 18, *Center for Institutional*

Reform and the Informal Sector, available online at http://pdf.usaid.gov/pdf_docs/PNABY546.pdf.

Himanshu and Abhijit Sen (2011). "Why not a Universal Food Security Legislation?", *Economic and Political Weekly,* 46 (12), pp. 38-47.

Hirway, Indira (2003), "Identification of BPL Households for Poverty Alleviation Programmes", *Economic and Political Weekly,* 38(45), November 8, pp. 4803-8.

Jha, Shikha and Srinivasan P.V. (1999), "Food Security and Price Stabilisation: Buffer Stocks *vs.* Variable Levies", *Economic and Political Weekly,* 34(47), November 20, pp. 3299-3304.

Krishna, Anirudh; Mahesh Kapila; Mahendra Porwal; and Virpal Singh (2003), "Falling into Poverty in a High-Growth State: Escaping Poverty and Becoming Poor in Gujarat Villages", *Economic and Political Weekly,* 38(49), December 6-12, pp. 5171-5179.

Meenakshi, J.V., and Vishwanathan, Brinda (2003). Calorie deprivation in rural India between 1983 and 1999/00: Evidence from unit record data. *Economic and Political Weekly,* 38(4), 369-375.

Nayyar, Deepak and Abhijit Sen (1993), *International Trade and the Agricultural Sector in India,* Paper presented at ISID-FAO Workshop, New Delhi, September.

Nayyar, R. (1991), *Rural Poverty: An Analysis of Inter-State Differences.* Bombay, India: Oxford University Press.

Pal, S.; D.K. Bahl; and Mruthynjaya (1993), "Government Interventions in Foodgrain Markets", *Food Policy,* 18(5), October.

Patnaik, U. (2007), Neoliberalism and poverty in India. *Economic and Political Weekly,* 42(30): 3132–3150.

Radhakrishna R. and K. Subbarao (1997), "India's Public Distribution System: A National and International Perspective", *World Bank Discussion Paper No. 380,* Washington D.C.: The World Bank.

Shah, Amita and Jignasu Yagnik (2007), "Estimates of BPL Households in Rural Gujarat: Measurement, Spatial Pattern and Policy Imperatives", *Paper presented at International Seminar on 'Revisiting Poverty Issues: Measurement, Identifications and Eradication Strategies',* Patna, July 20-22.

Sundaram, K. (2003), "On Identification of Households below Poverty Line in BPL Census 2002: Some Comments on the Proposed Methodology", *Economic and Political Weekly,* 38(9), March 1, pp. 896-898.

Swaminathan, Madhura (1999), "Understanding the Costs of the Food Corporation of India", *Economic and Political Weekly,* 34(52), December 25, pp. A-121-A132.

Swaminathan, Madhura (2000), *Weakening Welfare: The Public Provisioning of Food in India,* New Delhi: Left Word Books.

Swaminathan, Madhura and Nita Misra (2001), "Errors of Targeting:

Public Distribution of Food in a Maharashtra Village 1995-2000", *Economic and Political Weekly*, 36(28), June 30, pp. 2447-2454.

Venkatasubramanian, A. K., (2006). "The Political Economy of the Public Distribution System in Tamil Nadu", in Vikram K. Chand (ed.), *Reinventing Public Service Delivery in India*, New Delhi: Sage Publications.

4

A Regional Analysis of Rural Infrastructural Development in Karnataka

Soumya Manjunath

Introduction

Infrastructure investment is an important instrument employed by the developing countries to influence economic development (Krueger, 1992 Cited in Saeed and Honggang, 1999. p. 4). These investments become indispensable in rural areas as they have crucial linkages with development of the overall economy, poverty reduction and human development. The India Rural Infrastructure Report (1997) has emphasized that access to rural infrastructure has a strong positive association with rural economic development. In Karnataka, around 64 per cent of the population continue to live in rural areas and thus there is a need for greater emphasis on rural development (Karnataka Vision for Development, 2008). The Government of Karnataka has made efforts to invest in infrastructures as per the goals of the Five-Year Plans. However, the rapid urbanization and global forces have thrown up greater challenges. The increasing rural-urban divide and growing inter-regional disparities pose a threat to the developmental processes. As the demand for rural infrastructure continues to grow, resources have to be mobilized for new investments. The limited resources need to be carefully planned for the right kind of investments.

Against this backdrop, the present study attempts to examine the nature of rural infrastructural development across the districts of Karnataka over a period of three decades. The study seeks to identify the need of the regions with respect to infrastructural requirement in rural areas.

This chapter consists of seven sections. The second section deals with the data and the methodology used for the analysis. The third section deals with some conceptual issues of rural infrastructural development. The fourth section gives the meaning and various types of rural infrastructure used in the study. The next section presents the indicators of rural infrastructure development followed by discussion of the individual infrastructure types and the analysis of results. The sixth section constructs rural infrastructural development index for each of the districts using Principal Component Analysis and ranks the districts using the same. The final section sums up the results of the study.

I. Data and Methodology

This chapter is based on an analysis of rural infrastructural development at district level in Karnataka for the period between 1980-81 and 2009-10. Data on rural infrastructural development indicators have been collected and compiled from various issues of Statistical Abstract of Karnataka, Karnataka at a Glance, All India Census Reports, Quinquennial Livestock Census, Economic Survey of Karnataka, Karnataka Development Report and Karnataka State Human Development Report.

The selection of indicators to represent the variables was based on the availability and relevance of data across the districts over the 30 years. Though in certain instances, some other indicators could have best represented the chosen variables, problems with respect to data guided the process of finalising these indicators. The regional coverage considers 19 districts in total for the analysis as data for the newly created districts are not available for all the periods. Therefore, the data for newly created districts have been merged with that of their original districts.

Trend and correlation analysis were carried out for different time periods, TE 1980, TE 1990, TE 2000 and TE 2010 to analyse the regional differences using a sub-period analysis along with a view to examine the disparity in performance across districts in Karnataka. An index of rural infrastructural development was constructed for the period TE 2009-10, using principal component analysis and the districts were ranked on the basis of their performance in rural infrastructure development.

PCA was originally conceived by Pearson in 1901, and independently developed by Hotelling in 1933. Its main goal is to explain part of the variation in a set of observed variables on the basis of a few underlying dimensions. PCA has been widely used by researchers to construct development indices (Venkataramanan *et al.*, 1985; Gayathri, 1997; De and Ghosh, 2005; Chaminuka *et al.*, 2008; Chakraborty and Guha, 2009; De, 2010). To avoid one variable having an unrealistic influence on the principal components, the variables have been standardized. In order to remove the scale effects, we used the method of linearising the variables before computing the index (Nardo, 2005).

II. Some Conceptual Issues

The meaning of infrastructure has evolved over the years and some of the definitions have been reviewed here. The term infrastructure emerged during the Second World War indicating war logistics. In general, infrastructure refers to creation of public capital goods. Infrastructural facilities, according to Hirschman (1958), refer to those basic services without which primary, secondary and tertiary productive activities cannot function. In its wider sense, infrastructural facilities embrace all public services from law and order through education and public health to transportation, communications and water supply (Mabogunje, 1974; Kahn, 1979). According to the World development Report 1994 " infrastructure is an umbrella term for many activities referred to as "social overhead capital" proposed by such development economists as Paul Rosenstein-Rodan, Ragnar Nurkse and Albert Hirschman. Venkatachalam (2003) considered agricultural infrastructure to include all of the basic services, facilities, equipment, and institutions needed for the economic growth and efficient functioning of the food and fibre markets. Infrastructure Policy for the State of Karnataka 2007 referred to infrastructure as any public work relating to facilities for utilization of natural resources or provision of services, by way of physical structures or systems. The earlier definitions on infrastructure mainly dealt with creation of new infrastructure facilities in physical terms. However, the concept in recent years is more related to the service delivery of infrastructural facilities.

III. Classification of Rural Infrastructure

In the present study, rural infrastructure is used to refer to those facilities and services that largely determine/contribute to the development of rural economy. Since the overall objective is to see how provision of infrastructural services can affect agricultural development, the indicators chosen are those that influence agricultural sector either directly or indirectly. Consequently, the analysis is also restricted to examining the disparities in provision of these facilities at a disaggregated level in as much as it influences agricultural sector. The existing literature has shown that agricultural productivity is, to a great extent, determined by the availability of adequate roads, irrigation, market, credit, and power. These facilitating factors have been largely grouped under the term 'infrastructure'. The present study considers infrastructure to include both the facilities and the services that have a bearing on the agricultural development.

Arguably, various types of structures and services do not have the same kind of roles to play in agricultural development. As services flowing from various infrastructures are complementary, they do not stand isolated in their contribution to the agrarian economy. Thus, the synergy created by these infrastructures need to be augmented by developing a holistic understanding of the various infrastructures that directly and indirectly contribute to the agricultural development.

Our classification of rural infrastructure is guided by Kahn (1979) who has grouped rural infrastructural facilities into physical, social, and institutional infrastructure. In this study, rural infrastructure is broadly divided into three categories, viz., *Economic Infrastructure* (irrigation, electricity, transport, and communication), *Social Infrastructure* (education and health) and *Institutional Infrastructure* (market, banks and co-operatives). However, it is to be noted that this classification is not a water-tight compartment. The present categorization is intended to identify the infrastructure types because the channels through which they operate are different. We restrict our analysis here to identify the regional differences in infrastructural development.

IV. Indicators of Rural Infrastructural Development

Lack of adequate infrastructure in rural areas is widely acknowledged. However, adequacy of infrastructure is closely tied up with the optimum use of the existing infrastructure. Utilization of infrastructure is also the pathway through which infrastructure influences development of a region. Studying how well a unit, whether State or district, fares with regard to the infrastructural development needs to take into consideration how much the built up infrastructure is put to use. For example, irrigation has been widely recognized as an infrastructure that sought to be augmented by extending the length of canals. It is important that mere existence of canals is not taken as an indicator of development in irrigation facilities. A region may be said to be developed in irrigation infrastructure when both availability of canals and an optimum use of these canals for irrigation purposes are evident. As Hulten (1996) has stressed that additional capital formation would be of little help in stimulating economic growth if the capital stocks are not used effectively thereby stressing the need for utilization of the available infrastructure facilities.

Therefore, indicators of each type of infrastructure should reflect its availability of infrastructure and utilization. In the present study, the availability of infrastructure shows the potential infrastructure provisions made available to the economy and the utilization of infrastructure refers to the use of these facilities and services to their potential for the desired purposes. It is possible that a region may be endowed with a variety of infrastructure facilities and yet fall short of expected outcomes due to inefficient utilization. On similar lines, The HPCRRI report has pointed out that government needs to rectify the defects in the existing infrastructure instead of concentrating on new proposals only for adding to the existing figures. Underutilization could result from many factors like inaccessibility to the infrastructures, unaffordability or inefficient service delivery.

While most studies confirm the importance of building up and expanding infrastructure in the rural areas, little attention has been paid to how well these infrastructure have been utilized. It may be noted that universal access does not necessarily imply universal service. Universal service implies ensuring that each household consumes the infrastructure. In other words, each household has an electricity connection and it is physically and economically able to make calls and use roads for motorised transport. Thus, universal service is something more than universal access (India Rural Infrastructure Report, 1997).

Table 4.1 Outlines the classification of rural infrastructure and the indicators that are chosen to represent their availability and utilization.

Table 4.1: List of Variables of Rural Infrastructural Development

Sl. No.	Types of Infrastructure	Indicators	Variables	
			Availability	Utilization
(a)	Economic Infrastructure	Irrigation	Length of canals per lakh hectare of geographical area	Percentage of NIA by canals to NIA by all sources
		Electricity	No. of villages and hamlets electrified per lakh hectare of geographical area	Irrigation pumpsets electrified (on '000) per thousand hectare of Net sown area
		Transport	Total road length (kms) per lakh hectare of geographical area	No. of total registered motor vehicles per lakh rural population
		Tele-communication	No. of telephone exchanges per lakh hectare of geographical area	No. of telephones in use (hundreds) per lakh rural population
(b)	Social Infrastructure	Education	No. of primary schools per lakh hectare of geographical area	No. of students in primary schools per lakh rural population in the age group of 5-14 years
		Health	No. of Primary Health Centres per lakh hectare of geographical area	Number of cases of immunization (in thousands) per lakh rural population
(c)	Institutional Infrastructure	Markets	No. of regulated markets per lakh hectare of geographical area	Value of turnover (Rs. in crores) per regulated market
		Banks	No. of scheduled commercial banks including branches per lakh hectare of geographical area	Total credit (Rs. in crores) per lakh rural population
		Co-operatives	No. of primary agricultural credit cooperatives per lakh hectare of geographical area	Loans by agricultural credit co-operatives (Rs. in crores) per lakh rural population

Source: Author's compilation.

Economic Infrastructure

In our study, economic infrastructure includes irrigation, electricity, road and telecommunications infrastructure which seem to have a direct influence on agricultural development. Economic infrastructure has been recognised as one of the most important facilities required for economic development. "Development of physical infrastructure is essential for all economic activities to enable production and distribution of goods and services for human welfare" (KDR, 2005, p. 190). Ghosh and De (2004) point out that economic overhead capital is oriented primarily towards the direct support of productive activities or movement of economic goods. Emphasizing the need for investments in economic infrastructure, various authors have pointed out the need to expand these facilities as mere creation of economic infrastructure will not necessitate development.

Irrigation Infrastructure

Irrigation infrastructure is probably the most consequential one among the economic infrastructure as it assists the farmers as a production augmenting input and also acts a strategy for rural development (Spencer, 1994; Reddy, 1996; Kurian, 2001). In a drought prone State like Karnataka, development of irrigation facilities assume utmost importance for accelerating agricultural production (Kurian, 2001). In the study, irrigation infrastructure is being captured by variables such as length of canals (km) per lakh hectare of geographical area and percentage of net irrigated area by canal to net irrigated area by all sources. Canal irrigation is chosen to indicate irrigation infrastructure as we are considering only provisions by the government.

Power Infrastructure

Electrification in the rural areas is another vital infrastructure for agricultural development. Various authors have drawn attention to the fact that electricity as an input to agriculture also helps in dissemination of technology in rural areas and have further pointed out that use of motor pumps for agricultural use is sometimes limited by the availability of the power in the villages. (Felloni *et al.*, 2001; Thorat *et al.*, 2003; Modi, 2005). Rural electrification also has a direct impact on agricultural productivity through private investment in electric pumps (Barnes and Binswanger, 1986). Therefore, a system of viable and efficient reliable electricity services would result in increased productivity in agriculture and labour and at the same time lead to improvement in the delivery of health and education, access to communications. The number of villages and hamlets electrified per lakh hectare of geographical area and irrigation pumpsets electrified ('000) to hundred hectares of net sown area are used to represent the availability and utilization of rural electrification.

Transport Infrastructure

Rural road connectivity is a key component of rural development as it will enable access to economic and social services by reducing transportation cost, increasing productivity and incomes of the rural farmers (Rajeev, 2008). Rural transport can be viewed as an asset to any rural setting as it provides the farmers, access to their farm, the input and output markets thereby facilitating in production and distribution activities (Spencer, 1994; Binswanger *et al.*, 1989; Felloni *et al.*, 2001; and Thorat *et al.*, 2003). Transport infrastructure is captured by road length per lakh hectare of geographical area indicating road connectivity across the regions and its utilization is captured by number of registered motor vehicles per lakh rural population which denotes the use of the road services.

Telecommunication Infrastructure

A solid network of communication infrastructure is a key to improving agriculture (Hackler, 2003). Directly, ICT acts as a tool to boost agricultural productivity by providing services in terms of techniques of geographical information systems, soil testing services and remote sensing using satellite technologies. Indirectly, ICT enables reliable and timely information available and accessible to farmers as it is crucial for important decision making. In addition to facilitating farmers in improving the productivity of agriculture and allied activities, the potential of IT assumes importance in bringing about an overall qualitative improvement in life by providing timely and quality information inputs for decision making (Meera *et al.*, 2004; Tripathi, 2008; Mittal and Tripathi, 2009). According to India Rural Infrastructure Report (1997), telephone services can result in considerable savings on cost and time on travel. The study has used number of telephone exchanges per lakh geographical area to represent the availability of telecommunication infrastructure while number of telephones in use (in hundreds) per lakh rural population is used to represent the teledensity.

Road Density and Other Indicators

Availability of transport infrastructure is considered to be an important factor in the development of any economy, especially in the case of rural sector. Our analysis also gives credence to this view. As seen in Table 4.2, length of road correlates very strongly with a variety of other development-indicators.

Table 4.2: Correlations between Road Length and Other Indicators

Road density (km/lakh area)	*Correlation coefficient*	*Sig.*
Telephone exchanges per lakh ha area	.934**	.000
Regulated Markets per lakh area	.862**	.000
Commercial Banks per lakh area	.905**	.000
PAC per lakh ha area	.799**	.000
Primary Schools per lakh ha area	.918**	.000
PHCs per lakh ha area	.960**	.000
Telephones (hundreds) per lakh rural population	.868**	.000
Market turnover (Rs. crores) per lakh rural population	.692**	.001
Bank Credit (Rs. crores) per lakh rural population	.871**	.000
Per capita income	.717*	.001

**Significant at .01 level.

The last mile connectivity which is very crucial in the rural areas do seem to play an important role in making other infrastructure accessible to the population and at the same time fuel growth in indicators such as access to regulated markets, density of motor vehicles and telephones. For instance, there is a high degree of positive and significant correlation (.871) between creation of road and access to bank credit by the rural population. The correlation coefficient of per capita income .717 shows that there exists a positive and significant association between road density and per capita incomes. This means that those districts with better connectivity through road tend to have higher per capita incomes thereby emphasising the need to invest in providing better transport infrastructure. The impact of transport infrastructure, indisputably, cuts across different types of other infrastructure like credit, and market and establishes itself as a key player in the development of rural areas.

Institutional Infrastructure

Notwithstanding the importance of economic infrastructure, agriculture would still be crippled without provision of adequate resources for the producer through a set of institutional infrastructure. The institutional infrastructure comprising market, banks, and cooperatives are indispensable to further the growth in agriculture. Many studies have pointed out the resource-crunch of the farmers and the resulting handicap experienced by them in capitalizing the potential of the economic infrastructure.

Market Infrastructure

Market infrastructure is central for organising agricultural produce in the economy. Market access is critical for agriculture to become the main driver of pro-poor growth. (OECD, 2006, p. 30). Various authors have stressed the need to integrate farmers of the rural worlds into the global economy, by creating greater market opportunities which would assist the farmers in enhancing their incomes and to remove the inadequacies in the domestic and external markets especially in the context of liberalization (Thippaiah and Deshpande, 1998; Orden *et al.*, 2004; Mahmood *et al.*, 2009). In this book, market infrastructure is composed of number of regulated markets per lakh geographical area and value of turnover (Rs. in crore) per regulated market of the district.

Banking Infrastructure

Given the level of finances available to an average farmer in rural India, institutional infrastructure like banking and cooperatives are enabling resources to build on the foundation laid by the availability of economic infrastructure. To adopt modern technology which is capital intensive, provision of credit is essential, especially for marginal farmers. However, non-availability of adequate and timely financial sources can make the farmers dependent on unscrupulous non-institutional sources. Institutional credit can greatly influence private capital formation (Chand and Kumar, 2004), both directly and indirectly, which can add to the development of agricultural sector.

The derivation of benefits depends upon the density of markets as well as the distance of markets from the residence of the farmers indicating the importance of institutional infrastructure (Thippaiah and Deshpande, 1998). Credit delivery to the agriculture sector continues to be inadequate leading to a situation of excessive dependency on non-institutional sources of credit and also restricting use of technology and other critical inputs (Golait, 2007).

MARKET TURNOVER AND ROAD DENSITY

There exists a positive relationship between value of market turnover and road length. Development of road-infrastructure facilitates transport of goods from farms to the markets. With better road connectivity, the farmers would prefer to sell in regulated markets and reduction in transportation costs could possibly induce farmer to come to the regulated markets and thereby increasing the business activity of the regulated markets.

Table 4.3 depicts how the different districts fare when their road connectivity is juxtaposed with the value of turnover per

Table 4.3: Matrix between Market Turnover and Road Density

		Market Turnover per regulated market (Rs. crore)		
		< 25 crore	25-50 crore	>50 crore
Road density (Road length (km) per lakh ha of geographical area	< 1000 kms	Bidar, Bijapur	Bellary, Gulbarga, Mysore, Shimoga	Raichur
	1000-2000 km	Chikmagalur, Hassan, Kodagu, Kolar, Tumkur, U.Kannada	Chitradurga, Dharwad	—
	>2000 km	Belgaum, Mandya	D.Kannada	Bangalore

Source: Author's calculation.

regulated markets as on TE2010. Bidar and Bijapur occupy the space that converges on the lowest points in both variables. Bangalore that has the longest road network has also recorded a very high market turnover. It is interesting to note that though Belgaum and Mandya do not seem to suffer from road connectivity issues, their market turnover did not benefit much from the last mile connectivity.

MATRIX OF MARKET TURNOVER AND TOTAL CREDIT

There exists a positive relationship between market turnover and total credit. When farmers have better access to financial resources, they would prefer to conduct their transactions in regulated markets thereby increasing the business activity and the market turnover. The other factors, examined earlier, in combination with credit facility may prove to be crucial in helping districts to achieve better levels of market turnover in specific and to better levels of overall development.

In as much as institutional credit facility is made available to the rural population; it may create an atmosphere of non-dependence on non-institutional sources of borrowing credit, especially the exploitative moneylenders. This is expected to directly and indirectly contribute to the agricultural development. Table 4.4 presents the matrix of districts when assessed on their access to total credit from commercial banks and agricultural credit co-operative societies and their market turnover in TE 2010. Significantly, Raichur seems to have accessed very low amount of credit from commercial

Table 4.4: Matrix of Market Turnover and Total Credit

		Market Turnover per regulated market		
		< 25 crore	25 to 50 crore	> 50 crore
Total Credit (Rs. crore per lakh area)	< 150 crore	Bidar, Kolar, Mandya, Tumkur, Uttara Kannada	Chitradurga, Gulbarga	Raichur
	150 to 300 crore	Belgaum, Bijapur, Chikmagalur, Hassan, Kodagu	Dharwad, Mysore, Shimoga	—
	Above 300 crore	—	Bellary, D.Kannada	Bangalore

Source: Author's calculation.

banks and yet have recorded high levels of market turnover. It is only Bangalore that seems to make maximum use of total credit and at the same time reaches a high market turnover. The extraordinarily high figure for Bangalore could be because of the sizable urban population included in the district. The districts like Bijapur, Bidar, Hassan, Kolar, etc., have not accessed credit and at the same time have not been able to reach beyond a turnover of 25 crore per regulated market in TE2010.

Social Infrastructure

Provision of the above two types of infrastructure, while making basic services and facilities available to the farming population, assumes that the producers have the required skills and competencies to tap their full potential. Agricultural development also depends on the know-how of the producers to access the information, to use the information to the optimum level and the ability to use time and other resources to convert them to profit in agriculture. In this regard, the development of social infrastructure becomes important as it contributes to the development processes indirectly. For instance, education and health will augment human capital which influences agricultural productivity with respect to assimilation and implementation of information and technology.

Health Infrastructure

Provision of suitable health infrastructure is important to ensure quality of life of the human resources in the rural areas. An inadequacy in provision of cheap medical facilities through government health services is seen as a major reason for increased borrowing by marginal and small farmers (World Bank, 2007; Singh, 2010). This means that the resources available for other productive activities would reduce. In India, primary healthcare centres are seen as making medical services available to the farmers and their dependents (e.g., children) at affordable rates thereby significantly contributing to labour productivity. There is a high correlation between nutrition and labour productivity (Deolaikar, 2001). Skills, competencies, health and overall well-being of the farmers are, therefore, important variables to help the farmers to take full advantage of the economic and institutional infrastructure.

Education Infrastructure

Investment in education especially in rural areas is viewed as an important step towards eradication of rural illiteracy. Development and extension of technical and vocational education and training to farmers can be highly beneficial. This will help by enabling the farmers to make efficient and effective use of inputs and to discover innovative ways by which they can maximise the economic returns from their produce.

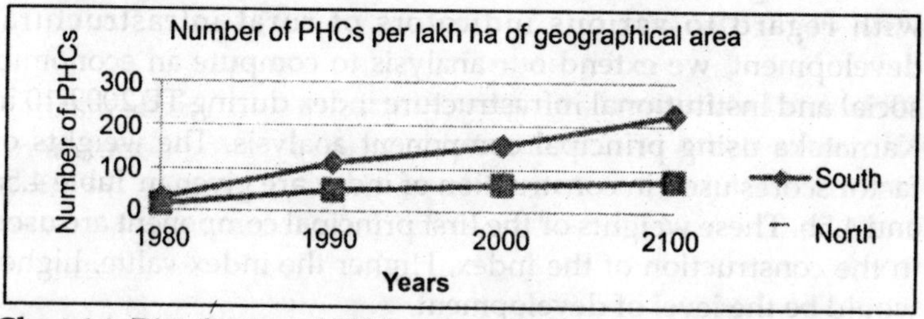

Chart 4.1: Distribution of PHCs across Northern and Southern Districts

Taking into account the distribution of primary health care centres per lakh hectares of geographical area across northern and southern regions of Karnataka as shown in Chart 4.1, the northern districts are lagging behind in the availability of primary health care centres which are mostly for the poorer sections. It is clear from the chart that investment by the government in provision of primary health care centres was more or less similar and the disparity is seen during the beginning of 1990s. This indicates the dearth of health care institutions in the northern part of the State.

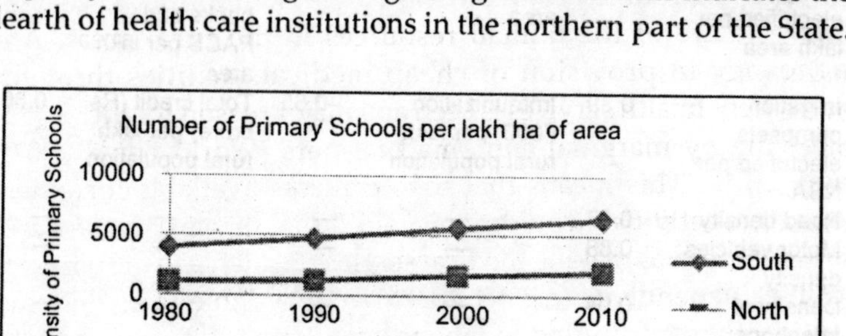

Chart 4.2: Distribution of Primary Schools across Northern and Southern Districts

Chart 4.2 shows the distribution of primary schools per lakh hectare of geographical area among the northern and southern districts of Karnataka. Again, there exists disparity between the northern and southern districts in number of primary schools. The development of education in northern districts of Karnataka over a period of time shows a need for greater investment in these areas.

V. Construction of the Rural Infrastructural Development Index

Considering the fact that the districts showed large scale disparities with regard to various indicators of rural infrastructural development, we extend our analysis to compute an economic, social and institutional infrastructure index during TE 2009-10 in Karnataka using principal component analysis. The weights or factor scores used in construction of index are given in Table 4.5a and 4.5b. These weights or the first principal component are used in the construction of the index. Higher the index value, higher would be the level of development.

Table 4.5a: Weights used in the Construction of Economic, Social and Institutional Infrastructure

Economic Infrastructure	*Weights*	*Social Infrastructure*	*Weights*	*Institutional Infrastructure*	*Weights*
Canal length per lakh geo area	0.15	Primary schools per lakh ha area	0.87	Market density	0.8
% NIA by canals to NIA	–0.44	Students per lakh children 5-14 years	–0.32	Market turnover per regulated market	0.65
Villages electrified per lakh area	0.81	PHC's per lakh area	0.94	Commercial banks and PACS per lakh area	0.93
Irrigation pumpsets electrified per NSA	0.39	Immunization ('000) per lakh rural population	–0.65	Total credit (Rs. crore) per lakh rural population	0.86
Road density	0.87	—	—	—	—
Motor vehicles density	0.88	—	—	—	—
Density of telephone exchanges	0.94	—	—	—	—
Teledensity	0.82	—	—	—	—

Source: Author's calculation.

Table 4.5b: Weights used in the Construction of Availability and Utilization Index

Availability index	*Weights*	*Utilization index*	*Weights*
Canal length per lakh ha geo area	0.53	% NIA by canals to NIA by all sources	–0.26
Villages electrified per lakh area	0.89	Irrigation pumpsets electrified per NSA	0.16
Road density	0.95	Motor vehicles density	0.99
Density of telephone exchanges	0.91	Teledensity	0.95
Market density	0.92	Market turnover per regulated market	0.92
Commercial banks and PACS per lakh area	0.96	Total credit (Rs. crore) per lakh rural population	0.99
Primary schools per lakh ha area	0.96	Students in primary schools	0.26
PHCs per lakh area	0.97	Immunization ('000) per lakh rural population	0.96

Source: Author's calculation.

The results of the PCA are given in Table 4.6. Based on these results, the districts were grouped into different categories along the various levels of development for each infrastructure type, economic, social and institutional. The classification categories were Highly developed, Moderately developed, and Developing. The basis of this grouping was the index score arrived through the PCA.

Table 4.7 presents the classification of all the districts by levels of economic, social and institutional infrastructural development during TE 2009-10. Despite performing well in economic and institutional infrastructure, Dakshina Kannada is moderately developed with respect to social infrastructure. Bangalore has remained consistently in the highly developed category in all the three types of infrastructure. Northern districts such as Bidar, Bijapur, and Gulbarga have remained in the developing category across the three types.

Since, the other intention of the analysis was to distinguish from availability and utilization of infrastructures; we have developed indices of availability and utilization of infrastructures for the period TE 2009-10. Further, the ratio of utilization to availability indices has been computed to arrive at the Overall

Table 4.6: Indices of Economic, Social and Institutional Index (TE 2009-10)

Rank	Economic infrastructure		Social infrastructure		Institutional infrastructure	
	Districts	Index	Districts	Index	Districts	Index
1.	Bangalore	34.88	Bangalore	8.7	Bangalore	18.75
2.	D.Kannada	27.74	Belgaum	7.08	Belgaum	12.54
3.	U.Kannada	26.56	Mandya	6.82	D.Kannada	12.37
4.	Kolar	26.54	Hassan	6.65	Dharwad	12.26
5.	Belgaum	26.37	Kolar	6.36	Chitradurga	11.36
6.	Tumkur	26.01	Chitradurga	6.29	Mysore	11.2
7.	Shimoga	25.07	D.Kannada	6.16	Shimoga	11.03
8.	Hassan	24.95	Tumkur	5.99	Bellary	11.01
9.	Chikmagalur	24.73	Mysore	5.9	Mandya	10.91
10.	Chitradurga	24.71	Chikmagalur	5.71	Hassan	10.89
11.	Mysore	24.49	U.Kannada	5.2	Raichur	10.87
12.	Mandya	24.11	Dharwad	5.1	Kodagu	10.79
13.	Dharwad	23.86	Shimoga	5.07	Kolar	10.38
14.	Kodagu	23.70	Raichur	4.81	Gulbarga	10.30
15.	Bellary	22.32	Gulbarga	4.78	Tumkur	10.27
16.	Raichur	21.84	Kodagu	4.77	Chikmagalur	10.27
17.	Bidar	21.68	Bidar	4.37	U.Kannada	9.91
18.	Bijapur	21.63	Bijapur	4.29	Bijapur	9.7
19.	Gulbarga	21.53	Bellary	4.06	Bidar	9.2

Source: Author's calculation.

Table 4.7: Classification of Districts by Levels of Rural Infrastructural Development

Levels of development	Economic infrastructure	Social infrastructure	Institutional infrastructure
Highly developed	Bangalore, D.Kannada,, U.Kannada, Kolar, Belgaum, Tumkur	Bangalore, Belgaum, Mandya, Hassan, Kolar, Chitradurga	Bangalore, Belgaum, D.Kannada, Dharwad, Chitradurga, Mysore
Moderately developed	Shimoga, Hassan, Chikmagalur, Chitradurga, Mysore, Mandya, Dharwad	D.Kannada, Tumkur,Mysore, Chikmagalur, U.Kannada, Dharwad, Shimoga	Shimoga, Bellary, Mandya, Hassan, Raichur, Kodagu, Kolar
Developing	Kodagu, Bellary, Raichur, Bidar, Bijapur Gulbarga	Raichur, Gulbarga, Kodagu, Bidar, Bijapur, Bellary	Gulbarga, Tumkur, Chikmagalur, U.Kannada, Bijapur, Bidar

Infrastructure Performance index across the districts for the period TE 2009-10.

Table 4.8 shows the indices of availability and utilization and the overall infrastructure index. A high value of availability index means greater distribution of infrastructural facilities within the districts. Similarly, a high value of utilization index indicates generally higher utilization indicators of the infrastructures. Districts such as Bangalore, Belgaum, Shimoga, Chitradurga, Hassan and Bidar do not seem to suffer from non-availability of infrastructures. However, Bidar has scored very low on its utilization. Despite the fact that Dakshina Kannada has scored low on availability index, its better development with regard to the utilisation index, it has scored relatively high.

Table 4.9 presents the districts based on their level of development in terms of their infrastructure performance. Dakshina Kannada and Dharwad have higher utilization out of

Table 4.8: Infrastructure Performance Index (TE 2009-10)

Rank	*Infrastructure Availability Index*		*Infrastructure Utilization Index*		*Infrastructure Performance Index*	
	Districts	*Index*	*Districts*	*Index*	*Districts*	*Index*
1.	Bangalore	41.75	Bangalore	34.52	D. Kannada	1.131
2.	Belgaum	33.79	D. Kannada	26.32	Dharwad	1.055
3.	Shimoga	31.63	Shimoga	24.76	Mandya	0.941
4.	Chitradurga	30.84	Bellary	24.69	Tumkur	0.909
5.	Hassan	29.23	Dharwad	24.36	Chikmagalur	0.881
6.	Bidar	28.29	Mysore	24.17	Bellary	0.879
7.	U. Kannada	28.29	U. Kannada	23.53	Bijapur	0.868
8.	Bellary	28.08	Kodagu	23.29	Mysore	0.867
9.	Mysore	27.89	Chitradurga	23.18	Raichur	0.865
10.	Kodagu	27.45	Kolar	22.9	Kodagu	0.848
11.	Kolar	27.02	Chikmagalur	22.71	Kolar	0.848
12.	Gulbarga	26.80	Tumkur	22.59	Gulbarga	0.833
13.	Raichur	25.98	Belgaum	22.55	U. Kannada	0.832
14.	Chikmagalur	25.79	Raichur	22.47	Bangalore	0.827
15.	Bijapur	25.00	Gulbarga	22.33	Shimoga	0.783
16.	Tumkur	24.86	Hassan	21.73	Bidar	0.764
17.	D. Kannada	23.27	Bijapur	21.7	Chitradurga	0.752
18.	Dharwad	23.08	Bidar	21.60	Hassan	0.743
19.	Mandya	21.73	Mandya	20.45	Belgaum	0.667

Source: Author's calculation.

Table 4.9: Classification of Districts based on Infrastructure Performance Index

Levels of Performance	*Infrastructure Performance Index*
Low Performance	D. Kannada, Dharwad, Mandya, Tumkur, Chikmagalur, Bellary
Moderate Performance	Bijapur, Mysore, Raichur, Kodagu, Kolar, Gulbarga
High Performance	Bangalore, Shimoga, Bidar, Chitradurga, Hassan, Belgaum

the resources made available indicating that more needs to be invested to make relevant resources available to them. Surprisingly, Bangalore recorded lower infrastructure performance despite ranking high on both the indices. Shimoga, Bidar, Chitradurga, Hassan, Belgaum suffer from lower utilization of these facilities.

VI. To Sum Up

The findings presented here are at the initial stage and the tables can lend themselves to further analysis to give more insights into the nature of rural infrastructural development and its pattern across the districts. The preliminary analysis of the data gives an overall picture of the development of various types of infrastructure in the districts. Road connectivity seem to play an important role in making other infrastructure accessible to the population and at the same time fuel growth in indicators like development of regulated markets, commercial banks and access to primary schools. Consistent with various other studies, transport and credit have reiterated themselves to be crucial in the growth of the rural economy. They not only affect the population directly but also contribute by indirectly augmenting the benefits of other types of infrastructures by making such facilities accessible. Key infrastructural investments like roads, electricity, credit, etc. have a ripple effect by which it promotes the growth of other sectors and invites the development of related infrastructure.

The initial analysis has revealed that penetration of telephones has been high among Bangalore, Dakshina Kannada while it has been low among Mandya and Mysore districts of southern Karnataka. The lower shares of the Northern Districts in irrigation infrastructure are an indication of the way allocation of resources for irrigation could proceed to tackle regional disparities. Southern districts seem to be more developed than the northern ones. Even among the southern regions, few districts such as Bangalore and D. Kannada dominate the picture. Among Northern districts, Belgaum and Uttara Kannada have relatively performed better. As per the Infrastructure Performance index, Dakshina Kannada and Dharwad have higher utilization out of the resources made available indicating that more needs to be invested to make relevant resources available to them. Shimoga, Bidar, Chitradurga, Hassan, Belgaum suffer from lower utilization of the infrastructure facilities. Realising the potential of the infrastructures would require availability of different infrastructure types together than in isolation.

The scheme of availability-utilization was used to examine how much of the infrastructure that is available was made use of, and this was made a part of the development-process. The infrastructure performance index showed that not all districts that enjoyed a high level of accessibility to various types of infrastructure were using them to the optimum levels. The study emphasises that realising the potential of infrastructures in rural areas would require provisions of different infrastructure types together than in isolation. The results of the study reveal that there exists a large scale variation in the levels of infrastructures across districts and also in levels of individual components of infrastructures.

Since rural infrastructure sector has forward and backward linkages to the economy, investments should be directed towards priority sectors and in lagging areas and at the same time efforts should be made to maintain and improve in areas where infrastructure is well developed. The results reveal large scale disparities between northern and southern parts of Karnataka. Even within the southern part, few districts such as Bangalore, Mandya and Mysore dominate the picture. Districts such as Bangalore, Belgaum, Shimoga, Chitradurga, Hassan and Bidar do not seem to suffer from non-availability of infrastructures. However, Bidar has scored very low on its utilization. Development in these districts would mean examining the reasons why their utilization-indicators scored less and applying greater focus on enhancing the utilization of the available infrastructure. Despite the fact that Dakshina Kannada has scored low on availability index, its better development with regard to the utilisation index, it has scored relatively high.

A key insight from the analysis that distinguishing utilization of infrastructure from mere availability can give a fresh perspective to the question of adequacy of infrastructure. With respect to the provision of different infrastructures, we find that more questions need to be asked about why the built-up infrastructure is underutilized. Underutilization needs to be addressed along with, if not instead of, adding on to the existing structures. This is important especially when the government is the only provider of most infrastructural facilities covered in our study. It is imperative to ensure appropriate and optimum utilization of the infrastructure since these require massive investments to build up and the State is constrained by budgetary limitations.

REFERENCES

Barnes, D., and Binswanger, H. (1986). Impact of Rural Electrification and Infrastructure on Agricultural Changes, 1966-1980. *Economic and Political Weekly*, Vol. 21(1), 26-34.

Binswanger, H.P.; Khandekar, S.R.; and Rosenswig, M. R. (1989). *The Impact of Infrastructure and Financial Institutions on Agicultural Output and Investment in India.* World Bank.

Chakraborthy, D., and Guha, A. (2009). Infrastructure and Economic Growth in India: Analysing the Village-Level Connectivity Scenario of the States. *Journal of Infrastructure Development*, 67-86.

Chand, R, and Kumar, P. (2004). Determinants of Capital Formation and Agriculture Growth: Some New Explorations, *Economic and Political Weekly*, V. 39(52): 5611-5616

De, P., and Ghosh, B. (2005). Effects of Infrastructure on Regional Income in the Era of Globalization: New Evidence from South Asia. *Asia Pacific Development Journal*, Vol. 12 (No.1), 81-107

Deoalikar, A.B. (2001). Nutrition and Labour Productivity in Agriculture: Estimates from Rural South India. *The Review of Economics and Statistics*, 406-413.

Fan, S.; Hazell, P.; and Thorat, S. (1999). *Linkages between Government Spending, Growth, Poverty in Rural India*. Washington, D.C.: International Food Policy Research Institute.

Felloni, F.; Wahl, T.; Wandschneider, P.; and Gilbert, J. (2001). *Infrastructure and Agricultural Prodcution: Cross-Country Evidence and Implications for China.* Washington State University.

Gayathri, K. (1997). Role of Infrastructure in the Industrial Development of Karnataka: A District Level Analysis. *Arthavijnana,* Vol. XXXIX (2), 185-205.

Golait, R. (2007). *Current Issues in Agriculture Credit in India: An Assessment.* Reserve Bank of India Occasional Papers, Vol. 28 (No. 1).

Government of Karnataka. (2007). Infrastructure Policy-2007 for the State of Karnataka. *Infrastructure Development Department.* Bangalore: Government of Karnataka.

Hulten, C.R. (1996). Infrastructure Capital and Economic Growth: How well you use it may be more important than how much you have. NBER Working Paper Series, Working Paper 5847, 1-37.

Kahn, A. 1979. *Social Policy and Social Services.* 2nd Edition. New York: Random House.

Kurian, N. (2001). Regional Disparities in India. Retrieved from Planning Commission of India: http://planningcommission.nic.in/reports/sereport/ser/vision2025/regdsprty.pdf

Mabogunje, A.L. 1974. *Infrastructure in Planning Process.* Town and Country Planning Summer School. England: University of London

Meera, S.N.; Jhamtani, A.; and Rao, D. (2004). *Information and Communication Technology in Agricultural Development: A Comparative Analysis of Three Projects from India.* ODI. New Delhi: Agricultural Research and Extension Network.

Mittal, S., and Tripathi, G. (2009). Role of Mobile Phone Technology in Improving Small Farm Productivity. *Agricultural Economics Research Review,* Vol. 22, 451-459.

Nanjundappa, D. (2002). *Report of the High Power Committee for Redressal of Regional Imbalances in Karnataka.* Government of Karnataka.

Narayanamoorthy, A., and Hanjra, M. A. (2006). Rural Infrastructure and Agricultural Output Linkages: A Study of 256 Indian Districts. *Indian Journal of Agricultural Economics,* Vol. 61(3), 444-459.

Pinstrup-Andersen, P., and Shimokawa, S. (2006). Rural Infrastructure and Agricultural Development. *Annual Bank Conference on Development Economics.* Tokyo.

Planning Commission. (2006). *Human Development Report.* Bangalore: Planning and Statistics Department, Government of Karnataka.

Planning Commission. (2007). *Karnataka Development Report.* New Delhi: Planning Commission, Government of India.

Rajeev, M. (2008). *Against Gravity? RIDF and the Challenges to Balanced Development of Infrastructure.* Monograph Series No. 14. Bangalore: Institute for Social and Economic Change.

Rajeev, M. (2008). *Rural Infrastructure Development Fund: Need for a Track Change.* Working Paper No. 195. Bangalore: Institute for Social and Economic Change.

Reddy, V.M. (1996). Irrigation Development Problems and Prospects. In

A. Aziz, and S. Krishna, *Regional Development: Problems and Policy Measures*. Bangalore: Institute for Social and Economic Change.

Rao, H. (1984). *Regional Disparities and Development in India.* New Delhi: Ashish Publishing House.

Saeed K; and Honggang Xu, (1999). *Infrastructure Development in a Dual Agricultural Economy: Implications for Economic Growth and Income Distribution*

Sangwan, S.S. (2010). *Infrastructure for Agricultural Development*. Mumbai: National Bank for Agriculture and Rural Development, Occasional Paper-53

Satish, P. (2007). Rural Infrastructure and Growth: An Overview. *Indian Journal of Agricultural Economics,* 62(1), 32-51.

Singh, N. (2010). Rural Healthcare and Indebtedness in Punjab. *Economic and Political Weeky,* Vol. XLV(11), 22-25.

Spencer, D.S. (1994). *Infrastructure and Technology Constraints to Agricultural Development in the Humid and Sub Humid Tropics of Africa.* Washington. EPTD Discussion Paper No. 3, IFPRI, Environment and Production Technology Division, Washington D.C.

The India Rural Infrastructure Report (1997): New Delhi: NCAER

Thippaiah, P., and Deshpande, R.S. (1998). Analysis of Market Infrastructure, Prices and Terms of Trade: A Case Study of Karnataka. *Indian Journal of Agricultural Economics,* Vol. 53 (No. 3), 359-369.

Thorat, S., and Sirohi, S. (2004). *Rural Infrastructure: A Millennium Study* (Vol. No. 4). New Delhi: Ministry of Agriculture, Government of India.

Thorat, S.; Chand, R.; and Bhalla, G. (2003). *Rural Public Investment in India: Lessons for Growth and Poverty Reduction.* New Delhi: International Food Policy Research Institute.

Tripathi, R., and Suresh, R. (2008). Trends of Production Infrastructure Development and its Impact on Economic Growth of Haryana. *Agricultural Situation in India,* 569-600.

Venkatachalam, K. (2003). *Infrastructure and Agricultural Development in Karnataka State.* Bangalore: Institute for Social and Economic Change

Venkataramanan, L.; Prahaladachar, M.; and Deshpande, R.S. (1985). *Dynamics of Rural Transformation in Karnataka 1956-76.* Bangalore: Institute for Social and Economic Change.

World Bank. (1994). *Infrastructure for Development.* World Development Report 1994. Washington D.C.: The World Bank.

World Bank. (2007). *Agriculture for Development.* World Development Report 2008. Washington D.C.: The World Bank.

5

Do Women have the Freedom to decide the Sex of her Child?

A Spatio-Temporal Analysis through the Transition of Small Family Size in India

Ritwika Mukherjee

Introduction

Parental preferences for desired sex composition of their children had been a major barrier to fertility decline in a developing patriarchal society like India. The recent NFHS round has shown a precipitous decline in fertility rate with ten States reporting replacement or below replacement fertility. The emerging trend of small family norms along with the need to accommodate the phenomena of son preference has led to a distorted Child Sex Ratio (Girls/1000 boys) consequent with a shift from parental conscious choice to more deliberate strategies of birth control under the new regime of sex selective abortions. The present study seeks to enquire how and to what extent the role of son preference has been intensified in the present context of two child family norm as an outcome of desired sex preference towards children.

Review of Literature

A great body of literature has been flooded dealing with the declining Child Sex Ratio in India of which an one of the most significant works has been forwarded by Monica Das Gupta (1987) where she heralded an important finding of sex selective discrimination to be more acute among the higher birth order of girls. Such an adverse situation is empirically investigated in her work through the higher post-neonatal mortality among girls when the environmental and care related factors are more susceptible to societal manipulation. The progressive deterioration of the survival chances of girls in instances from second or third birth order (whether the first child is a boy or a girl) is surprising in view of the fact that their mother's level of education have been rising steadily over time. More interestingly such discrimination is more prevalent among educated younger mothers than uneducated younger or older mothers (30-49). Having supported these facts through female neglect in access to nutrition and health care through selective discrimination in consumption patterns (food and clothes) and the frequency of treatment in the first five years of life, the basic contention is that even with progress of education, awareness and improvement in treatment of women they still are the structural marginalized sections of the society. The strong patriarchy in such societies bears them as an additional economic burden in their families' discontinuing the family lineage a non-security for parents in their old age.

That the most important determinant assumes to be the cultural variables as could be found in the above study is well documented by Dyson and Moore (1983) where they highlighted the patterns of regional demography in India. Their basic contention was the North-South divide in demographic performances and female autonomy could be the result of long term historical consistency of dichotomous regional patterns of demographic performances. With this view they developed a sociological model of different gender relations inherent in North and South culture by pointing out the implications of strong kinship relations and patrilineal exogamous marriage patterns in the North and *vice versa*.

Christian Seidl (1995) investigates the impact of preferences for male offspring to female offspring upon the sex ratio of the population. Asymmetric procreation behaviour of this kind is modelled by assuming that a female's procreation ceases only after at least one son or one daughter is born. It is shown that such asymmetric procreation behaviour has no effect on the sex ratio of the society, but influences rather the growth rate of the population. Finally, problems concerning the inter-relationship between the sex ratio, the pattern of procreation, and the marriage regime in stationary populations are investigated.

Sudha and Rajan (2003) presented evidence from the census of India to show that abnormally masculine estimated SRB grew more prevalent between 1981 and 1991; and female disadvantage in child mortality risks persisted. Statistical analyses suggested that women's status indicators are associated with partial protection to daughters; women's work participation more so than female literacy. Male work participation and urbanisation over the decade are associated with decreasing female disadvantage in child mortality, suggesting that modernisation may be associated with substitution of pre- for post-natal sex selection. Changes in cultural factors also suggest links to growing female disadvantage. That is, gender bias remains firm.

Now coming to the context of the role of family planning in determining the size of the family useful literature forwarded by James (1999) highlighting the recent 'revolution of family life' in India, and the southern States in particular may not conform to the classical demographic transition theory and other theories of fertility primarily attempted to capture the conditions necessary for a change in the reproductive behaviour of people. Understanding such a dramatic decline in fertility achieving the replacement level or less such as in Kerala and Tamil Nadu has steered attention to the search of new development variables that can explain the forces of change on the demographic front, one of which is the female literacy. The author considers the state of Andhra Pradesh which have shown a tremendous decline in fertility in the recent years, yet unaccompanied by any suggestive improvement in social development as exhibited by low female literacy, infant mortality rate and levels of urbanisation. Hence, in a nutshell, it is possible that the generous welfare measures undertaken by the government of Andhra Pradesh in poverty alleviation particularly in the 1980s have not only reduced poverty but also have had some impact on the fertility decisions of the people. This, along with the changes in the rural labour market, labour organisation, and other related factors could have created a favourable climate for a decline in fertility, even with a low level of social development.

Das (2004) sought to trace the antecedents that have caused the phenomenon of missing females and tries to understand the factors behind the increased manifestation of gender bias. The analysis of two rounds of NFHS, conducted during the last decade in the country, suggested that loss of female children may be attributed to sex selective abortion and a resultant more masculine sex ratio at birth, since other factors such as sex differential in mortality and the undercount of females are found to have a minimal effect. This phenomenon is typical of societies with a strong son preference, experiencing fertility transition, wherein the conflicting desires of limiting family size and simultaneously to have at least one son, put pressure on couples to resort to sex selective abortion for the fulfilment of both desires. The recent spread of clinics offering sex determination tests and abortion services in India has facilitated the increased use of these techniques.

Discussion

Cross-Sectional and Longitudinal Analysis of Child Sex Ratio

At a very cursory look the district-wise variations of Child Sex Ratio shows a clear North-West and South-East divide (Figures 5.1, 5.4 and 5.7). The distinction is much stronger in rural areas (Figures 5.2, 5.5 and 5.8) while the urban counterparts (Figures 5.3, 5.6 and 5.9) show a gradual dilution of the sharp differences reflecting certain commonalities of the nature of daughter aversion. The situation of daughter discrimination is very high in urban areas well equipped with the modern technologies for not having to bear an unwanted child. This distinction is further strengthened in 2001 (Figure 5.4) and the gaps between the worst and best performing districts have increased considerably. Very little positive changes in Child Sex Ratio could be observed among the worst performing districts of Punjab, Haryana, Delhi, Himachal Pradesh, etc. located in the north-western part in 2001 but these districts seem to have improved a lot in 2011 (Figures 5.10, 5.11 and 5.12) with about ten points increase in Child Sex Ratio values of what was in 2001. While Rajasthan which showed some signs of improvement in 2001, the condition got worsened in 2011, this calls for evaluation of the regional dynamics and policy implications which will be discussed in the later sections. One clear picture emerging from the spatio-temporal distribution is that some of the conventionally daughter disadvantaged districts like those comprising of Punjab and Haryana are actually performing better in the recent decade as shown by signs of positive changes in Child Sex Ratio while new emerging districts particularly those of Maharashtra are taking the lead role of disappearing women.

The condition of Child Sex Ratio has been worsened over the years following a steep jump from 1991 to 2001 the decline being more prominent in the urban areas. Figures 5.12, 5.13 and 5.14 clearly shows the adverse condition of Child Sex Ratio from 1991 onwards even though the overall Sex Ratio is on the rise. Thus traditional patriarchy blended with the modern trends of burden-free children conjointly took shape in a strong daughter aversion where the possibilities of pre birth sex determination and safe methods of daughter elimination are more than the rural counterparts. Even among the rural areas, those in proximity to urban areas portray more adverse nature than the remotest villages where the hierarchical network connectivity and spatial spread are constrained by absolute distance followed by weaker waves of diffusion of innovation.

Tables 5.1, 5.2 and 5.3 clearly shows the deteriorating performance of the States over the years in terms of Child Sex Ratio as the States transited from no district having less than 800 Child Sex Ratio values, to reaching the 800 mark in 2001 and 2011. States like Jammu and Kashmir, Punjab, and Haryana, etc. have got some of their districts below the 800 mark in 2001 which, however, improved to some extent in 2011. An interesting trend from the analysis comes out that almost all the States excepting south Indian States have shown a progressive reduction in more than 950 values and the values have steeply declined from 1991 to 2011. This decline is even sharper in urban areas. Most of the values are concentrated in 800 to 900 classes depicting a clear shift to a more worsened situation of female-male ratio. States like Maharashtra which had its values concentrated in 900 to more than 950 classes in 1991 shows a relative shift in maximum values concentrated in less than 900 categories. This clearly pinpoints towards a regional shift in the performance of Child Sex Ratio and a gradual dilution of the traditional North South divide of daughter elimination.

The districts which come under the bottommost quintile of Child Sex Ratio show the majority from UP, Rajasthan, Haryana,

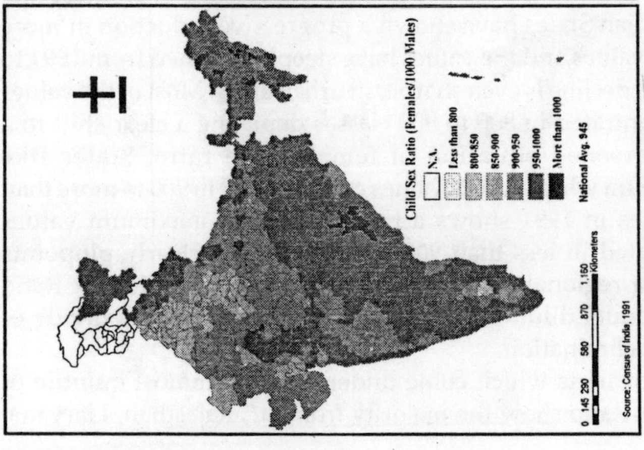

Fig. 5.1: District-wise Child Sex Ratio (1991)

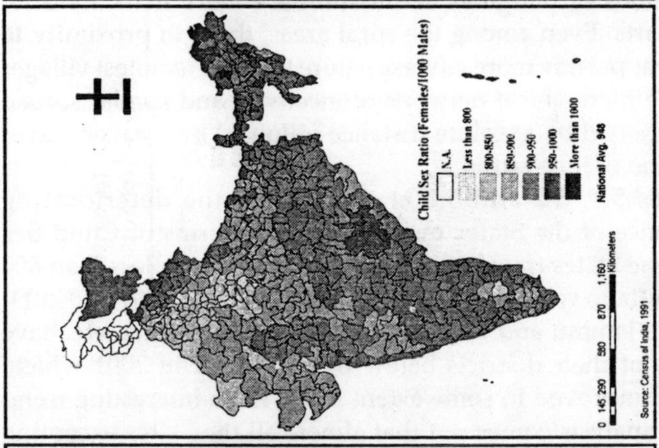

Fig. 5.2: District-wise Child Sex Ratio (Rural) (1991)

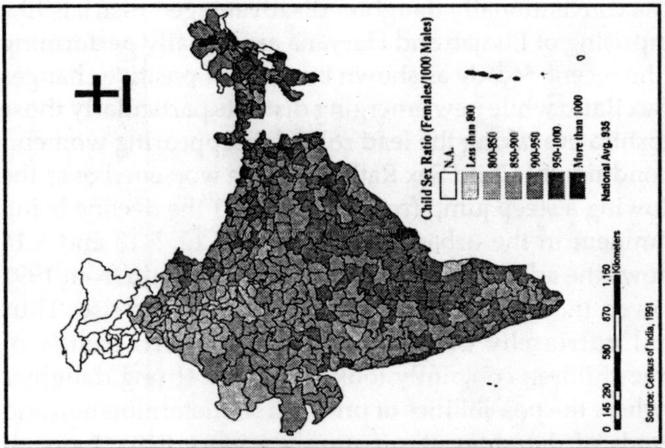

Fig. 5.3: District-wise Child Sex Ratio (Urban) (1991)

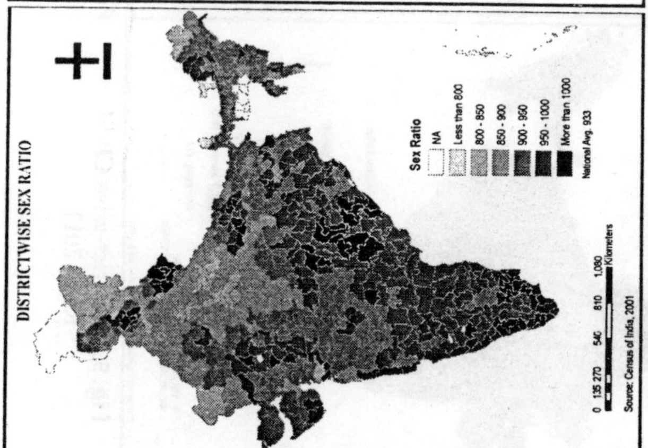

Fig. 5.4: District-wise Sex Ratio 2001

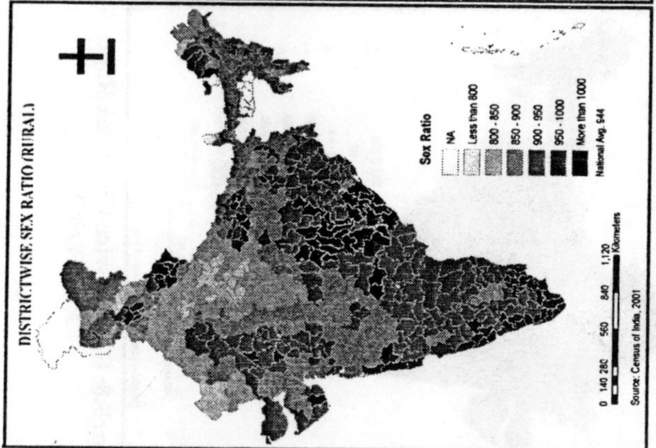

Fig. 5.5: District-wise Sex Ratio (Rural) 2001

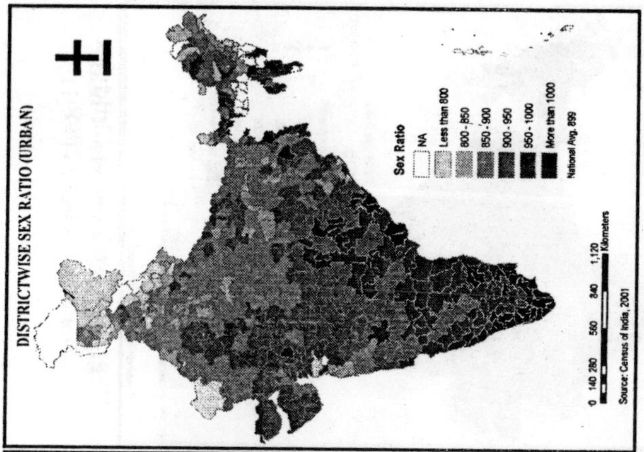

Fig. 5.6: District-wise Sex Ratio (Urban) 2001

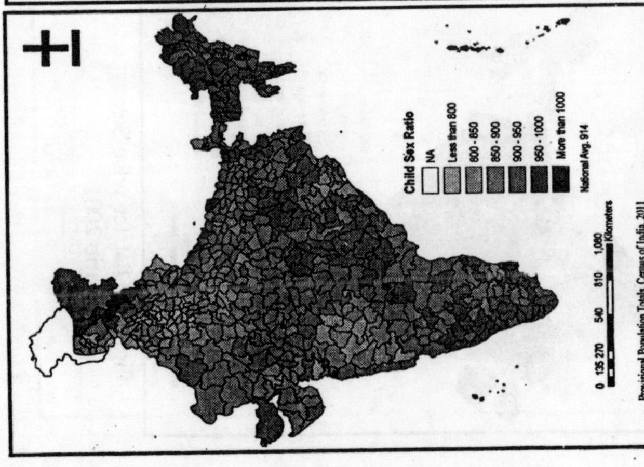

Fig. 5.7: District-wise Child Sex Ratio 2011

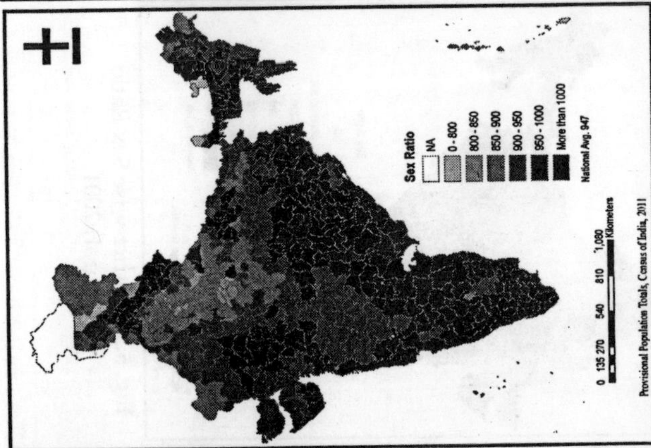

Fig. 5.8: District-wise Child Sex Ratio Rural (2011)

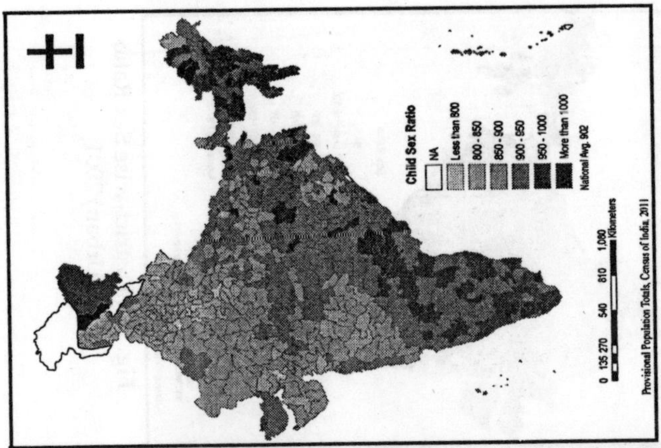

Fig. 5.9: District-wise Child Sex Ratio (Urban) 2011

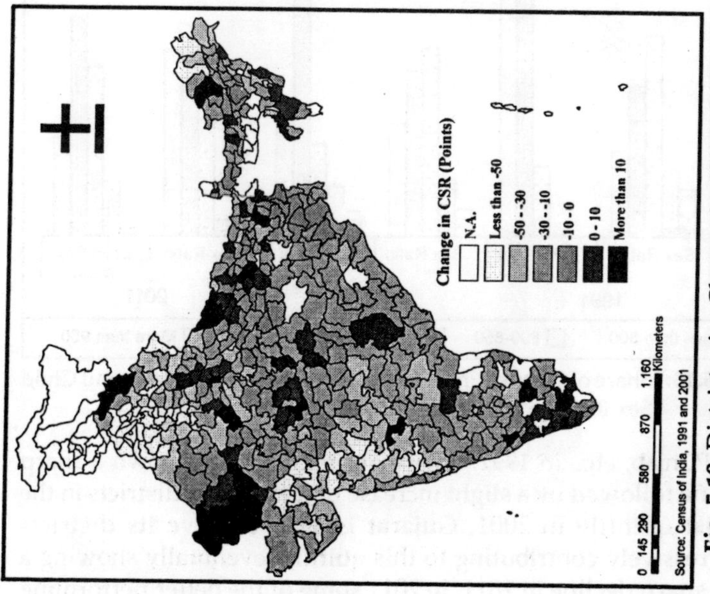

Fig. 5.10: District-wise Change in Child Sex Ratio (1991-2001)

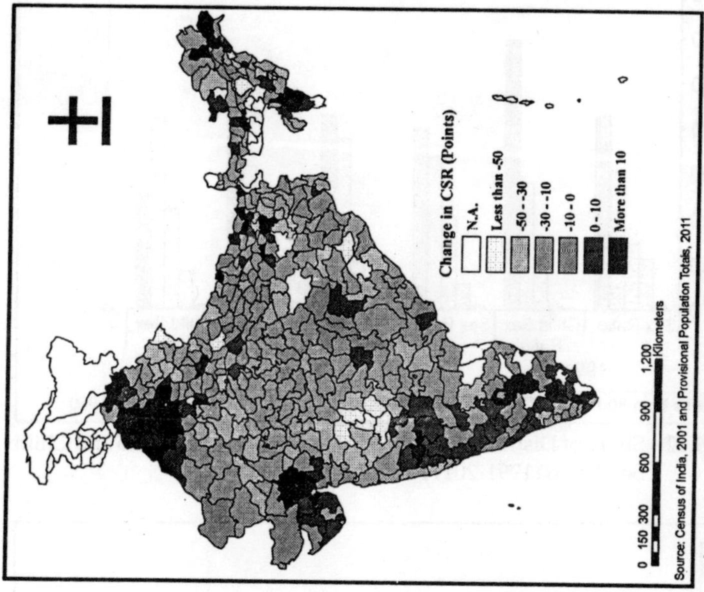

Fig. 5.11: District-wise Change in Child Sex Ratio (2001-2011)

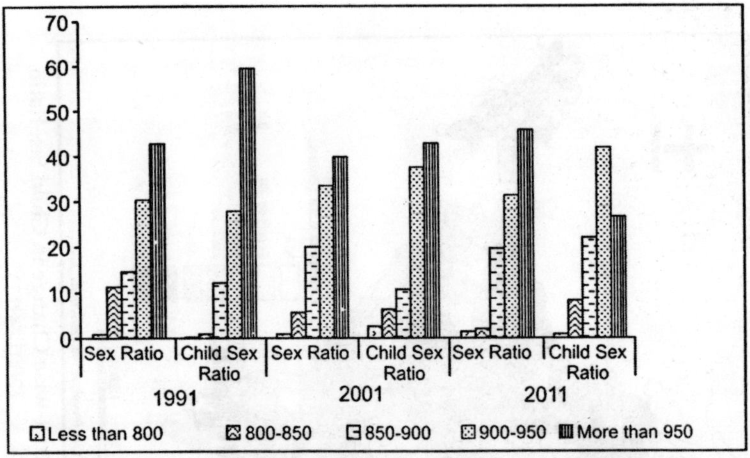

Fig. 5.12: Share of Districts in Different Categories of Sex Ratio and Child Sex Ratio (1991-2011)

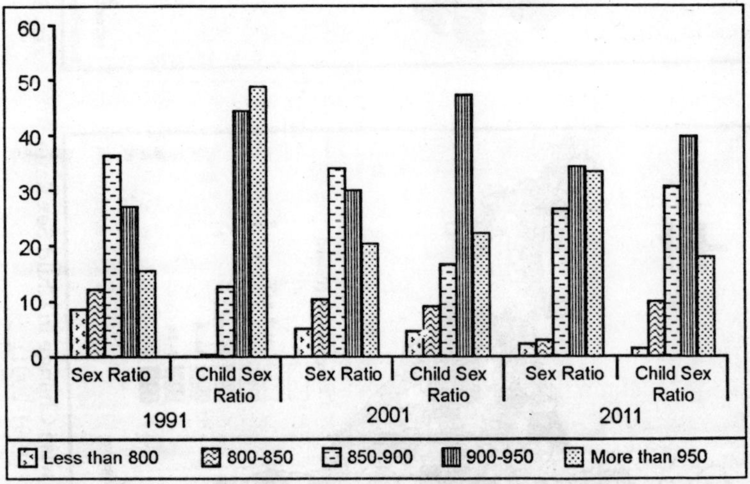

Fig. 5.13: Share of Districts in Different Categories of Sex Ratio and Child Sex Ratio in Urban Areas (1991-2011)

and Punjab, etc., in 1991. Rajasthan in 2001 have shown a sharp decline followed by a slight increase of its share of districts in the lowest quintile in 2001. Gujarat is seen to have its districts progressively contributing to this quintile eventually showing a very sharp decline in 2011. In 2011 some of the better performing

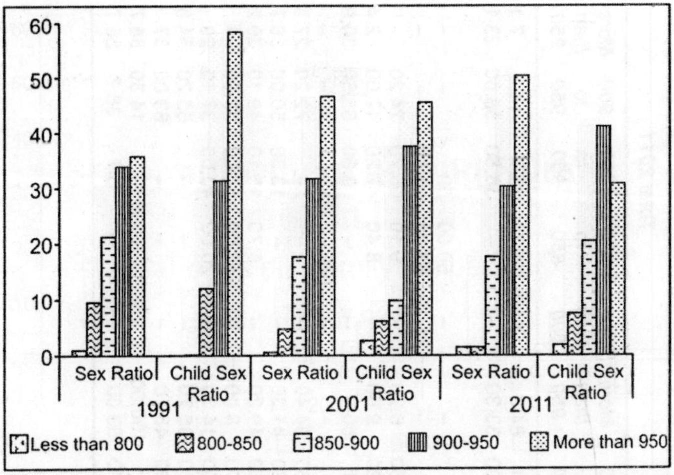

Fig. 5.14: Share of Districts in Different Categories of Sex Ratio and Child Sex Ratio in Rural Areas (1991-2011)

States like Maharashtra which had none districts in the bottommost quintile of Child Sex Ratio have shown a clear upshot in 2011 and so for the case of Jammu and Kashmir (Figure 5.15). While those States which had an increased number of districts in the lowest 20 per cent of Child Sex Ratio in 2001 like UP, Gujarat, Himachal Pradesh, etc., have in fact got their relative share reduced in the recent decade.

From the above analyses three facts have become clear, firstly, temporal worsening of the condition of Child Sex Ratio. Secondly, that the decline is much stronger in urban areas than in rural areas. Thirdly, regional shifts of this adverse condition. The third finding is well evident in the following Table showing rank correlation of different districts in order to enquire whether there have been any relative shifts in the temporal ranking of the States from 1991 to 2011.

Between 1991 and 2001 the correlation values depict no major changes in the relative performance of the States except to some extent in urban areas where the centres of sex determination clinics have already started cropping up (Table 5.4). Between 2001 and 2011 significant changes in rankings of districts took place in rural areas especially those parts lying in close proximity to urban areas where accessibility to these clinics are easier as well as diffusion

Table 5.1: State-wise Share of Districts in Different Categories of Child Sex Ratio

States	Total 1991					Total 2001					Total 2011				
	Less than 800	800 to 850	850 to 900	900 to 950	More than 950	Less than 800	800 to 850	850 to 900	900 to 950	More than 950	Less than 800	800 to 850	850 to 900	900 to 950	More than 950
Jammu & Kashmir	–	–	–	–	–	14.3	–	–	21.4	64.3	7.10	35.70	35.7	14.3	7.1
Himachal Pradesh	–	–	–	33.30	66.70	–	25	16.70	25.00	33.30	–	–	38.50	38.50	23.1
Punjab	–	–	100.0	–	–	52.9	47.1	–	–	–	–	50.00	50	–	–
Haryana	–	–	100.0	–	–	26.3	68.4	5.30	–	–	21.10	63.20	15.80	–	–
Rajasthan	–	–	24.10	55.20	20.70	–	3.10	28.10	62.50	6.20	–	9.10	66.70	24.20	–
UP+Uttarakhand	–	–	20.60	58.70	20.60	–	1.20	28.90	60.20	9.60	–	8.40	42.20	47.00	2.4
Bihar+Jharkhand	–	–	–	26.20	73.80	–	–	–	49.1	50.9	–	–	3.60	65.50	30.9
N.E.States	–	–	–	–	–	–	–	–	–	–	–	–	–	–	–
West Bengal	–	–	–	–	100.0	–	–	–	5.60	94.40	–	–	–	72.20	27.8
Orissa	–	–	–	15.40	84.60	–	2.70	2.70	53.30	41.30	–	–	13.30	50.00	36.7
MP+Chhattisgarh	–	2.20	8.70	41.30	47.80	–	3.30	3.30	44.30	49.20	–	5.70	15.10	49.10	30.2
Gujarat	–	–	10.00	65.00	25.00	–	16.00	44.00	32.00	8.00	–	12.00	52.00	32.00	4
Maharashtra	–	–	–	34.50	65.50	–	2.90	22.90	60.00	14.30	–	20.00	40.00	37.10	29
Andhra Pradesh	–	–	–	–	100.0	–	–	–	4.30	95.70	–	–	–	65.20	34.8
Karnataka	–	–	–	–	100.0	–	–	–	51.90	48.10	–	–	–	63.00	37
Kerala	–	–	–	21.40	78.60	–	–	–	–	100.00	–	–	–	14.30	85.7
Tamil Nadu	–	5.00	–	25.00	70.00	–	–	13.30	26.70	60.00	–	–	6.7	36.7	56.7

Table 5.2: State-wise Share of Districts in Different Categories of Child Sex Ratio (Rural)

States	Rural 1991					Rural 2001					Rural 2011				
	Less than 800	800 to 850	850 to 900	900 to 950	More than 950	Less than 800	800 to 850	850 to 900	900 to 950	More than 950	Less than 800	800 to 850	850 to 900	900 to 950	More than 950
Jammu & Kashmir	–	–	–	–	–	–	14.3	–	14.3	71.4	7.1	35.7	28.6	21.4	7.1
Himachal Pradesh	–	–	–	33.30	66.70	–	16.7	16.7	25.00	41.70	–	–	33.30	33.30	33.3
Punjab	–	–	100.0	–	–	52.9	47.1	–	–	–	–	50.00	50	–	–
Haryana	–	–	100.0	–	–	26.3	63.20	10.5	–	–	26.30	52.60	21.10	–	–
Rajasthan	–	–	25.90	55.60	18.50	–	–	28.1	59.40	12.50	–	9.40	65.60	25.00	–
UP+Uttarakhand	–	–	15.90	65.10	19.00	–	–	26.5	62.70	10.80	–	6.00	38.60	53.00	2.4
Bihar+Jharkhand	–	–	–	26.20	73.80	–	–	–	45.50	54.5	–	–	1.80	63.60	34.5
N.E. States	–	–	–	–	–	–	–	–	–	–	–	–	–	–	–
West Bengal	–	–	–	–	100.0	–	–	–	–	–	–	–	–	47.10	52.9
Orissa	–	–	–	15.40	84.60	–	–	–	40.00	–	–	–	13.30	43.30	43.3
MP+Chhattisgarh	–	2.20	6.70	46.70	44.40	–	3.30	3.30	44.30	49.20	–	4.90	11.50	47.50	36.1
Gujarat	–	–	21.10	57.90	21.10	–	8.00	32.0	48.00	12.00	–		44.00	52.00	4
Maharashtra	–	–	–	50.00	50.00	–	6.10	21.2	48.50	24.20	–	18.2	33.3	36.4	9.1
Andhra Pradesh	–	–	–	4.30	95.70	–	–	–	4.50	95.50	–	–	–	63.60	36.4
Karnataka	–	–	–	10.00	90.00	–	–	–	51.90	48.10	–	–	–	55.60	44.4
Kerala	–	–	–	21.40	78.60	–	–	–	–	100.00	–	–	–	7.10	92.9
Tamil Nadu	–	4.80	–	23.80	71.40	–	3.40	10.3	34.50	51.70	–	–	13.8	34.5	51.7

Table 5.3: State-wise Share of Districts in Different Categories of Child Sex Ratio (Urban)

States	*Urban 1991*					*Urban 2001*					*Urban 2011*				
	Less than 800	*800 to 850*	*850 to 900*	*900 to 950*	*More than 950*	*Less than 800*	*800 to 850*	*850 to 900*	*900 to 950*	*More than 950*	*Less than 800*	*800 to 850*	*850 to 900*	*900 to 950*	*More than 950*
Jammu & Kashmir	–	–	–	–	–	14.3	21.4	21.4	28.6	14.3	–	28.6	42.9	14.3	14.3
Himachal Pradesh	–	–	50.00	50.00	–	–	60.0	40.00	–	–	–	20.00	60.00	20.00	–
Punjab	–	7.7	92.3	–	–	64.7	35.3	–	–	–	–	50.00	50	–	–
Haryana	–	–	87.50	12.50	–	47.4	52.60	–	–	–	26.30	68.40	5.30	–	–
Rajasthan	–	3.4	27.6	65.5	3.4	–	12.5	46.90	40.60	–	–	21.90	75.00	3.10	–
UP+Uttarakhand	–	–	11.10	65.10	23.80	2.4	6.0	43.4	44.6	3.6	3.6	10.8	53.0	31.3	1.2
Bihar+Jharkhand	–	–	–	38.10	61.90	–	–	5.50	85.50	9.1	–	–	27.30	67.30	5.5
N.E.States	–	–	–	–	–	–	–	–	–	–	–	–	–	–	–
West Bengal	–	–	–	29.40	70.60	–	–	–	50.00	50.00	–	–	5.60	66.70	27.8
Orissa	–	–	–	46.20	53.80	–	–	3.30	63.30	33.30	–	6.70	20.00	66.70	6.7
MP+Chhattisgarh	–	–	10.90	60.90	28.30	–	4.90	13.10	77.00	4.90	–	4.90	27.90	60.70	6.6
Gujarat	–	–	20.00	70.00	10.00	–	12.50	41.70	41.70	4.20	4.00	16.00	72.00	8.00	–
Maharashtra	–	–	–	76.7	20.0	–	2.90	37.10	60.00	–	–	11.4	60.0	28.6	–
Andhra Pradesh	–	–	–	–	91.30	–	–	–	21.70	78.30	–	–	–	65.20	34.8
Karnataka	–	–	–	–	61.90	–	–	–	63.00	37.00	–	–	–	66.70	33.3
Kerala	–	–	–	–	85.70	–	–	–	7.10	92.90	–	–	–	14.30	85.7
Tamil Nadu	–	–	–	42.90	57.10	–	–	–	33.30	66.70	–	–	–	33.3	66.7

Table 5.4: Rank Correlation Coefficients of Child Sex Ratio

Years	Total	Rural	Urban
1991 and 2001	0.819	0.837	0.685
2001 and 2011	0.885	0.648	0.844
1991 and 2011	0.748	0.571	0.651

Note : All the Correlations are Statistically Significant at 1 percent level.

of the modern methods of sex selection are constantly taking place. This shifting is more prominent from 1991 to 2011 statistically significant at 1 per cent level. Some of the explorations of the above analysis have already shown the traditionally disadvantaged States like Punjab and Haryana have done better in the recent decade while Maharashtra have a progressive decline in Child Sex Ratio showing a tendency of North-South dilution across the social space of daughter elimination.

Empirical Evidence through Female Neglect and Pre-Birth Elimination

This section seeks for the mechanisms of the adverse condition of Child Sex Ratio guided by the twin processes of female neglect and sex selective abortions. Whether or not these factors have been operative and by what extent is a matter of enquiry in the present subset. The Child Sex Ratio transition in India has undergone a transition from neglect and infanticide of the girl child to more focused sex selective abortions both indicative of daughter aversion, and are nothing but the variants towards the common goal depending upon the purpose of choice of elimination. Ideally as more males are born than females and male foetus susceptible to greater mortality than females, the Sex Ratio at Birth (SRB) of 950 boys per 1000 girls is considered to be normal. However, in India barring a few States like West Bengal and Andhra Pradesh in 1998-00, Tamil Nadu in 2001-03, Chhattisgarh and Kerala in 2004-06 and 2006-08, no other States have recorded more or equal to the ideal values (Table 5.5). The SRB of India as a whole is stationed at 897 in 1998-00 showing little improvement in 2007-09 (913). This overall increase in SRB values is mainly contributed by the so called worst performers in SRB during the earlier period

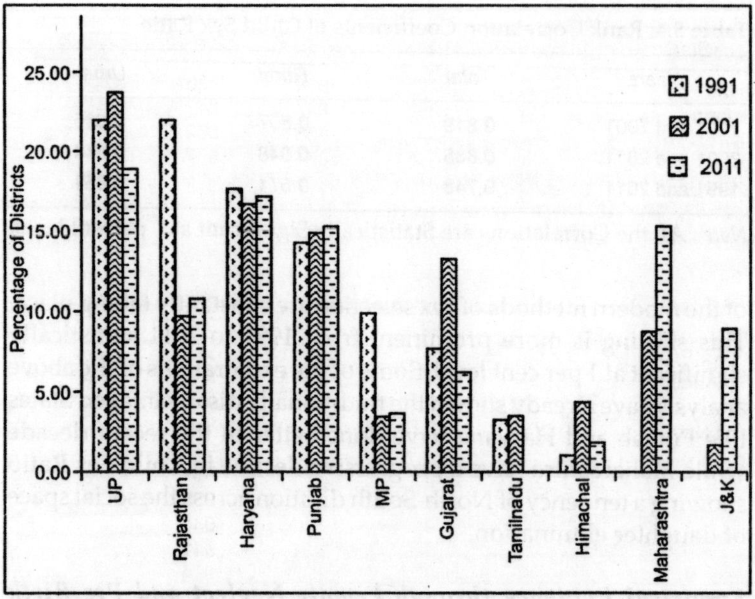

Fig. 5.15: Ralative Contribution of Districts from Different States Falling in the Bottommost Quintile of Child Sex Ratio (1991-2011)

such as the States of Punjab, Haryana, Himachal Pradesh, Gujarat, MP, etc., showing an appreciable improvement over the periods. However, the pushing effects of these States is also lagged by the pulling effect of those who is critical SRB has declined such as Rajasthan, Maharashtra, Tamil Nadu, etc. The regional picture points essentially to the dilution of the processes of sex selective abortions for which a proxy had been taken through SRB either by realization of the potential worth of today's girl and tomorrow's bride or through effective policy implications.

Female neglect captured by Age specific death rate of less than 4 age group show a clear cut differentiation of Northern *vis-à-vis* Southern States (Table 5.6), the latter showing a lesser female male ratio of mortality projected by greater prestige and status upholded of a girl child. Nearly all of Northern India excepting West Bengal reveals excess girl child mortality associated with the high economic and cultural burden of bearing a girl child.

Table 5.5: State-wise Sex Ratio at Birth

States	*1998-00*	*2001-03*	*2004-06*	*2006-08*	*2007-09*
Punjab	792	776	808	836	836
Haryana	797	807	837	847	849
J&K	—	—	838	862	870
UP	868	853	874	877	874
Rajasthan	877	855	855	870	875
Delhi			847	877	882
Maharashtra	913	887	879	884	896
Gujarat	851	862	865	898	904
India	898	883	892	909	913
Bihar	896	861	881	914	917
Andhra Pradesh	960	932	917	917	919
Jharkhand	—	—	888	922	921
MP	907	922	913	919	926
Tamil Nadu	931	953	955	936	929
Assam	984	904	920	933	931
Orissa	928	934	934	937	941
Himachal Pradesh	902	803	872	938	944
Karnataka	942	943	917	935	944
WB	952	937	931	941	944
Kerala	930	892	922	964	968
Chhattisgarh	—	—	961	975	980

Source: SRS Bulletins, Registrar General of India.

Fertility Transition under Strong Son Preference

Results from the Multivariate Model

In order to trace out the differentials in desire for having children in terms of the family size and a number of socio-demographic factors, a binary logistic regression analysis (Table 5.7) has been attempted. However, as the nature of these determinants vary regionally and across rural to urban context, three separate models have been worked out to show the changing scenario of desired family size along with their necessary covariates as a whole and according to changing place of residence (i.e., rural or urban). The dependent variable in this case is the desire for having more children and this factor is examined in the context of the number of existing children and their sex as well as a host of other socio-demographic factors. The main objective of this exercise is to enquire the necessary intention of households to limit their

Table.5.6: Female Male Ratio of Age Specific Death Rate

States	Age groups	F/M Ratio 1997	2000	2003	2006
Andhra Pradesh	Below 1	0.96	0.94	0.96	0.94
	1 to 4	0.84	1.37	0.86	0.62
	0 to 4	0.96	1.01	0.95	0.92
Assam	Below 1	1.05	1.27	0.90	1.02
	1 to 4	1.40	0.99	1.25	1.12
	0 to 4	1.13	1.25	0.98	1.02
Bihar	Below 1	0.96	0.94	1.02	0.92
	1 to 4	1.54	1.64	1.48	1.75
	0 to 4	1.09	1.09	1.08	1.15
Gujarat	Below 1	1.03	1.05	1.04	1.11
	1 to 4	1.98	1.53	1.14	1.19
	0 to 4	1.19	1.13	1.13	1.14
Haryana	Below 1	1.02	1.11	1.22	1.10
	1 to 4	2.52	1.57	2.04	1.58
	0 to 4	1.27	1.21	1.36	1.14
Himachal Pradesh	Below 1	0.94	0.76	0.82	1.16
	1 to 4	1.50	1.70	1.07	1.80
	0 to 4	1.04	0.88	0.80	1.21
Karnataka	Below 1	1.08	0.71	1.03	1.09
	1 to 4	1.20	1.23	1.11	0.57
	0 to 4	1.10	0.80	1.01	1.04
Kerala	Below 1	1.13	0.87	1.08	1.14
	1 to 4	1.38	1.13	1.67	1.20
	0 to 4	1.17	0.94	1.12	1.13
MP	Below 1	0.87	1.14	1.09	1.04
	1 to 4	1.37	1.62	1.30	1.55
	0 to 4	0.98	1.22	1.15	1.12
Maharashtra	Below 1	0.79	1.08	1.66	1.01
	1 to 4	1.27	1.44	1.41	0.77
	0 to 4	0.88	1.13	1.61	0.96
Orissa	Below 1	1.00	0.92	0.92	1.06
	1 to 4	1.00	1.51	1.03	1.08
	0 to 4	1.01	1.00	0.97	1.04
Punjab	Below 1	1.34	1.42	1.14	1.28
	1 to 4	1.61	1.46	1.44	1.70
	0 to 4	1.40	1.36	1.23	1.36
Rajasthan	Below 1	1.26	1.13	1.10	0.92
	1 to 4	1.37	1.86	1.41	1.59
	0 to 4	1.28	1.26	1.11	1.11
Tamil Nadu	Below 1	1.21	1.07	0.98	0.97
	1 to 4	0.94	1.13	1.31	0.54
	0 to 4	1.20	1.08	1.03	0.93
UP	Below 1	1.12	1.07	1.18	1.04
	1 to 4	1.87	1.65	1.56	1.52
	0 to 4	1.29	1.20	1.25	1.12
WB	Below 1	0.91	0.89	1.05	0.99
	1 to 4	0.96	0.94	1.13	0.76
	0 to 4	0.92	0.90	1.03	0.98
India	Below 1	1.02	1.02	1.09	1.01
	1 to 4	1.49	1.49	1.36	1.36
	0 to 4	1.12	1.11	1.13	1.09

Source: SRS Bulletins, Registrar General of India.

Table.5.7: Summary of Regression Analysis

Background Variables	*Desire to have more children*		
	Odds Ratio		
	Total	*Rural*	*Urban*
No. of living children (Ref. more than 2)			
Less than or equal to 2	2.121*	2.180*	1.510***
	(0.335)	(0.363)	(2.093)
Sex-specific Birth Order (Ref. female)			
1	1.269*	1.416*	–0.525***
	(0.214)	(0.229)	(0.001)
2	–1.086*	–1.045*	–1.195***
	(0.219)	(0.231)	(0.678)
3	–1.064*	–1.185*	0.580
	(0.212)	(0.226)	(0.896)
4	0.378	0.454**	0.702
	0.202)	(0.084)	(0.893)
5+	0.268	0.335	–0.165
	(0.200)	(0.214)	(0.973)
For those currently married women (15-49) who has less than or equal to two living children			
Household Structure (Ref. Non-Nuclear)			
Nuclear	0.496***	0.512	0.461***
	(0.242)	(0.256)	(0.110)
Wealth Index (Ref. Poorest)			
Poorer	2.943	2.628	3.512
	(2.085)	(2.375)	(3.813)
Middle	2.785	2.531	4.140
	(2.086)	(2.376)	(3.825)
Richer	1.492	1.158	2.739
	(2.110)	(2.409)	(3.730)
Richest	1.948	2.017	3.332
	(2.125)	(2.494)	(3.640)
Caste (Ref. General)			
SC	0.235	0.231	3.370
	(0.291)	(0.301)	(2.685)
ST	0.009	0.022	0.137
	(0.243)	(0.257)	(1.180)
OBC	0.561	0.571***	0.467
	(0.311)	(0.017)	(1.179)
Mother's Education (Ref. No Education)			
Primary	0.699**	1.579**	0.560*
	(1.794)	(1.989)	(0.002)
Secondary	2.215	3.814***	0.572*
	(2.769)	(1.089)	(0.003)
Higher	3.746***	6.649***	0.906*
	(2.123)	(2.327)	(0.001)

(Contd.)

Table 5.7 *(Contd.)*

Background Variables	*Desire to have more children*		
	Odds Ratio		
	Total	*Rural*	*Urban*
Partner's Education (Ref. No Education)			
Primary	3.614***	3.156***	0.353
	(1.156)	(1.909)	(3.631)
Secondary	3.024	2.459	1.236***
	(2.158)	(3.912)	(0.653)
Higher	3.360***	3.072***	3.040***
	(1.101)	(1.705)	(1.013)
Mother's Work (Ref. No Work)			
Currently Working	0.212***	0.100	0.340***
	(0.001)	(0.153)	(0.003)
Worked Last Year	0.332	0.123	0.754
	(0.445)	(2.123)	(1.897)
MEI (Ref. Low)			
Medium	0.999***	2.828***	1.482**
	(0.326)	(1.037)	(0.377)
High	0.274***	2.250***	0.318*
	(0.113)	(1.012)	(0.003)
Constant	–5.278	–4.258	–39.039*
	(3.010)	(3.545)	(1.662)
–2 log likelihood	793.746	701.055	57.468

Significance Levels: *1 per cent, **5 per cent, ***10 per cent.
Standard Errors in parentheses.
The MEI includes the following indicators:

(i) Adult women literacy (15-49 years).
(ii) Percentage of adult women (15-49) having exposure to some kind of mass media.
(iii) Percentage of currently married women who alone or jointly with their husbands decide how their own earnings are used.
(iv) Percentage of men who say that wives should have the final say alone or jointly with the husband in six major decisions (Decisions include major household purchases, visits to the wives' family or relatives jointly or alone, permitted to go to the market alone, wives own decision making ability for her own health care, what to do with the money the wife earns and wives decision making ability for using contraceptives).
(v) Percentage of Female headed households.

family size depending upon the sex and number of the existing children that has obvious implications on the conscious choice of sex selection, especially in the regime of small family norms. It is notable that a number of socio-demographic factors discussed here also have significant relation with the changes in family size itself; therefore, the differential probabilities that may occur in response to these factors can be interpreted as the indirect effects of family size, or more specifically, the small family norm itself.

Results from the three separate models have been shown in Table 5.7. It can be seen that the probability of wanting more children is usually higher in the case of the families that already have two or less than two living children, although this tendency is much lower in urban areas rather than their rural counterparts. The results are statistically significant and strongly support the urban households' larger intention to go by the small family norms, mainly driven by the rising opportunity cost of child bearing and child rearing. Nevertheless, this analysis require deeper enquiry in terms of gendered preferences in family size limitation. The sex-specific birth order of the children has shown an interesting result in this regard. It can be observed that the chances to desire for more children are likely to be much higher in the case of female siblings in the first birth order than the males, although the situation reverts in the case of the two higher birth orders. These results are also statistically significant and a strong indicator of the sex selective ways of family size limitation. Another significant finding is that unlike the overall picture or the rural background, families residing in the urban areas show lower intention to have more children if the first child is a girl rather than a son. In other words, the probability of desiring another child is less in the case of a single daughter rather than a single son in the urban areas, whereas the rural and overall scenarios show a reverse trend. In addition to this, it is also found that the progressive disintegration of families in the urban areas, coupled with the perceived trade-off between the number of children and their personal achievements has resulted more qualitative development of children rather than any sex preference. Therefore, it can be seen that after controlling only for the currently married women who have already less than or equal to two living children, the nuclear families in urban areas, unlike their rural counterparts, are likely to have less desire for additional children due to these reasons. However, higher value of women in terms of education and labour services provided are additional facts that drive this. This is portrayed by the fact that higher level of parental education, especially mother's education in the urban areas results lower chances of wanting more children than their rural counterparts, which is statistically significant. It is also notable that in rural areas, mothers having higher level of education show larger likelihood of having additional children than their less educated counterparts. This is nothing but the result of the diffusion of the knowledge factor which acts reversely in the rural areas, thereby guiding the parents about the processes and factors of family size limitation and related daughter aversions. Same factor can be seen in the case of the education of their counterparts. Factors like income or wealth profile and caste of the households have not shown any significant results, although the poorest and richest parts have shown higher chances of wanting additional children in presence of two or less existing children than their middle counterparts, especially in the rural areas. The rationale behind this is different for the two classes; for the richer ones it is the greater due to larger son-preference rooting from economic and cultural factors whereas for the poorer section, it is much due to lesser penetration of family planning practices and increase in the family labour force. The working mothers, both in rural and urban areas, are supposed to have lower chances for desiring more children while already having two or less children, although for urban it shows a more significant effect. The empowerment level of mothers, that consists a host of factors incorporates the literacy and awareness profile of the mothers as well as their decision making ability in the family, has shown interesting results. It can be seen that in urban areas, mothers with higher level of empowerment have shown statistically significant lower chances of desiring additional children, whereas in rural areas, the situation is reverse. It is the same rationale of knowledge diffusion which is manifested into more conscious choice of family size limitation, keeping into view the sex of the existing child. Henceforth, it can be opined that the modernization factors have acted differentially in these cases which somehow prolongs the factor of daughter aversion in the conscious scope of family size limitation. The additional factor of technology and pre-birth elimination techniques have simply acted as a catalyst in these processes.

Concluding Remarks

The Child Sex Ratio has declined sharply for most of the major States of India in the recent decade. Such a phenomenon could be attributed to the strong cultural preference mediated by the modern technologies of sex preference especially in the urban areas who are the forerunners of the adoption of small family norms. The study traced a dilution of the traditional north-south divide of son preference supported by the converging trend of Child Sex Ratio and Sex Ratio at Birth, a proxy of sex selective abortions. States that have attained replacement level fertility like Maharashtra and Tamil Nadu seem to catch up with their Northern counterparts like Punjab and Haryana in terms of pre-birth elimination of female foetus. The growths of the small family norms have thus become indistinguishable for planning for sons, and certainly not for only daughters. On the other extreme sSates with considerably large family size daughters predominate who are mostly unwanted with a desire of having sons. The phenomenon of son preference is found to be strongest among the middle classes due to better life chances and rising opportunity costs. A strong instance of rural-urban convergence can also be seen due to the gradual diffusion of sex-selection technologies across space. Therefore, the study concludes the continuity of the past with the present situations of girl child elimination through infanticide and neglect transmuted into a more focused pre-birth elimination. Women are passive speakers to decide upon the pre-birth elimination largely conditioned by its male counterparts.

REFERENCES

Bhat, M. (2003), On the Trail of Missing Indian Females: II: Illusion and Reality, *Economic and Political Weekly*, 37(52): 5244-5263.

Bose, A. (2001), Fighting Female Foeticide: Growing Greed and Shrinking Child Sex Ratio, *Economic and Political Weekly*, 36(36): 3427-3429.

Das, N.P. (2004), Intensified Masculinity of the Child Sex Ratio in India: A Phenomenon of Sex Selective Abortion, iussp2005.princeton.edu/download.aspx?submissionId = 50265

Das Gupta, M. (1987), Selective Discrimination against Female Children in Rural Punjab, North India, *Population and Development Review*, 13(1): 77-100.

Dyson, T. and Moore, M. (1983), On Kinship Structure, Female Autonomy, and Demographic Behaviour in India, *Population and Development Review*, 9(1): 35-60.

James, K.S. (1999), Fertility Decline in Andhra Pradesh: A Search for Alternative Hypotheses, *Economic and Political Weekly*, 34(8): 491-499.

Mayer, P. (1999), India's Falling Sex Ratios, *Population and Development Review*, 25(2): 323-343.

Murthi, M.; Guio, A.; and Dreze, J. (1995), Mortality, Fertility, and Gender Bias in India: A District-Level Analysis, *Population and Development Review*, 21(4): 745-782.

Seidl, C. (1995), The Desire for a Son is the Father of Many Daughters: A Sex Ratio Paradox, *Journal of Population Economics*, 8(2): 185-203.

Sudha, S. and Rajan, I. (2003), Persistent Daughter Disadvantage: What Do Estimated Sex Ratios at Birth and Sex Ratios of Child Mortality Risk Reveal?, *Economic and Political Weekly*, 38(41): 4361-4369.

Yadav, B. (2001), Haryana's 'Setting Daughters', *Economic and Political Weekly*, 36(45): 4257-4259.

6
Problem of Farm Viability and Agrarian Crisis
A Study of West Bengal

Rajib Dey

Introduction

The Indian economy entered in the Neo Liberal Policy Regime in 1991 as a part of structural adjustment reform by IMF. The direct and immediate impact of this policy in agriculture was, first of all, a cut in food and fertilizer subsidy and there was a rise in fertilizer price. The prices of nitrogenous fertilizer were increased by 40 per cent in July 1991 and subsequently the rise was reduced to 30 per cent in August 1991 (Rao, 1998). The prices of phosphatic and potassic fertilizers doubled following the decontrol in the early 1990s. A large section of poor, small and middle farmer found it extremely difficult to bear this higher price. Particularly, the IMF directed structural adjustment policy as a part of financial liberalization also curbed the provision of institutional credit (Bhattacharyya and Bhattacharyya, 2007). Given the fact that the increased price of fertilizer and decreased access to credit, the peasantry in large faced a hand to mouth situation. The latest Situation Assessment Survey of Farmers 2005 of NSSO (National Sample Survey Organisation) observes that the average Monthly Per Capita Expenditure (MPCE) of a farm household has been just Rs. 503 (US$ 11.32) in 2003 across regions, classes and income groups, with 27 per cent of farmers not liking farming while 40 per cent felt that given the option they would prefer other career owing to poor earnings. According to (National Sample Survey

Organisation) NSSO report on 'Indebtedness of Farmers Household' stated that out of 89.35 million farmer households, about 43.42 million (48.6%) were indebted. This is nearly half the farm households in the country.

The farmers in most of the regions in India are fed up with crop cultivation because they have not been able to recover even the cost of cultivation. The (SAS) Situation Assessment Survey carried out on various aspects of farming by the Ministry of Agriculture clearly showed that over 40 per cent of farmers are willing to get out of farming because it had become non-viable [Narayanamoorthy (2007)].

During the post-liberalisation period (1990-93 to 2003-06), the growth rates of both agricultural output and of land yields slowed down as compared with the pre-liberalisation period. At the all-India level, while the output growth rate decelerated to 1.74 per cent per annum from 3.37 per cent per annum, the yield growth rate decelerated to 1.52 per cent per annum from 3.17 per cent per annum in the earlier period and the diversification towards oilseeds has slowed down considerably.

The most important feature during 1990-93 to 2003-06 is that agricultural growth decelerated sharply at the all-India level and in all regions. At the all-India level, the output growth decelerated to 1.74 per cent per annum during 1990-93 to 2003-06. The main reason for the deceleration of growth during the post-reform period was a visible deceleration in investment in irrigation and other rural infrastructure [Bhalla and Singh (2009)].

Patnaik, U. (2005) clearly stated that there is not over supply of foodgrains, but a decline in foodgrains supply and an even more drastic decline of effective demand for foodgrains especially in rural India owing to an abnormally fast loss of purchasing power during 1998-2004 and poverty is very high on the basis of current data affecting at least three-quarters of rural and over two-fifths of the urban population.

The New Economic Policy of early 90s open up the economy in an environment of freer operation of the market. As a result, the fertilizer subsidy was partially withdrawn, the public investment and expenditure were slashed down and there was a partial withdrawal of subsidies of food and credit, particularly the priority sector lending. Hence, New Economic Policy intensified the ongoing process of the differentiation of the peasantry [Bhattacharyya (2008)].

Aerthayil (2008) stated that with the Structural Adjustment Programme (SAP) in 1991, the policy of globalisation was concretely introduced in India. Based on this policy and the directives of the World Bank, International Monetary Fund and World Trade Organisation, the Indian economy was substantially overhauled. The Export-Import policy was liberalised; the import and customs duties of many products were drastically lowered or totally dropped so that they could be imported without any restriction. The government started reducing its investment in agriculture and the industrial sector allowing the private sector to take over. The restructuring of the public distribution system really affected the availability of foodgrains to the poor at subsidised rates. All such measures had implications for the farm sector.

According to the Mid-term Appraisal of the Tenth Five-Year Plan (2002-07), the rate of growth of the GDP in agriculture and allied sectors was just one per cent per annum during the year 2002-05. As a result, per capita availability of foodgrains decreased; the growth rate of population became higher than that of foodgrains, and India started to import foodgrains at a much higher price than that in the domestic market.

In the post-reform period the government reduced different types of subsidies to agriculture, and this has increased the production cost of cultivation. According to Ramesh Chand, an economist, cutback in subsidy and control of fertilisers over the last few years has adversely affected the agricultural sector. It has increased the input cost and made agriculture less profitable. Since the decrease in subsidy to agriculture is part of the regulations of the WTO, it is related to the policy of globalisation.

After 1991, the lending pattern of commercial banks, including nationalised banks, to agriculture drastically changed with the result that loan was not easily available and the interest was not affordable. This has forced the farmers to rely on moneylenders and thus pushed up the expenditure on agriculture. The National Commission for Agriculture, headed by Dr. M.S. Swaminathan, also pointed out that removal of the lending facilities and concessions of banks during the post-reform period have accelerated the crisis in agriculture. When the farmers were not able to pay back loan with high interest, they fell into the debt trap. Studies show that most of the farmers' suicides were due to the debt trap. It is part of the policy of privatisation that banks, even nationalised banks, look for profit over their social responsibilities to the people.

There has been a decline in the trend growth rate of production as well as productivity for almost all crops from the mid-nineties. Further, the value of output from agriculture has been declining from late nineties. Second, there is an excessive dependence of a large section of the population on agriculture (in 2004-05 nearly 64 per cent of the rural persons were from households whose members major activity status was either self-employed in agriculture or agricultural labour). This also indicates that rural non-farm employment opportunities are limited. Third, with declining size-class of holding and an increasing preponderance of marginal holdings (63% as per 2000-01 agricultural census) along with poor returns from cultivation indicates that income for farm households is very low. Fourth, the much talked about green revolution had a greater focus on rice and wheat under irrigated condition bypassing crops and regions under rainfed or dry land conditions (which is three-fifths of the 141 million hectares of net sown area in the country during 2003-04). There has been a failure to capitalise on the vast network of institutes to provide and regulate new technology (including the usage of biotechnology), and a virtual absence of extension service. Fifth, the neglect of agriculture in plan resource allocation has led to a decline of public investments in irrigation and other related infrastructure. Sixth, supply of credit from formal sources to the agricultural sector is inadequate leading to greater reliance on informal sources at higher interest burden. Last, but not the least, with changing technology and market conditions the farmer is increasingly being exposed to the uncertainties of the product as well as factor markets [Mishra (2007)].

By using household level data from the 48th and 59th rounds (1992 and 2003-04) of the NSSO, finds that (within the limitations of the data) more than 40 per cent of households in rural India do not own land, as much as 15 million acres is in ownership holdings of more than 20 acres, and inequality in ownership has worsened between 1992 and 2003-04 [Rawal (2008)].

Mazumdar (1999), Ramachandran and Swaminathan (2001), Shetty (2004) in their studies explored that policy fatigue with reference to agricultural credit is prime culprit of Agrarian crisis in India.

The agrarian crisis and the threatened decimation of the peasantry are casually connected with the process of growth, which is the accepted agenda of all mainstream political formations. The marginalized peasantry, and the landless poor depending on agriculture and allied activities for their livelihood are the first and the worst victims of the unfolding logic of the growth [Shukla, 2007)].

Regarding the objectives, this study aims to comprehend the real situation of farm viability and to compare cultivators income with poverty level.

Methodology

This study covered four districts of West Bengal and was carried out by the author in different time periods from July 2010 to March 2011. The districts were selected purposively. The following districts were Birbhum, Burdwan, Hooghly, Murshidabad, Birbhum for paddy, Burdwan for paddy, mustard and potato, Hooghly for paddy, potato and mustard; Murshidabad for paddy and jute. In each district, 2-3 major crops were identified, which were cultivated by marginal farmers. Based on the major crops identified in the districts at least one village was selected for each major crop. Care was taken to select village with different socio-economic, cultural and geographical background. From each of the selected district two villages that were distantly located were identified. The sample villages were directly selected from the district-wise village-level 2001 census disaggregated data. We have selected the household randomly (SRSWOR). The total number of households was 221.

We have used the NSSO definition to identify farmer and farmer household. Any person who possessed some land and was engaged in agricultural activities on any part of that land during the reference year was accepted as a farmer and any household which had at least one farmer member was accepted as a farmer household.

Our study have used Patnaik's E. criterion (For detail see Appendix A). Side by side the standard classification used by the Government of India's National Sample Survey Office (NSSO) that is acreage-group analysis for classification of peasants.

The farm-size grouping is self-explanatory. Five categories of households were constructed:

1. No land operated; that is, landless households.
2. Some land operated, but less than 2.5 acres.
3. Operated land in excess of 2.5 acres but less than or equal to 5 acres.
4. Operated land in excess of 5 acres but less than or equal to 10 acres.
5. Operated land in excess of 10 acres (Above 10 acres groups).

Scholars such as A.K. Sen (1966) and Thorner (1980) argue that farm sizes reflect the economic status of peasants and thus an analysis based on acreage sizes is, essentially, a class-based analysis. Patnaik, on the other hand, took a more classic Marxist approach to rural class differentiation. She measured differentiation of the peasantry in terms of labour use. She developed a labour exploitation index, or E-criterion, in order to obtain an empirical approximation to the analytical concept of the class status of the household based on labour use. The labour-exploitation index measured the farming family's use of outside labour through hiring in or employing tenants and, conversely, the dependence of the family members on working for others; both considered in relation to the extent of self-employment on their own farm. Under certain simplifying assumptions, this is identical to the surplus labour appropriated (or parted with), relative to surplus labour generated in self-employment. Patnaik argued that this index allowed a more precise study of the (class) dynamics of agrarian change. The six agrarian classes based on the labour-exploitation index are (Patnaik 1976, 1987):

- *Landlord*: Buyer of labour, not working on own land.
- *Rich Peasant*: Net buyer of labour, buying in more than spent on working own land.
- *Middle Peasant*: Net buyer of labour, but of fewer days than spent on working own land.
- *Small Peasant*: Net provider of labour, but of fewer days than spent on working own land.

- *Poor Peasant*: Net provider of labour, more days than spent on working own land.
- *Landless Worker*: Provider of labour, not working own land.

The labour-exploitation index seeks to give an empirical approximation to the analytical concept of the class status of the household. The class-status is essentially determined by the extent of the use of outside labour or to the extent the family works for others, relative to the extent of self-employment It is identical, under certain simplifying assumptions with the surplus labour appropriated or parted with, relative to surplus labour with self-employment.

$$E–x/Y–\{(H_i–H_o) + (L_o–L_i)\}/F$$

Where

H_i = Labour-days hired on the operational holding of the household.

H_o = Family labour days hired out to others.

L_i = Labour days worked on leased in land (whether by family or hired labour).

L_o = Labour days similarly worked on land leased out by the household.

F = Labour days worked by household worker on the operational holding.

'The index is a ratio, or a pure number, which can have positive or negative values depending on whether the household is a net employer of outside labour or is itself on balance working for others (as labourer or tenant). The range of values of *E* is from plus infinity to minus infinity, for at the two poles of the rural class structure, there will be diametrically opposite types of households for whom *F* will be zero or near zero: first, the big landlords have such a large resource endowment that they perform no manual labour themselves, but rely entirely on employing others' labour, and the landless labourers, with zero resource endowment; hence, zero self employment, who are entirely dependent on working for other" (Patnaik, 1988; p. 305). Classes within the cultivating peasantry are identified by looking at the degree of working for others or of employing others' labour, relative to self employment. For this purpose certain limits are set upon the values of the *E*-ratio, which are given, in the Appendix A. All subsequent use of class categories refers to the definitions given in the Table 6.2 taken from Patnaik (1976, 1987).

The survey data on the distribution of the (i) assets (land and non-land); (ii) outputs; (iii) surplus/deficit; and (iv) value-added. There are significant differences between the results obtained from the two types of grouping.

A complete list of households belonging to different occupational groups is available from the village papers lying at local Panchayat office. Among all rural households belonging to different occupational groups, we have taken only the household belonging to the cultivator category. From this category of households, simple random sample is drawn without replacement. We have used MS excel, access for analysing the data.

Asset Structure

In the reform era, West Bengal's agrarian economy has experienced class-differentiation with the arrival of more sophisticated technology. The previous studies of Bhattacharyya (2001), Rakshit (2010) advocated that Neo-liberal Policy intensified the ongoing process of differentiation of the peasantry in West Bengal. The outcome has been a greater ownership concentration in terms of land and non-land asset structure, in the upper grade of the rural class structure. Our study (see methodology) was undertaken after two decades of reform era, which was possible to represent the current scenario in rural West Bengal relating to asset composition.

Table 6.1: Acreage-wise Percentage Distribution of Major Assets

Farm Size	*%age of Different Types of Asset to Total Value of Asset*			*%age of Different Types of Asset to their Respective Total*		
	All Mechanical Asset	*Livestock Asset*	*Total Asset*	*All Mechanical Asset*	*Livestock Asset*	*Total Asset*
0	43.12	56.88	100	0.07	0.25	0.12
0.01-1.25	38.49	61.51	100	8.14	34.18	15.32
1.25-2.5	64.79	35.21	100	19.77	28.22	22.10
2.5-5.0	78.84	21.16	100	39.58	27.90	36.35
5.0-10.0	90.01	9.99	100	32.44	9.45	26.10
Total	72.42	27.58	100	100	100	100

Table 6.2: Class-wise Percentage Distribution of Major Assets

Economic Class	%age of Different Types of Asset to Total Value of Asset			%age of Different Types of Asset to their Respective Total		
	All Mechanical Asset	*Livestock Asset*	*Total Asset*	*All Mechanical asset*	*Livestock Asset*	*Total Asset*
Landless	43.12	56.88	100	0.07	0.25	0.12
Poor	36.11	63.89	100	0.94	4.39	1.89
Small	48.67	51.33	100	3.07	8.51	4.57
Middle	76.34	23.66	100	59.45	48.39	56.40
Rich	71.34	28.66	100	36.46	38.46	37.01
Total	72.42	27.58	100	100	100	100

Looking at the productive assets other than land in the survey region. Table 6.1 and Table 6.2 represent the percentage distribution of non-land asset structure by farm size and economic class, non-land asset classification has been organised under two broad categories: (i) Mechanical assets, and (ii) Livestock assets. Mechanical assets consists of simple machines such as the plough, sickle, spade and labour displacing modern implements such as tractors and submersible pumps, storage and transport equipment, including cold storage facilities.

The acreage grouping asset distribution shows that as we move from zero acre to 5.0-10.0 acre group percentage of mechanical asset to total value of their asset increases. The sample indicates that 90 per cent of mechanical assets to total is controlled by 5.0-10.0 acre groups whereas 0.01-1.25 acre group owned only 38 per cent approximately. Turning to percentage of livestock asset to total value of their asset the trend decreases from lower to higher acreage groups. Only approximately 10 per cent of livestocks to total is controlled by 5.0-10.0 acres group and 62 per cent approximately is owned by 0.01-1.25 acres group. Similarly, same result we found for percentage of mechanical asset to their respective total and percentage of livestock asset to their respective total.

The economic class-wise asset distribution shows that as we move from landless to rich peasant class percentage of mechanical asset to total value of asset increased from landless to middle peasant class and then it decreased to rich peasant class.

The sample result clearly revealed that middle peasants owned highest percentage of mechanical assets to total, i.e., 76 per cent approximately whereas poor peasants owned only 36 per cent. Looking at the percentage of livestock assets to total value of their assets, the sample result revealed that it decreased from landless to middle peasant, only 23 per cent of livestock assets to total is owned by middle peasants and 64 per cent of livestock assets to total is owned by poor peasants. Similarly, same result we found for percentage of mechanical asset to their respective total whereas we found an interesting result that percentage of livestock asset to their respective total increased from landless to middle peasant and then it decreased to rich peasant class.

This clearly indicates that there is a high level of non-land asset concentration in the higher acreage groups and higher economic classes. Thus, there is a high level of differentiation within the peasantry in terms of non-land asset holding.

Non-land Asset Structure

Now, we turn to the land asset structure in the survey region. The facts regarding land tenure-owned and operated as well as the percentage of holding by economic class and farm size is revealed in Tables 6.3 and 6.4. The structure of land according to acreage grouping analysis shows that percentage of holding decreased from lower to higher acreage groups. Approximately 42 per cent of holding is controlled by 0.01-1.25 acres whereas only 4 per cent approximately is controlled by 5.0-10.0 acres group. Percentage distribution of owned land increased from 0.01-1.25 acres to 2.5-5.0 acres group and then it decreased to 5.0-10.0 acres group. Percentage distribution of operated land increased from 0.01-1.25 acres to 2.5-5.0 acres group and then it decreased to 5.0-10.0 acres group. The structure of land according to economic class analysis shows that percentage of holding increased from landless to middle peasants and then it decreased to rich peasants. Approximately 48 per cent of holding is controlled by middle peasants whereas approximately 5 per cent of holding is controlled by poor peasants. Percentage distribution of owned land increased from landless to middle peasants and then it decreased to rich peasants. Percentage distribution of operated land increased from landless to middle peasants and then it decreased to rich peasants. This depicts that there is also a high level of land asset concentration in higher acreage group and higher economic class.

Thus, there is a high level of differentiation within the peasantry in terms of land asset holding. There is also low inequality between percentage distribution of owned land and percentage distribution of operated land according to economic class and farm size.

Land Asset Structure

Table 6.3: Acreage-wise Structure of Land

Farm Size	Percentage of holding	Percentage Distribution of Owned Land	Percentage Distribution of Operated Land
0	7.24	0.00	0.00
0.01-1.25	42.08	17.77	16.55
1.25-2.5	26.70	24.85	27.63
2.5-5.0	19.46	37.96	38.52
5.0-10.0	4.52	19.41	17.29
Total	100.00	100.00	100.00

Table 6.4: Economic Class-wise Structure of Land

Economic Class	Percentage of Holding	Percentage Distribution of Owned Land	Percentage Distribution of Operated Land
Landless	7.24	0.00	0.00
Poor	5.43	2.47	3.80
Small	10.41	6.68	7.50
Middle	47.96	46.95	50.60
Rich	28.96	43.90	38.10
Total	100.00	100.00	100.00

Composition of Percentage Distribution of Input Cost

Looking at the survey results represented by the Table 6.5 relating to the composition of percentage distribution of different input cost. We observed that there was a distinct concentration of different input cost incurred by middle and rich peasants. Nearly 50 per cent and 40 per cent of all the different categories (i.e., from cost on seeds to land rental) of cost incurred are distributed among the middle and rich peasants respectively. Middle peasant class appears to incur the higher input costs in all categories. In these cost categories, i.e., from cost on seeds to land rental, the distribution of the respective costs incurred among the primarily exploiting classes (rich peasant) ranges between 35 and 45. On the other hand, when modern implements is considered the percentage increases to 60 per cent for middle peasant. This points to the fact that the economically richer classes generally use expensive inputs. The economically poorer classes cannot afford the costly inputs and thus rely more on traditional inputs and livestock assets for undertaking agricultural production. For a better comparison, we project the distribution of different types of costs incurred among the middle peasant. Distribution of cost percentage are as follows: seeds—48.30 per cent; fertilizer—47.35 per cent; pesticides—51.92 per cent; modern implement—60.88 per cent; traditional implement—45.32 per cent; irrigation cost—53.32 per cent; livestock maintenance cost—47.17 per cent; purchased material input—52.52 per cent; material input—52.28 per cent. Thus, concentration of input costs on modern implements among the middle peasant in the survey region confirms that there was fair amount of differentiation has occurred. One thing is clear from the data that the self employed and labour exploiting classes incurs the majority of cost of inputs out of the aggregate cost that which is spent by all households in whole region. Similarly, acreage-wise distribution of the same data reflects same trend.

Problem of Farm Viability and Poverty

It is widely accepted that a serious crisis arises in the countryside of India after reform era. The crisis is clearly marked by the continuous and widespread deceleration in agricultural growth rate. Narayanamoorthy (2007) stated that peasantry in most of the regions in India are fed up with crop cultivation since they have not been able to convalesce even the cost of cultivation. Even the Situation Assessment Survey (SAS) revealed that over 40 per cent of farmers are willing to escape from farming since it had become non-viable.

For the depiction of Farm Non-Viability, we calculated some variables that project economic Surpluses/Deficits accruing to the peasant classes/acreage group. The variables stressed were net output and surpluses like Gross value added (GVA), farm labour

Table 6.5: All Regions, Acreage-wise Percentage Distribution of Different Input Cost

Farm Size	Seed Cost	Organic fertiliser	Chemical Fertiliser	Fertiliser Total Cost	Pesticide Total Cost	Modern Imple-ments	Traditional Implements
0	0.00	0.00	0.00	0.00	0.00	0.00	0.00
0.01-1.25	22.22	20.92	19.42	19.52	17.91	5.26	38.36
1.25-2.5	31.87	28.70	28.18	28.20	30.13	18.78	29.36
2.5-5.0	31.76	34.44	35.91	35.82	37.88	40.90	26.37
5.0-10.0	14.15	15.95	16.49	16.46	14.08	35.06	5.91
Total	100.00	100.00	100.00	100.00	100.00	100.00	100.00

Farm Size	Irrigation Cost	Livestock Maint-enance Cost	Purchased Material Input Cost	Material Input Cost	Labour Cost	Land Rental	Total Cost
0	0.00	0.00	0.00	0.00	0.00	0.00	0.00
0.01-1.25	16.52	35.00	22.23	22.72	19.14	11.96	21.97
1.25-2.5	29.33	27.04	24.56	24.72	25.78	36.53	25.19
2.5-5.0	39.90	29.51	34.10	33.86	38.17	40.40	34.57
5.0-10.0	14.25	8.46	19.11	18.70	16.91	11.11	18.26
Total	100.00	100.00	100.00	100.00	100.00	100.00	100.00

Economic Class-wise Percentage Distribution of Different Input Cost

Economic Class	Seed Cost	Organic Fertiliser	Chemical Fertiliser	Fertiliser Total Cost	Pesticide Total Cost	Modern Implement	Traditional Implement
Landless	0.00	0.00	0.00	0.00	0.00	0.00	0.00
Poor	1.46	1.66	2.29	2.26	1.73	0.06	10.01
Small	7.94	9.62	7.00	7.13	8.92	2.56	8.33
Middle	48.30	45.98	47.41	47.35	51.92	60.88	45.32
Rich	42.30	42.74	43.30	43.25	37.43	36.50	36.35
Total	100.00	100.00	100.00	100.00	100.00	100.00	100.00

Economic Class	Irrigation Cost	Livestock Maintenance Cost	Purchase Material Input Cost	Material Input Cost	Labour Cost	Land Rental	Total Cost
Landless	0.00	0.00	0.00	0.00	0.00	0.00	0.00
Poor	1.48	4.31	2.47	2.72	1.62	5.47	2.67
Small	7.26	8.27	6.18	6.25	5.07	10.23	6.23
Middle	53.32	47.17	52.52	52.28	50.96	64.22	52.48
Rich	37.94	40.25	38.83	38.75	42.36	20.08	38.63
Total	100.00	100.00	100.00	100.00	100.00	100.00	100.00

surplus (FLS)/deficit and farm disposable surplus (FDS)/deficit. In order to represent the distress, our study investigated:

- Firstly, the gross value of crop output and net output class and group-wise.
- Secondly, surplus and deficit accruing to each class and group.
- Thirdly, gross output and value added, farm labour and farm disposable surplus class and group-wise.

(1) Value of agricultural production = Gross output of all crops + value of by-product and livestock production.

(2) Gross value added (GVA) of all crops = Value of agricultural production – Total material input cost.

(3) Farm labour income (FLI) = Gross value added (GVA) of all crops – wages (kind and cash).

(4) Farm labour surplus or deficit (FLS) = Farm labour income (FLI) – imputed value of family labour income.

(5) Total income = Agricultural income (A) + Non-Agricultural income (B). Where agricultural income is the sum of: (i) Farm labour income (A_1); (ii) Income from agricultural wages (A_2); (iii) Income from hiring out equipments, etc. (A_3); (iv) Non-cultivation income from rent (A_4).

Therefore, $A = A_1 + A_2 + A_3 + A_4$. And non-agricultural income is the sum of: (i) Income from salaries, pension, and remittances (B_1); (ii) Non-cultivation income from other sources (B_2). Therefore, non-agricultural Income = $B = B_1 + B_2$.

(6) Farm-disposable income (FDI) = Farm-labour income (FLI) – Rents paid.

(7) Total disposable income = Farm disposable income (FDI) + Non-agriculture income + Agricultural wage+ Rents + Income from Hiring out.

(8) Farm-disposable surplus or deficit = Farm disposable income-Imputed value of family labour. (Patnaik 1987, Rakshit 2010).

To obtain the real production and surplus/deficit in the survey region, We have used Tables 6.6 and 6.7 to portray Agricultural

Production and Farm Labour Surplus according to economic class and farm size.

Gross value of crop output per holding increased from poor peasants to rich peasants, similarly same trend is noticed for Gross value of crop output per acre. This indicates that exploiting class (rich peasants) have a greater amount of crop output than the exploited class (poor peasants). Relative measures Gross output per rupee of material input cost and Gross Value Added per rupee of material input cost are 0.56 and –0.18 respectively. In other words for each rupee of material input cost GO obtained is more than rupee one whereas GVA obtained is negative.

Farm Labour Surplus or Deficit is calculated by deducting from farm-labour income from the imputed value of family labour income.

Farm Labour Surplus and Deficit presented in relative terms per holding, per acre and they are negative for all classes. We found that it shows a uniform pattern of downward fluctuation in the exploited and self employed classes. This is shown in Fig. 6.1. In the Figure 6.1 horizontal axis measures Economic Class and vertical axis measures Farm Labour Surplus/Deficit per acre per holding. Thus, all peasant class is the sufferer in terms of realization of surplus.

Table 6.6: All Regions

Class	*Gross Value of Crop Output per Holding*	*Gross Value of Crop Output per Acre*	*Gross Output Per rupee of Material Input Cost*	*Gross Value Added per rupee of Material Input Cost*	*Farm Labour Surplus per Holding*	*Farm labour surplus per Acre*
Landless	0.00	0.00	0.00	0.00	3814.38	0.00
Poor	13220.08	10569.02	0.40	–0.31	–19216.33	–15362.82
Small	23925.30	18584.33	0.61	–0.04	–19547.02	–15183.43
Middle	38241.25	20288.15	0.54	–0.23	–37782.96	–20045.02
Rich	53174.56	22619.95	0.61	–0.13	–29703.78	–12635.71
Total	36948.72	20679.38	0.56	–0.18	–29525.72	–16524.89

In Table 6.7 the gross value of crop output per holding increased from 0.01-1.25 per acre to 5.0-10.0 per acre, whereas Gross value of crop output per acre decreased from 0.01-1.25 per acre to 2.5-5.0 per acre and then it increased to 5.0-10.0 per acre. Relative

Table 6.7: All regions

Farm size	Gross value of crop output per holding	Gross value of crop output per acre	Gross output per rupee of material input cost	Gross value added per rupee of material input cost	Farm labour surplus per holding	Farm labour surplus per acre
0	0.00	0.00	0.00	0.00	3814.38	0.00
0.01-1.25	16322.64	23221.75	0.46	–0.22	–23499.64	–33432.25
1.25-2.5	37629.86	20346.06	0.62	–0.09	–25986.48	–14050.61
2.5-5.0	69178.16	19557.27	0.61	–0.17	–42541.16	–12026.76
5.0-10.0	145283.90	21277.67	0.54	–0.29	–103827.50	–15206.14
Total	36948.72	20679.38	0.56	–0.18	–29525.72	–16524.89

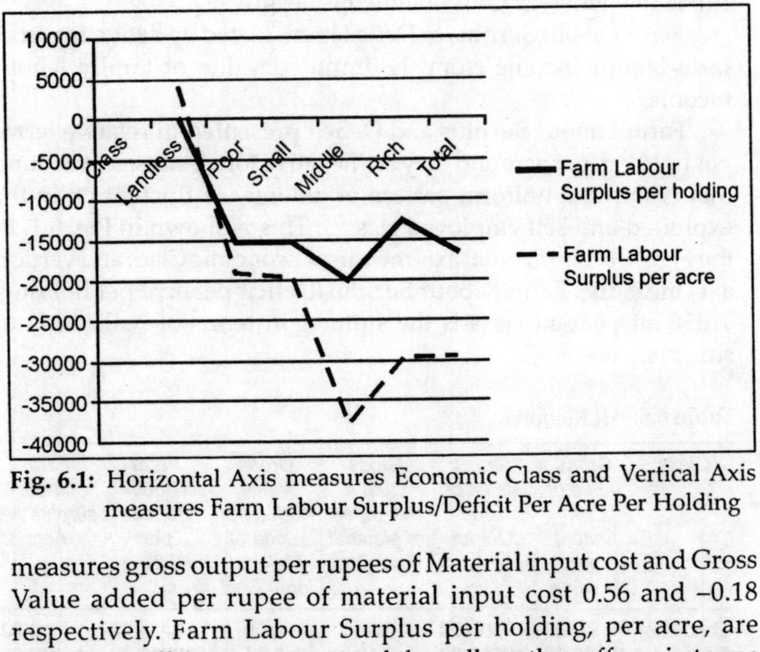

Fig. 6.1: Horizontal Axis measures Economic Class and Vertical Axis measures Farm Labour Surplus/Deficit Per Acre Per Holding

measures gross output per rupees of Material input cost and Gross Value added per rupee of material input cost 0.56 and –0.18 respectively. Farm Labour Surplus per holding, per acre, are negative in all acreage group and they all are the sufferer in terms of realization of surplus.

Turning to different categories of income in Tables 6.8 and 6.9 by farm size and economic class. Farm Labour Income per holding is negative from 0.01-1.25 acres to 5.0-10.0 acres. Similarly, Farm Labour Income per acre is also negative for all acreage group. Non-Agricultural Income per holding increased from 0.01-1.25 acres to 5.0-10.0 acres and Non-Agricultural Income per acre decreased from 0.01-1.25 acres to 5.0-10.0 acres. Non-Agricultural Income

Table 6.8: All Regions—Acreage-wise Different Categories of Income

Farm size	*Farm labour income per hold*	*Farm labour income per acre*	*Non-agri income per hold*	*Non-agri income per acre*	*Agri-income per hold*	*Agri-income per acre*	*Total income per hold*	*Total income per acre*
0	3814.38	0.00	1659.38	0.00	13614.38	0.00	15273.75	0.00
0.01-1.25	–15841.04	–22536.58	19763.44	28116.87	–11725.55	–16681.60	8037.89	11435.27
1.25-2.5	–15059.78	–8142.66	23912.71	12929.34	–12193.85	–6593.08	11718.86	6336.26
2.5-5.0	–30235.93	–8547.96	37634.53	10639.61	–27105.93	–7663.08	10528.60	2976.53
5.0-10.0	–92262.50	–13512.38	68515.00	10034.42	–88772.50	–13001.24	–20257.50	–2966.83
Total	–20468.25	–11455.63	25243.60	14128.28	–16494.86	–9231.81	8748.74	4896.48

Table 6.9: All regions—Class-wise Different Categories of Income

Economic Class	*Farm labour income per hold*	*Farm labour income per acre*	*Non-agri income per hold*	*Non-agri income per acre*	*Agri- income per hold*	*Agri-income per acre*	*Total income per hold*	*Total income per acre*
Landless	3814.38	0.00	1659.38	0.00	13614.38	0.00	15273.75	0.00
Poor	–15122.58	–12090.01	1945.83	1555.63	–2639.25	–2109.99	–693.42	–554.36
Small	–9872.02	–7668.24	4917.39	3819.66	1006.24	781.61	5923.63	4601.27
Middle	–26292.87	–13949.17	32792.26	17397.30	–24354.29	–12920.69	8437.98	4476.61
Rich	–21702.22	–9231.92	30310.23	12893.69	–19892.38	–8462.03	10417.86	4431.66
Total	–20468.25	–11455.63	25243.60	14128.28	–16494.86	–9231.81	8748.74	4896.48

per holding and per acre are both positive whereas Agricultural Income per holding and per acre are both negative. In other words, income from agriculture is not less than non agricultural sector, but it is negative and peasants are looking non-agricultural sector for survival. Total Income per holding is negative for 5.0-10.0 acres. Similarly, Total Income per acre is negative for 5.0-10.0 acres.

Looking at the different categories of income by economic class. Farm Labour Income per holding and per acre are both negative for all peasant group. Non-Agricultural Income per holding and per acre increased from poor to middle peasants and then it decreased to rich peasants. Agricultural Income per holding and per acre is positive for small peasants and it is negative for poor, middle and rich peasants. Total Income per holding increased from poor to rich peasants.

Finally, we again come to the newer concept of surplus and deficit that is Farm Disposable Surplus or Deficit. What is distinguishing about Farm Disposable Surplus or Deficit in comparison to Farm Labour Surplus is that only rent payment is additionally deducted when we are discussing about Farm Labour Surplus.

In Table 6.10 Farm Disposable Surplus per holding and per acre are negative for all acreage group. In other words, all acreage groups are the worst sufferer in terms of realization of surplus.

Table 6.10: Farm Disposable Income and Farm Disposable Surplus/ Deficits

(All regions and acreage-wise)

Farm Size	*FDS per Acre*	*FDS per Holding*	*FDS per Worker*	*TDI per Acre*	*TDI per Holding*
0	0.00	3814.38	2653.48	0.00	15273.75
0.01-1.25	–34355.00	–24148.24	–17143.41	10512.52	7389.28
1.25-2.5	–15738.75	–29108.68	–19296.77	4648.12	8596.66
2.5-5.0	–13366.07	–47278.60	–30802.73	1637.21	5791.16
5.0-10.0	–16026.29	–109427.50	–84175.00	–3786.98	–25857.50
Total	–17801.87	–31807.35	–21830.51	3619.50	6467.11

In Table 6.11 We depict Economic Class-wise Farm Disposable Surplus per acre and holding.

Farm Disposable surplus per acre and per holding is negative for all classes, we found that it shows a uniform pattern of

Table 6.11: Farm Disposable Income and Farm Disposable Surplus/ Deficit All Regions Economic Class-wise

Economic Class	*FDS per Acre*	*FDS per Holding*	*FDS per Worker*	*TD per Acre*	*TDI per Holding*
Landless	0.00	3814.38	2653.48	0.00	15273.75
Poor	–17200.93	–21515.50	–9930.23	–2392.47	–2992.58
Small	–16925.41	–21789.63	–10663.01	2859.29	3681.02
Middle	–21665.64	–40837.68	–28667.51	2855.98	5383.26
Rich	–13308.82	–31286.13	–26697.49	3758.54	8835.52
Total	–17801.87	–31807.35	–21830.51	3619.50	6467.11

downward fluctuation in the self employed and exploited classes. This is shown in Fig. 6.2, in the Figure 6.2 horizontal axis measures Economic Class and vertical axis measures Farm Disposable Surplus/Deficit per acre and per holding. A crisis in agriculture affects adversely all the classes and farm size.

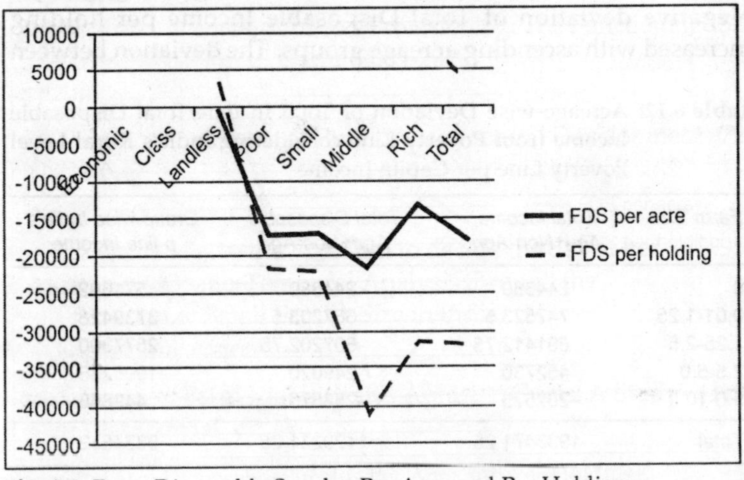

Fig. 6.2: Farm Disposable Surplus Per Acre and Per Holding

For comparison of cultivators' income with poverty level we have undertaken the deviation of the calculated total income and total disposable income separately from the poverty line income of West Bengal and India. The latest estimate on this per capita poverty line income is by Planning Commission, Government of India filed an affidavit before the Supreme Court on September 2011. For India the estimated poverty line per capita income is

Rs. 781 per month and Rs. 800 for West Bengal. We have calculated groupwise per capita income per annum by multiplying the number of members in each group with the poverty line per capita income. For comparisons of West Bengal's poverty line see Appendix-B. In Table 6.12, we have shown the deviation of Total Income and Total Disposable Income from poverty line and per holding according to acreage group analysis. When we compare them with total income according to calculation indicated before with respect to India's per capita poverty line income, we find all the acreage groups have negative deviation. The negative deviation decreases with the ascending acreage groups. There is also negative deviation per holding for all acreage groups. Here negative deviation increased from zero to 0.01-1.25 acre and then it decreased to 1.25-2.5 acre and again it increased to 5.0-10.0 acre groups. There is a negative deviation of Total Disposable Income from poverty line and it decreased with ascending acreage groups. Negative deviation of Total Disposable Income per holding increased with ascending acreage groups. The deviation between

Table 6.12: Acreage-wise Deviation of Total Income/Total Disposable Income from Poverty Line considering India's Rural Level Poverty Line per Capita Income

Farm Size	*Total Income Agri+Non-Agri*	*Total Disposable Agri+Non-Agri*	*Group-wise India's p-line Income*
0	244380	244380	571692
0.01-1.25	747523.5	687203.5	3739428
1.25-2.5	691412.75	507202.75	2577300
2.5-5.0	452730	249020	1996236
5.0-10.0	–202575	–258575	449856
Total	1933471.25	1429231.25	9334512

Farm size	*Deviation WRT TI*		*Deviation WRT TDI*	
	From P-Line	*Per Holding*	*From P Line*	*Per Holding*
0	–327312	–20457.00	–327312	–20457.00
0.01-1.25	–2991904.5	–32171.02	–3052224.5	–32819.62
1.25-2.5	–18885887.25	–31964.19	–2070097.25	–35086.39
2.5-5.0	–1543506	–35895.49	–1747216	–40632.93
5.0-10.0	–652431	–65243.10	–708431	–70843.10
Total	–7401040.75	–33488.87	–7905280.75	–35770.50

Total Income and Total Disposable Income from poverty line income and per holding reveals that all acreage groups goes below the India's poverty line income. We find similar result when we compare Total Income and Total Disposable Income from West Bengal poverty line, per holding given in Appendix B.

In Table 6.13 we have shown the deviation of Total Income and Total Disposable Income from poverty line and per holding Economic class analysis. When we compare them with total income according to calculation indicated before with respect to India's per capita poverty line income, we find all the Economic class have negative deviation, negative deviation increased from landless to middle peasants and then it decreased to rich peasants. Negative deviation per holding increased from landless to small peasants and then it decreased to rich peasants. Similar deviation is noticed for Total Disposable Income. Negative Deviation increased from landless to middle peasants and then it decreased to rich peasants. Negative Deviation per holding increased from landless to small peasants and then it decreased to rich peasants.

Table 6.13: Economic Class-wise Deviation of Total Income/Total Disposable Income from Poverty Line considering India's Rural Level Poverty Line Per Capita Income

Economic Class	*Total Income Agri+Non-Agri*	*Total Disposable Agri+Non-Agri*	*Group-wise India's p-line Income*
Landless	244380	244380	571692
Poor	–8321	–35911	477972
Small	136243.5	84663.5	1124640
Middle	894425.75	570625.75	4686000
Rich	666743	565473	2474208
Total	1933471.25	1429231.25	9334512

Economic Class	*Deviation wrt TI from P-Line*	*Per Holding*	*Deviation wrt TDI from P line*	*Per Holding*
Landless	-327312	-20457.00	-327312	-20457.00
Poor	-486293	-40524.42	-513883	-42823.58
Small	-988396.5	-42973.76	-1039976.5	-45216.37
Middle	-3791574.25	-35769.57	-4115374.25	-38824.29
Rich	-1807465	-28241.64	-1908735	-29823.98
Total	-7401040.75	-33488.87	-7905280.75	-35770.50

Conclusion

The Survey results clearly depicted that Farm is not non viable but it is in a very ghastly state. We have shown that even the non-agricultural income is unable to sustain the agricultural farm. In the reform era peasants are unable to recover the cost of production due to inhuman rise in input cost. Peasants are facing losses in agriculture by being unable to recover the cost of production.

This study finds a significant degree of Farm Labour Deficit and Farm Disposable Deficit among all peasants and also among all acreage groups. They are unable to realize the surplus.

There is a high level of non-land asset concentration in the higher acreage groups and higher economic classes, whereas there is also a high level of land asset concentration in higher acreage group and higher economic class. Thus, there is a high level of differentiation within the peasantry in terms of land asset holding and non-land asset holding.

Finally, it is interesting to note that the comparison of different poverty level income with farm labour income and farm disposable income have increased the magnitude of negative divergence. We found that all acreage and economic class are far below the West Bengal and India's poverty line income. This clearly explores the fact that under the reform era the economic status of all peasant groups has worsened so badly such that even the non-farm activities cannot supplement their farm labour income and farm disposable income to sustain themselves in the neo liberal policies adopted by the Government of India after 1991.

A crisis in agriculture affects adversely all the classes and farm size. The most momentous incident is that it affects the rich farmers as well. This well to do farmers obtained significant degree of negative farm labour income and farm disposable surplus. They are unable to realize the surplus like poor, small and middle peasants.

This is in spite of the fact that there is a high level of concentration of assets among the exploiting classes (rich farmers). Even the non-agricultural income of the upper echelons in the agrarian class structure are unable to recuperate their situation. They are in a very nastiest condition. The survey study revealed that the economic position of all economic classes are in a very depressed state after two decades of reform era. Thus, we believe that a resolution to the agrarian distress must involve the following measures which uplift the peasantry from the current anguish by–

- enhancing investment in strengthening the resource base of agriculture;
- developing agricultural market and eliminating local traders and middleman;
- introducing co-operative farming;
- creating rural employment;
- developing rural infrastructure; and
- developing agricultural research and technology.

REFERENCES

Aerthayil, Mathew (2008), 'Agrarian Crisis in India is the Creation of the Policy of Globalisation', *Mainstream,* Vol. XLVI, No. 13, 16 March 2008.

Bhalla, G.S. and Singh, Gurmail (2009), 'Economic Liberalisation and Indian Agriculture: A State-wise Analysis', *Economic and Political Weekly,* Vol. XLIV, No. 52, December 26, 2009.

Bhattacharyya, S. (2008), "Class differentiation, Liberalization Policy and Labour Absorption: Some Paradoxes of Efficiency with and without Agrarian Capitalism in Two Agro-ecological Regions in West Bengal. K.K. Bagchi, Abhijeet, (eds). *Agrarian Crisis, Farmers Suicides and Livelihood Security of Rural Labour in India.* Vol. 1, 2008.

Bhattacharyya, S. (2001), 'Capitalist Development, Peasant Differentiation and the State: Survey Findings from West Bengal, *Journal of Peasant Studies,* Volume 28, No. 4, July 2001, pp. 95-126.

Majumdar, N.A. (1999): 'Reviving Rural Credit', *Economic and Political Weekly,* Vol. 34, No. 25, June 19, pp. 1577-79.

Mishra, S. (2007), *'Risks, Farmers' Suicides and Agrarian Crisis in India,* www.igidr.ac.in/pdf/publication/wp-2007-014/pdf.

Narayanamoorthy, A. (2007), 'Deceleration in Agricultural Growth, Technology Fatigue or Policy Fatigue?'*Economic and Political Weekly,* Vol 42, No. 25, June 23-29, 2007.

Patnaik, Utsa (2005), 'Theorizing Food Security and Poverty in the Era of Economic Reforms' *Social Scientist,* Vol. 33, Nos. 7-8, July-Aug. 2005.

Patnaik, Utsa (1987), *'Peasant Class Differentiation: A Study in Method with Reference to Haryana',* Delhi, Oxford University Press.

Rakshit, Santanu (2010). 'Agrarian Transition' Diversity in Nature, Notion and Observations—A Survey of Theoretical Expositions and Empirical Studies with Reference to India and West Bengal, *Research in Social Stratification and Mobility, Elsevier, Science Direct,* Volume 28, Issue 4, December 2010.

Rakshit, Santanu (2011), 'Capital Intensification, Productivity and Exchange' – A Class-Based Analysis of Agriculture in West Bengal in the Current Millennium, *Jou.nal of Agrarian Change,* Volume 11, No. 4, October 2011, pp. 505-535.

Ramachandran, V.K. and Madhura Swaminathan (2001): Does Informal Credit Provide Security? Rural Banking Policy in India, International Labour Organisation, Geneva, Switzerland (*www.ilo.org/ses).*

Rawal, Vikash (2008), 'Ownership Holding of Land in Rural India, putting the Record Straight', *Economic and Political Weekly,* Vol. 43, No. 10, March 8-14, 2008.

Shetty, S.L. (2004), 'Distributional Issues in Bank Credit: Multi-pronged Strategy for Correcting Past Neglect', *Economic and Political Weekly,* July 17, pp. 3265-69.

Shukla, S.P. (2009), 'In Search of Radical and Inclusive Politics' *Economic and Political Weekly,* Vol. 44, No. 8, February 21-27, 2009.

Appendix A

Patnaik's E-Criterion

According to Marxian class differentiation, In commodity production era, rich peasants increasingly employ the labour of others, thereby appropriating surplus that contributes in turn to the accumulation process. The latter progress is itself premised on the sale of labour-power by poor peasants who, required to work for others, are thereby increasingly subjected to exploitation. The self-employed petty commodity producers, the middle peasants of Lenin, are in a vulnerable position. While a few of them succeed in transforming themselves into rich peasants, the majority are always under the constant threat of 'depeasantization', or being pushed down into the ranks of the semi-proletariat. At the top end of the rural class structure, and more or less distinct from the peasantry, stands the landlord, defined by 'possession of substantial means of production and non-involvement in any manual labour, living entirely by appropriating surplus labour of others'. At the bottom end is the landless labourer who, since he possesses no means of production, is obliged to live entirely by selling his labour-power.

The following limits are specified to the value of *E* in order to classify households into a set of mutually exclusive and all-exhaustive categories (sub-category not specified here are not ruled out)

Class Category	*Defining Characteristics*	*Value of* $E = X/F$	*Reason*
1. Landless labourers	No self-employment; working entirely for others.	$(E \rightarrow -\infty)$	$F = 0$ $X < 0$ and large
2. Poor peasants (tenants and labourers with small holdings.	Working for others exceeds self-employment	$(E \leq -1)$	$F > 0$, $X < 0$ $\lvert X \rvert \geq F$

Class Category	Defining Characteristics	Value of E = X/F	Reason
3. Small peasants	No employment of/or working for others; self-employment exceeds working for others	$(0 \geq E > -1)$	$F > 0$ $X \leq 0$ $\lvert X \rvert < F$
4. Middle peasants	Self-employment predominates, combined with the employment of a small amount of others' labour	$(1 > E > 0)$	$F > 0$ $X > 0$, $X < F$
5. Rich peasants	Self-employment equalled by the amount of labour-power purchased	$(E \geq 1)$	$F > 0$, $X > 0$ $X \geq F$
6. Landlords	No manual labour expended in the form of self-employment; large amounts of outside labour employed	$(E \rightarrow \infty)$	$F = 0$, $X > 0$, and large

Source: Utsa Patnaik (1987), Peasant Class Differentiation: A Study with Method with Reference to Haryana.

Appendix B

Acreage-wise Deviation of Total Income/Total Disposable Income from Poverty Line considering West Bengal Rural Level Poverty Line Per Capita Income

Farm Size	*Total Income Agri+Non-Agri*	*Total Disposable Agri+Non-Agri*	*Group-wise West Bengal P-Line Income*
0	244380	244380	585600
0.01-1.25	747523.5	687203.5	3830400
1.25-2.5	691412.75	507202.75	2640000
2.5-5.0	452730	249020	2044800
5.0-10.0	–202575	–258575	460800
Total	1933471.25	1429231.25	9561600

Farm Size	*Deviation WRT TI from P-Line*	*Per Holding*	*Deviation WRT TDI from P-Line*	*Per Holding*
0	–341220	–21326.25	–341220	–21326.25
0.01-1.25	–3082876.5	–33149.21	–3143196.5	–33797.81
1.25-2.5	–1948587.25	–33026.90	–2132797.25	–36149.11
2.5-5.0	–1592070	–37024.88	–1795780	–41762.33
5.0-10.0	–663375	–66337.50	–719375	–71937.50
Total	–7628128.75	–34516.42	–8132368.75	–36798.05

Economic Class-wise Deviation of Total Income/Total Disposable Income from Poverty Line considering West Bengal Rural Level Poverty Line Per Capita Income

Economic Class	*Total Income Agri+Non-Agri*	*Total Disposable Agri+Non-Agri*	*Group-wise West Bengal P-Line Income*
Landless	244380	244380	585600
Poor	–8321	–35911	489600
Small	136243.5	84663.5	1152000
Middle	894425.75	570625.75	4800000
Rich	666743	565473	2534400

Economic Class	Deviation WRT TI from P Line	Per Holding	Deviation WRT TDI from P Line	Per Holding
Landless	–341220	–21326.25	–341220	–21326.25
Poor	–497921	–41493.42	–525511	–43792.58
Small	–1015756.5	–44163.33	–1067336.5	–46405.93
Middle	–3905574.25	–36845.04	–4229374.25	–39899.76
Rich	–1867657	–29182.14	–1968927	–30764.48
Total	–7628128.75	–34516.42	–8132368.75	–36798.05

7

Question of Sustainable Development in Agriculture and Rural Credit

A Study of West Bengal in New Millennium

Nikhil Kumar Mandal

1. Introduction

Based on a primary field survey in rural West Bengal and secondary sources of information, here we would like to discourse on the informal credit market. This study particularly focuses on village level class structure and state of peasant class differentiation in an atmosphere of pro-poor interventionist policies pursued since early eighties and the introduction of contradictory policies of market economic reform that Government of India adopted since early nineties and West Bengal had to accept it. Though the main concern of this study is the informal credit market, but in a market economic regime the structure of the credit market is generally determined by the pattern of inter-class distribution of all basic means of production such as land and non-land assets (machinery and transport, storage and irrigation, etc.). This, in turn, is associated with a differentiated structure of labour, input use, cropping pattern, production/productivity and market orientation across classes (Bhattacharyya, 2001). In other words the extent of peasant class differentiation fixes the structure of rural credit. It is defined with respect to control over the basic means of production. On the other hand, the process of usury capital can worsen the already existing unequal distribution (Bhaduri, 1973, 1977; Prasad,

1974). In this regard we can say that the structure of credit is both the cause and consequence of the existing class structure.

Here we deal with the dominance of the few people over the major markets of the rural economy that includes the ownership of the major means of production, viz, assets-land and non-land, irrigation and credit. There are two sources of credit, one is organised credit market controlled by banking system with some uniform interest rates and other is unorganised market, regulated by private lenders. There is no uniform interest rate in the latter market. Here we also analyse the distribution of the inflow of rural credit at the national level and West Bengal by secondary sources, side by side it enquires the distribution of rural credit market in West Bengal by ground level data. The main objective of rural banking after bank nationalization was agricultural growth and alleviation of rural poverty. Here it is also evaluated how far this objective has been achieved. This paper displayed that the institutional credit failed to lift any class/group of household above the poverty line in the post-liberalization period. In other words the growth rate of agriculture has been arrested by the formal credit in rural West Bengal. The maximum number of farmers compelled to go to the informal credit market. This market is controlled by the money lender with exorbitant rate of interest. This study deals with problem of Sustainable Development in agriculture in West Bengal, as well as India during the reform period.

2. Methodology

This study is based on field survey data conducted in the year 2004-05 in ten sample villages which are selected from two blocks of Murshidabad district. The Murshidabad district is purposively selected from all other districts. At least two major reasons can be put forward for this selection. First of all, this being purely agricultural district and we can comfortably analyse the impact of credit as the other factors like impact of industrialization cannot be mixed up. Secondly, it is a relatively backward district and there is much scope to analyse developmental impact of credit. One hundred (100) households are surveyed separately in each Block. Two sample Blocks have been selected on the basis of level of economic development. One Block is Jalangi which is the most advanced region and other is Berhampore Block which seems to be the most backward region among 26 Blocks in the Murshidabad district. The following developmental variables have been chosen to identify the Blocks with high and low level of development:

1. Percentage of irrigated area to total cultivated area.
2. Percentage of villages having one or more educational institutions.
3. Percentage of rural population served by medical amenities.
4. Percentage of rural population served by puacca road.
5. Percentage of rural population served by power supply.
6. Percentage of cultivated area to total area.
7. Percentage of rural population served by market/*haat*.
8. Percentage of rural population served by drinking water.
9. Percentage of rural population served by Posts and Telegraph.
10. Percentage of rural population served by communications.

The rationale behind conducting field survey is that not enough secondary sources of data are available. Data for the supply of credit have been obtained from the secondary sources. The field survey data gives us an idea of the differentiated demand for credit influenced by the class structure of the rural economy. The secondary sources do not furnish any class-wise distribution of data. This is another reason for conducting a primary field survey. Two criteria (E-criteria and standard acreage criteria) are used throughout this chapter. According to E-criteria developed by Utsa Patnaik, the six categories of economic classes can be reduced to three broad categories, namely, **exploited classes** (landless or LLS and poor peasant or PP), **self-employment classes** (small peasant or SP and middle peasant or MP) and **labour hiring or exploiting classes** (rich peasant or RP and landlord or LLD).

The Marxist concept of the process of class differentiation is that, under a regime of commodity production, the rich peasant class increasingly employs the labour of others and thereby appropriates surplus. A poor peasant on the other hand is increasingly obliged to work for others and is thereby increasingly subjected to exploitation. The self-employed are in a vulnerable position. While a few of them might be able to transform themselves into rich peasant, the majority of them are always under the constant threat of being pushed down into the ranks of the semi-proletariat. At one of the two poles of the rural class structure, and more or less distinct from the peasantry, stands the landlord, defined by 'possession of substantial means of production and non-involvement in any manual labour, living entirely by appropriating surplus labour of others'. The landless labourer has no self-employment, for he possesses no means of production at all and is obliged to live entirely by selling his labour.

The labour-exploitation index seeks to give an empirical approximation to the analytical concept of the class status of the household. The class-status is essentially determined by the extent of the use of outside labour or to the extent the family works for others, relative to the extent of self-employment. It is identical, under certain simplifying assumptions with the surplus labour appropriated or parted with, relative to surplus labour with self-employment.

$$E = X/Y = \{(H_i - H_o) + (L_o - L_i)\}/Y$$

Where,

X = (net labour days hired in) + (net labour days appropriated through rent);

H_i = Labour days hired on the operational holding of the household;

H_o = Family labour days hired out to others;

L_i = Labour days worked on leased in land (whether by family or hired labour);

L_o = Labour days similarly worked on land leased out by the household; and

Y = Labour days worked by household workers on the operational holding.

'The index is a ratio, or a pure number, which can have positive or negative values depending on whether the household is a net employer of outside labour or is itself on balance working for others (as labourer or tenant). The range of values of E is from plus infinity to minus infinity, for at the two poles of the rural class structure, there will be diametrically opposite types of households for whom F will be zero or near zero: first, the big landlords have such a large resource endowment that they perform no manual labour themselves, but rely entirely on employing others' labour; and the landless labourers, with zero resource endowment, hence, zero self-employment, who are entirely dependent on working for others' (Patnaik, 1987; p. 305).

Cross Classification of the Number of Households

Acreage Groups	*Land-less*	*Poor Peasant*	*Small Peasant*	*Middle Peasant*	*Rich Peasant*	*Landlord*	*Total*
0.00	24	0	0	0	0	0	24
0.01 to 2.5	0	60	35	23	19	4	141
2.5 to 5	0	2	3	6	12	6	29
5 to 10	0	0	0	2	3	1	6
10 to 15	0	0	0	0	0	0	0
15 & above	0	0	0	0	0	0	0
Total	24	62	38	31	34	11	200

3.1 Institutionalisation of Rural Credit Market

Table 7.1 shows a comparative picture of source-wise distribution of agricultural credit in West Bengal *vis-à-vis* India between 1971 and 2002-03. It has been seen from Table 7.1 that the percentage of institutional credit outstanding registered a steady increase in West Bengal from 33 per cent in 1971 to 65.3 per cent in 1981 to 82 per cent in 1991 and then declined massively at 58 per cent in 2002-03. The same increases for India as a whole were 31.7 per cent in 1971, 63.2 per cent in 1981 and 66.3 per cent in 1991, followed a decline at 57.7 per cent in 2002-03. Thus institutional credit marked a steep expansion since the nationalisation of banks in India and maintained the increase till 1991 and declined thereafter. West Bengal followed the same trend, though registered much greater expansion in the institutional credit than the national average particularly during eighties. Among the institutional sources commercial and co-operative bank show expansion during seventies, though the magnitude of expansion was much greater for the commercial bank in West Bengal as well as in all India. However during 1981 to 1991 the co-operative society/bank experienced a decline in percentage share, though the magnitude of decline was relatively less in West Bengal. The most unfortunate thing was that during 1991 to 2002-03 the co-operative bank's share declined both in West Bengal and India by almost the same proportion (19.2% and 19.6%). On the other hand during this period the share of commercial banks credit remained stagnant at around 35 per cent but in West Bengal it declined substantially from 37.7 per cent to 28.5 per cent. Among the non-institutional sources there was a decline in the share of the three main exploiting classes, namely landlord, agriculturist moneylender and professional moneylender till 1991 which was considerably large in West Bengal compared to that of all-India; but these proportions increased to a great extent after that. It might be noteworthy that over time the share of landlord and agricultural moneylender started to decline steadily from 1971 and ultimately came to nil level in 2002-03 both in West Bengal and India. But the share of professional moneylenders increased from 3.4 per cent in 1991 to 13 per cent in 2002-03 in West Bengal and from 10.7 per cent in 1991 to 25.7 per cent in 2002-3 at all India. The share of traders is increased more in West Bengal (from 1.5% in 1991 to 10.7% in 2002-03) than at all India (from 2.2% in 1991 to 5.2% in 2002-03). The share of relatives and friends, on the other hand, almost doubled in West Bengal (from 8.9% 1991 to 15.4% in 2002-03) and as well as at the national level (from 4.6 % in 1991 to 8.5% in 2002-03), despite a steady fall since 1971 in both national and the State level. It might be mentioned that the relatives and friends are the main sources of the interest free credit in rural areas. Some scholars put some doubt about the actual intention of the relatives and friends. According to them some implicit valuation is often attached to the interest free loan (Basu, 1984). This is possible because different markets in the rural areas are interlinked. However, almost all the major micro and macro level studies reached at the conclusion that the market interlinkage had almost been disappeared in rural West Bengal in consequence of the emerging influence of capitalism in agriculture and an active pro-poor State intervention (Bhaumik, 1993; Khasnabis, 1995; Bhattacharyya, 2005). Thus, a comparatively higher share of relatives and friends does not necessarily indicate an evil for the economy.

3.2 Comparison between NSSO and Ground Level Data

The NSSO of India conducted the latest indebtedness survey for all Indian States in the 48th round (1991) and 59th round (2003).

Table 7.1: Sourcewise Percentage Distribution of Outstanding Credit for Cultivator Household in Rural Area : West Bengal-and India

	West Bengal				India			
	1971	*1981*	*1991*	*2003*	*1971*	*1981*	*1991*	*2003*
I. Institutional	33.00	65.30	82.00	58.00	31.70	63.20	66.30	57.70
1. Government	16.30	7.30	13.30	10.30	7.10	3.90	5.70	2.50
2. Co-operative society/ Bank	15.10	24.80	23.70	19.20	22.00	29.80	23.60	19.60
3. Commercial Bank	1.30	30.10	37.70	28.50	2.40	28.80	35.20	35.60
4. Insurance & Provident Fund	0.30	2.50	7.20	0.00	0.20	0.70	1.80	0.00
II. Non-institutional	67.00	34.70	17.80	42.00	68.30	36.80	30.60	42.30
5. Landlord	3.70	1.10	0.20	0.00	8.10	3.70	3.70	0.00
6. Agricultural Moneylender	12.50	5.10	2.90	0.00	23.00	8.30	6.80	0.00
7. Professional Moneylender	15.60	5.30	3.40	13.00	13.10	7.80	10.70	25.70
8. Trader	9.40	5.10	1.50	10.70	8.40	3.10	2.20	5.20
9. Relatives/Friends	24.10	15.00	8.90	15.40	13.10	8.70	4.60	8.50
10. Doctor,Lawyer, etc.	0.00	0.00	0.00	0.70	0.00	0.00	0.00	0.90
11. Others	1.70	3.10	0.80	2.30	2.60	5.20	2.60	2.10
Unspecified	0.00	0.00	0.20	0.00	0.00	0.00	3.10	0.00
Total (Inst. + Non-inst.)	100.00	100.00	100.00	100.00	100.00	100.00	100.00	100.00

Source: Different Rounds of NSSO.

The NSSO data shows that the percentage shares of the institutional credit for the West Bengal are 82.00 (1991) and 58.00 (2003) in Table 7.1, while in our primary field survey it is 39.02 per cent in 2004-05 which is shown in Table 7.2. The NSSO data reflects a massive fall (about one quarter, –19%) in percentage of institutional credit to the total during the period of financial liberalization. The share of the commercial banks in total outstanding credit in our survey is 31.97 per cent (2004-05), which is below the corresponding shares in NSSO 37.70 per cent (1991) but it is above 28.5 per cent (2003)). NSSO data reflects about a 3 per cent decline in commercial bank credit as a direct fallout of financial liberalization. Markedly different is the share of the co-operative-society/bank in the case of NSSO, 23.70 per cent in 1991 and 19.2 per cent in 2003 as against 7.05 per cent 2004-05 in our survey. Therefore, both in our field survey and NSSO data the percentage of co-operative bank declined. The share of Government also declined in NSSO data (from 13.30% to 10.3%) during 1991-2003, which non-existed in our field survey. Among the non-institutional sources, the professional moneylender is a relatively high share (31.31% in 2004-05) in primary field survey as against NSSO (3.40 % in 1991 and 13% in 2003).

In other words during the period of financial liberalization the professional moneylender become larger more than 100 per

Table 7.2: Source-wise Percentage Distribution of Outstanding Credit

Sources	*All*	*Advanced*	*Backward*
1. Intitutional			
Government	0.00	0.00	0.00
Co-operative	7.05	10.93	3.26
Commercial Bank	31.97	42.70	21.43
Others	0.00	0.00	0.00
Total	39.02	53.62	24.69
2. Non-institutional			
Landlord	0.09	0.13	0.05
Agr money lender	5.72	10.24	1.81
Pro money lender	31.31	13.81	48.09
Traders	13.18	12.70	13.57
Relatives and Friends	10.69	9.50	11.80
Others	0.00	0.00	0.00
Total	60.98	46.38	75.31
Total (1 +2)	100.00	100.00	100.00

cent according to the NSSO report. The share of the 'relative and friend' is below in our primary field survey (10.69% in 2004-05), while the same increased according to the NSSO (8.90% in 1991 and 15.4% in 2003). The share of the trader was negligible at 1.5 per cent in 1991 which increased to 10.7 per cent in 2003 in the case of NSSO. In our field survey the same jumped to 13.18 per cent in 2004-05. The meagre existence of the landlord (0.2% in 1991) in the case of NSSO disappeared in 2003. There is no reason why a micro study based on only 12 villages and 200 households should provide a common picture with a NSSO survey based on 8,000 villages and 64,000 households in 1991 and 6,638 villages and 51,770 households in 2003. The common thread of story between the NSSO survey and our study is that during the post-liberalization there is retrogression in the institutionalization of the rural credit, the commercial bank is not sufferer to that process, though its share declined to about 4 per cent in our field survey against 28.5 per cent NSSO data in 2003.

Looking into the regional break-up, some interesting observations emerge. The share of institutional credit to total in the region advanced is 53.62 per cent while it is only 24.69 per cent in the backward region. Looking into the different components of institutional credit we have found that percentage of commercial bank credit massively in both the areas, while the percentage of co-operative credit is second. The percentage of that becomes 10.93 per cent in advanced area compared to only 3.26 per cent in the backward region but in the advanced region of that is 42.70 per cent compared to 21.43 per cent in backward region. Within the non-institutional sources the share of the professional moneylender increased marginally in the backward region, while declined marginally in the advanced region. The professional moneylender's share remains around 48 per cent in the backward and about 14 per cent in the advanced region.

Table 7.2 shows among non-institutional sources the professional money lender, traders, relatives and friends, agricultural money lender and landlords registered 31.31 per cent, 13.18 per cent, 10.69 per cent, 5.72 per cent, and 0.09 per cent, respectively. Some scholars pointed out like Bhattacharyya 2005 that there is a new dimension story of insurance policy. The relatives and friends act as an insurance with each other, which generally makes transactions at nil rate of interest. It may be presumed that in the post-liberalization period this kind of personal insurance weakened for many reasons. The prime reason might be that owing to the increased vulnerability of living condition, the cases of default on personal loan increased. In other words, the relatives and friends can no more be taken into confidence that they will repay the loan. However, during the post-liberalization decade traders became second player in the informal credit market. This might be because in the virtual collapse of PDS system in post-liberalization, the traders emerged as a very powerful actor in the rural sector, which was able to raise their profit to a very high level. They might invest their swelled up and accumulated fund in the credit market. The performance of 'others' categories become nil. Thus, during the post-liberalization period role of professional money lenders is very important because their percentage in the informal credit market is 31.31 per cent out of total credit market in combined region. It may be supposed to be true that professional money lenders acted as the good judge who repaid the loan in course of time, as likely as not that they conducted their creditor day to day and collected monthly gross interest amount only, not principal. The share of institutionalisation of the credit market in the advanced region is greater than backward area. This share is 53.62 per cent compared to 24.69 per cent in the respective areas. It may be explained by the fact that the Narasimham Committee moved a step ahead by recommending a drastic reduction of priority sector lending from 40 per cent to 10 per cent of the total lending of the institution credit network.

4. The Peasant Class Differentiation in Rural Households

The theory of peasant class differentiation was developed by Lenin (1977), originally published in 1899 in opposition of the populist theory of homogeneous peasantry by Narodniks. According to the latter any attempt of capitalist development would annihilate the homogeneous peasantry, called for economic distress in their life and eventually collapse the home market. Lenin refuted this proposition and showed that the capitalism had already developed in Russian countryside which bifurcated the Old Russian peasantry into two distinct classes—bourgeoisie and proletariats. According to Lenin differentiation of the peasantry created home market for capitalism in Russia. The populist tradition again resurrected during 1920s Soviet Union in the hands of Chayanov (1966) who put forward the concept of a homogeneous peasantry and a process of biological differentiation associated with it. According to Chayanov there is a direct relation between farm size, family size and economy distress. Sen (1966) extended Chayanovian notion and pointed out that lower farm sizes characterised by family labour farm are more efficient than the capitalist farm belong to the higher farm sizes. Patnaik (1979) refuted these populist claim by showing that the so called family labour farms are in fact

Table 7.3A: Economic Classwise Percentage Distribution of Household Number, Assets, Owned Land, Operated Land, Irrigated Area, Input, Output, Product Marketed, Institutional and Non-institutional Credit

	% of Hhl.	Assets	Owned Area	Opertd Area	Irrigated Area	Input	Output	Product Marketed	Inst. Credit	Non-inst. Credit
All regions										
		(0.286)	(0.410)	(0.371)	(0.367)	(0.349)	(0.427)	(0.543)	(0.317)	(0.087)
LLS	12.00	4.20	0.55	0.00	0.00	0.00	0.00	0.00	4.41	12.33
PP	31.00	20.16	14.12	16.86	17.20	19.05	13.90	7.34	19.62	39.16
SP	19.00	12.85	14.25	15.42	15.69	15.77	14.61	11.04	10.34	19.41
MP	15.50	18.97	22.02	23.67	23.31	21.16	21.30	21.24	19.60	8.07
RP	17.00	36.59	35.30	31.33	30.86	32.48	33.71	37.23	32.60	19.12
LLD	5.50	7.24	13.76	12.71	12.94	11.54	16.48	23.15	13.44	1.91
Total	100.00	100.00	100.00	100.00	100.00	100.00	100.00	100.00	100.00	100.00
Advanced region										
		(0.290)	(0.360)	(0.326)	(0.326)	(0.347)	(0.376)	(0.415)	(0.341)	(0.094)
LLS	12.00	2.46	0.28	0.00	0.00	0.00	0.00	0.00	1.22	2.85
PP	18.00	6.30	5.99	7.94	7.91	6.70	5.37	3.50	10.99	21.41
SP	13.00	8.26	7.64	10.04	10.05	8.95	8.86	8.42	1.30	12.41
MP	20.00	21.67	22.68	22.01	22.01	21.71	21.56	21.28	22.74	15.62
RP	26.00	50.19	43.21	40.01	40.02	43.44	41.33	40.41	43.91	42.59
LLD	11.00	11.13	20.19	20.00	20.01	19.20	22.89	26.39	19.84	5.11
Total	100.00	100.00	100.00	100.00	100.00	100.00	100.00	100.00	100.00	100.00
Backward region										
		(0.073)	(0.314)	(0.331)	(0.304)	(0.271)	(0.276)	(0.285)	(0.066)	(0.158)
LLS	12.00	7.44	1.11	0.00	0.00	0.00	0.00	0.00	11.10	18.00
PP	44.00	45.92	31.51	32.43	34.19	37.64	35.85	34.81	37.75	49.76
SP	25.00	21.37	28.40	24.80	26.02	26.02	29.39	29.79	29.35	23.60
MP	11.00	13.96	20.60	26.56	25.69	20.35	20.62	20.89	12.99	3.55
RP	8.00	11.31	18.38	16.20	14.09	15.99	14.14	14.50	8.82	5.08
LLD	0.00	0.00	0.00	0.00	0.00	0.00	0.00	0.00	0.00	0.00
Total	100.00	100.00	100.00	100.00	100.00	100.00	100.00	100.00	100.00	100.00

LLS+PP = Exploited classes; SP+MP = Self-employed classes;
RP+LLD = Labour hiring classes

pauperized (and differentiated) agricultural labour with some tiny plot of land. The so called efficiency based on per acre land would vanish in thin air if we consider per unit labour as criterion of efficiency. Bhattacharyya (2001) and Rakshit (2005) also supported Patnaik's points

Table 7.3A displayed high concentration among the different markets. The labour hiring classes (only 22.5 % households) have control over different markets such as assets (44%), land (49%), input (44%), output (50%), product marketed (60%) and credit market (46%). On the other hand, exploited classes (33% households) holds only 24 per cent in assets, 15 per cent in owned land, and 7 per cent in product marketed etc., the landless labourers and poor peasant together can be referred as exploited as they are basically dependent on the earnings of others, from the sell of their labour to others. The Gini-coefficient of these markets are 0.286 (assets), 0.410 (Owned Land), 0.349 (Input), 0.427 (Output), 0.543 (product marketed) and 0.317 (Ins. Credit Market) in the combined region. This means that each market prevails differentiated in the rural economy in West Bengal.

There is no clear conclusion from Table 7.3B since maximum number of households belong to the acreage group (0.01 to 2.50 acres), they are called marginal peasant. But there is class differentiation in different markets in West Bengal. In combined region the values of Gini-coefficient are 0.299 in assets, 0.367 in owned, 0.388 in operated, 0.374 in irrigated land, 0.341 in inputs, 0.389 in output, 0.513 in product marketed, 0.149 in institutional credit and 0.014 in non-institutional credit markets.

5. Problem of Sustainable Development

5.1 The Estimation of Households' Income and Poverty Line

In this section we attempt to highlight the sustainable growth of agricultural with institutional credit after bank nationalization. The main objective of rural banking was agricultural growth and alleviation of rural poverty after bank nationalization period (1969). The challenge has been made in this study to review how far this objective has been achieved. In our study income of households from agriculture is defined as Farm Labour Income. The non-agricultural income has to be added to the Farm Labour

Table 7.3B: Acreage Group-wise Percentage Distribution of Household Number, Assets, Owned land, Operated land, Irrigated Area, Input, Output,Product Marketed, Institutional and Non-institutional Credit

	% of Hhl.	Assets	Owned Area	Opertd Area	Irrigated Area	Input	Output	Product Marketed	Inst. Credit	Non. Credit
All region										
		(0.299)	(0.367)	(0.388)	(0.374)	(0.341)	(0.389)	(0.513)	(0.149)	(0.014)
0.00	12.00	4.19	0.55	0.00	0.00	0.00	0.00	0.00	4.41	9.40
0.01 to 2.5	70.50	52.03	51.95	50.85	51.79	55.68	50.43	36.33	68.01	76.95
2.5 to 5	14.50	34.67	34.44	34.92	34.51	33.27	36.76	48.05	24.07	12.54
5 to 10	3.00	9.11	13.06	14.23	13.71	11.05	12.81	15.62	3.52	1.12
Total	100.00	100.00	100.00	100.00	100.00	100.00	100.00	100.00	100.00	100.00
Advanced region										
		(0.370)	(0.383)	(0.415)	(0.415)	(0.402)	(0.412)	(0.484)	(0.180)	(0.062)
0.00	12.00	2.44	0.28	0.00	0.00	0.00	0.00	0.00	1.22	2.46
0.01 to 2.5	62.00	37.94	41.92	39.20	39.18	39.69	38.67	30.20	60.51	71.84
2.5 to 5	21.00	46.91	40.18	41.59	41.60	44.25	44.62	52.64	33.99	23.11
5 to 10	5.00	12.71	17.62	19.21	19.22	16.07	16.70	17.16	4.27	2.59
Total	100.00	100.00	100.00	100.00	100.00	100.00	100.00	100.00	100.00	100.00
Backward region										
		(0.089)	(0.245)	(.(286)	(0.252)	(0.252)	(0.201)	(0.206)	(0.025)	(0.037)
0.00	12.00	7.44	1.11	0.00	0.00	0.00	0.00	0.00	11.10	13.55
0.01 to 2.5	79.00	78.23	73.41	71.19	74.85	79.75	80.63	80.22	83.77	80.00
2.5 to 5	8.00	11.92	22.17	23.28	21.52	16.75	16.54	15.21	3.21	6.22
5 to 10	1.00	2.41	3.32	5.53	3.63	3.50	2.82	4.57	1.92	0.23
Total	100.00	100.00	100.00	100.00	100.00	100.00	100.00	100.00	100.00	100.00

Income to achieve the total income of households; this income is compared to the poverty level income. The main items of non-agricultural income that accrues to the sample households is from (a) salaries and pensions; (b) the saie of human labour power; (c) the sale of inputs and the hire of equipment; and (d) income from all non-cultivating sources. The last item includes incomes from sales of tree, retail trade and petty business. It is salary, pension and other incomes, which constitute the main share. This may be due to the diversified non-agricultural activities which have come up following the agricultural growth (Chandrasekhar, 1993). On the other hand after the 'operation barga' the sharecropping has suddenly become a dead profession for the landlord class who are now reluctant to enter into new contract. This might be the reason behind the small value of the rent income.

The poverty lines of West Bengal and India for the year 2004-05 estimated from the Report of Expert Group on Estimation of

Table 7.4A: Economic Class-wise Total Income of Household and the Deviation of Total Income from the Poverty Line

	Farm Lab. Income	Income from wages	Income from salary	Hire income	Non-cultivation income	Total income	Considering WB's poverty line			Considering India's poverty line		
							Poverty line income	D/S from pov.line	Per Hhs D/S	Poverty line income	D/S from pov./line	Per Hhs D/S
All regions												
LLS	98470.00	236850.00	24920.00	0.00	58545.00	418785.00	542073.12	-123288.12	-5137.01	504138.48	-85353.48	-3556.40
PP	236707.00	422320.00	172220.00	4000.00	130112.00	965359.00	1359776.64	-394417.64	-6361.57	1264618.56	-299259.56	-4826.77
SP	263899.00	29265.00	271325.00	4000.00	85150.00	653639.00	799328.16	-145689.16	-3833.93	743390.64	-89751.64	-2361.69
MP	388666.50	13860.00	342700.00	5000.00	119880.00	870106.50	739608.24	130498.26	4209.62	687849.96	182256.54	5879.24
RP	587885.75	3410.00	309690.00	67100.00	122610.00	1090695.75	822297.36	268398.39	7894.07	764752.44	325943.31	9586.57
LLD	216052.00	0.00	743000.00	0.00	19850.00	978902.00	280224.24	698677.76	63516.16	260613.96	718288.04	65298.91
Total	1791680.25	705705.00	1863855.00	80100.00	536147.00	4977487.25	4543307.76	434179.49	2170.90	4225364.04	752123.21	3760.62
Advanced regions												
LLS	17285.00	125825.00	11720.00	0.00	17160.00	171990.00	248067.36	-76077.36	-6339.78	230707.44	-58717.44	-4893.12
PP	127032.00	116150.00	69825.00	0.00	58020.00	371027.00	367507.20	3519.80	195.54	341788.80	29238.20	1624.34
SP	113955.00	4805.00	158350.00	0.00	27350.00	304460.00	257255.04	47204.96	3631.15	239252.16	65207.84	5015.99
MP	349121.00	2520.00	304050.00	3600.00	99180.00	758471.00	482353.20	276117.80	13805.89	448597.80	309873.20	15493.66
RP	382620.75	2160.00	296240.00	67100.00	97610.00	845730.75	601793.04	243937.71	9382.22	559679.16	286051.59	11001.98
LLD	216052.00	0.00	743000.00	0.00	19850.00	978902.00	280224.24	698677.76	63516.16	260613.96	718288.04	65298.91
Total	1206065.75	251460.00	1583185.00	70700.00	319170.00	3430580.75	2237200.08	1193380.67	11933.81	2080639.32	1349941.43	13499.41
Backward regions												
LLS	81185.00	111025.00	13200.00	0.00	41385.00	246795.00	294005.76	-47210.76	-3934.23	273431.04	-26636.04	-2219.67
PP	109675.00	306170.00	102395.00	4000.00	72092.00	594332.00	992269.44	-397937.44	-9044.03	922829.76	-328497.76	-7465.86
SP	149944.00	24460.00	112975.00	4000.00	57800.00	349179.00	542073.12	-192894.12	-7715.76	504138.48	-154959.48	-6198.38
MP	39545.50	11340.00	38650.00	1400.00	20700.00	111635.50	257255.04	-145619.54	-13238.14	239252.16	-127616.66	-11601.51
RP	205265.00	1250.00	13450.00	0.00	25000.00	244965.00	220504.32	24460.68	3057.59	205073.28	39891.72	4986.47
LLD	0.00	0.00	0.00	0.00	0.00	0.00	0.00	0.00	0.00	0.00	0.00	0.00
Total	585614.50	454245.00	280670.00	9400.00	216977.00	1546906.50	2306107.68	-759201.18	-7592.01	2144724.72	-597818.22	-5978.18

Table 7.4B: Acreage Group-wise Total Income of Household and the Deviation of Total Income from the Poverty Line

Group	Farm Lab .Income	Income from wages	Income from salary	Hire income	Non-cultivation income	Total income	Considering WB's poverty line			Considering India's poverty line		
							Poverty line income	D/S from pov.line	Per Hhs D/S	Poverty line income	D/S from pov.line	Per Hhs D/S
All regions												
0.00	98470.00	236850.00	24920.00	0.00	58545.00	418785.00	542073.12	-123288.12	-5137.01	504138.48	-85353.48	-3556.40
0.01 to 2.5	874868.00	447615.00	842485.00	12400.00	341592.00	2518960.00	2990589.84	-471629.84	-3344.89	2781306.36	-262346.36	-1860.61
2.5 to 5	603998.25	21240.00	865500.00	63100.00	112210.00	1666048.25	748795.92	917252.33	31629.39	696394.68	969653.57	33436.33
5 to 10	214344.00	0.00	130950.00	4600.00	23800.00	373694.00	261848.88	111845.12	18640.85	243524.52	130169.48	21694.91
Total	1791680.25	705705.00	1863855.00	80100.00	536147.00	4977487.25	4543307.76	434179.49	2170.90	4225364.04	752123.21	3760.62
Advanced regions												
0.00	17285.00	125825.00	11720.00	0.00	17160.00	171990.00	248067.36	-76077.36	-6339.78	230707.44	-58717.44	-4893.12
0.01 to 2.5	715588.00	125635.00	593765.00	4400.00	194200.00	1633588.00	1240336.80	393251.20	6342.76	1153537.20	480050.80	7742.75
2.5 to 5	417450.75	0.00	847500.00	63100.00	84010.00	1412060.75	532885.44	879175.31	41865.49	495593.76	916466.99	43641.29
5 to 10	157469.00	0.00	130200.00	3200.00	23800.00	314669.00	215910.48	98758.52	19751.70	200800.92	113868.08	22773.62
Total	1206065.75	251460.00	1583185.00	70700.00	319170.00	3430580.75	2237200.08	1193380.67	11933.81	2080639.32	1349941.43	13499.41
Backward regions												
0.00	81185.00	111025.00	13200.00	0.00	41385.00	246795.00	294005.76	-47210.76	-3934.23	273431.04	-26636.04	-2219.67
0.01 to 2.5	261007.00	321980.00	248720.00	8000.00	147392.00	987099.00	1750253.04	-763154.04	-9660.18	1627769.16	-640670.16	-8109.75
2.5 to 5	186547.50	21240.00	18000.00	0.00	28200.00	253987.50	215910.48	38077.02	4759.63	200800.92	53186.58	6648.32
5 to 10	56875.00	0.00	750.00	1400.00	0.00	59025.00	45938.40	13086.60	13086.60	42723.60	16301.40	16301.40
Total	585614.50	454245.00	280670.00	9400.00	216977.00	1546906.50	2306107.68	-759201.18	-7592.01	2144724.72	-597818.22	-5978.18

Proportion and Number of Poor, Planning Commission (2004-05) are Rs. 382.82 per capita per month for West Bengal and Rs 358.03 per capita per month for India respectively (Himanshu, 2007). Multiplying total number of members of the households for each class/group with the poverty line we estimate the total poverty line income for each category per month and it is further multiplied by 12 which gives us yearly total poverty line income for each category shown in Table 7.4A and Table 7.4B. Comparing the poverty line income with the total income we calculate the surplus or deficit for each category. To get a comparable picture we take per household surplus or deficit of total income from the poverty line. The result we have is quite an expected one.

Considering the poverty line for West Bengal as well as India for the combined region only the top two labour hiring classes and middle peasant are registering the above poverty line income. The poverty lines for West Bengal and India, however, give a relatively consistent pattern for the size-group category. The acreage groups up to 2.5 acres register a deficit and beyond it a surplus.

Looking into the inter-class/group variation as one moves from the lower to the higher categories, the magnitude of deficit declines and after a point surplus starts to emerge and the magnitude of surplus increases. For example the per household deficit from poverty line (West Bengal) decreases from Rs. (–) 6361.57 for poor peasants to Rs. (–) 3833.93 for small peasants while middle peasants register a surplus of Rs. 4209.62. On the other hand per household deficit from poverty line (India) shows a sharp decrease from Rs. (–) 4826.77 for the poor peasants to Rs. (–) 2361.89 for small peasant and surplus of Rs. 5879.24 for middle peasants, to Rs. 9586.57 for rich peasant, to Rs. 65298.91 for the landlord. The magnitude of deficit (taking West Bengal's poverty line) of the landless is 134 per cent that of small peasant. The advanced region registers an overall surplus above poverty line per holding Rs. 119333.81 and Rs.13499.41with respect to West Bengal and India's poverty line respectively in comparison to the backward region that registers a deficit of the amount per holding (–) 7592.01 and Rs. (–) 5978.18 respectively.

The average per household income in agriculture is negative after deviation from their poverty line income in backward region. This is the main focus of our findings that question of sustainable

Table 7.5A: Economic Class-wise per Holding Credit Plus Surplus/Deficit from Poverty Line

	West Bengal				*India*			
	Per hhs D/S	*IC Plus S/D*	*NI Plus S/D*	*AC Plus S/D*	*Per hhs D/S*	*IC Plus S/D*	*NI Plus S/D*	*AC Plus S/D*
All regions								
LLS	–5137.01	–80688.12	59886.88	102486.88	–3556.40	–42753.48	97821.52	140421.52
PP	–6361.57	–204717.64	175877.36	365577.36	–4826.77	–109559.56	271035.44	460735.44
SP	–3833.93	–689.16	172230.84	317230.84	–2361.89	55248.36	228168.36	373168.36
MP	4209.62	319998.26	255728.26	445228.26	5879.24	371756.54	307486.54	496986.54
RP	7894.07	538648.39	560673.39	830923.39	9586.57	596193.31	618218.31	888468.31
LLD	63516.16	828677.76	727627.76	857627.76	65298.91	848288.04	747238.04	877238.04
Total	2170.90	1401229.49	1952024.49	2919074.49	3760.62	1719173.21	2269968.21	3237018.21
Advanced regions								
LLS	–6339.78	–68077.36	–59902.36	–51902.36	–4893.12	–50717.44	–42542.44	–34542.44
PP	195.54	75519.80	124877.80	196877.80	1624.34	101238.20	150596.20	222596.20
SP	3631.15	100704.96	117504.96	171004.96	5015.99	118707.84	135507.84	189007.84
MP	13805.89	425117.80	364647.80	513647.80	15493.66	458873.20	398403.20	547403.20
RP	9382.22	486687.71	485322.71	728072.71	11001.98	528801.59	527436.59	770186.59
LLD	63516.16	828677.76	727627.76	857627.76	65298.91	848288.04	747238.04	877238.04
Total	11933.81	1848630.67	1760078.67	2415328.67	13499.41	2005191.43	1916639.43	2571889.43
Backward regions								
LLS	–3934.23	–12610.76	119789.24	154389.24	–2219.67	7963.96	140363.96	174963.96
PP	–9044.03	–280237.44	50999.56	168699.56	–7465.86	–210797.76	120439.24	238139.24
SP	–7715.76	–101394.12	54725.88	146225.88	–6198.38	–63459.48	92660.52	184160.52
MP	–13238.14	–105119.54	–108919.54	–68419.54	–11601.51	–87116.66	–90916.66	–50416.66
RP	3057.59	51960.68	75350.68	102850.68	4986.47	67391.72	90781.72	118281.72
LLD	0.00	0.00	0.00	0.00	0.00	0.00	0.00	0.00
Total	–7592.01	–447401.18	191945.82	503745.82	–5978.18	– 286018.22	353328.78	665128.78

development in agriculture in West Bengal as well as India. Indian farmers do not find it viable in agricultural sector due to regular increase prices of means of production in post-reform era in India."

Looking into inter-class distribution in the advanced region shows all economic class above the poverty line except landless class in West Bengal and India in comparison to the backward region that only rich peasant constitutes surplus value of per holding from poverty line.

Considering acreage group-wise distribution of the deviation from the poverty line we found that only landless class registers a deficit value [Rs. (–) 6339.78 for West Bengal's poverty line and Rs. (–) 4893.12 for India's poverty line] in the advanced region are positive. All the classes except the landless constitute positive value in the advanced region. On the other hand the landless and the size group 0.01 to 2.5 acres register a deficit value and top two groups register positive value in West Bengal and India in the backward region.

5.2 Rural Credit and Poverty Alleviation

The main objective of the bank nationalization was agricultural growth and alleviation of rural poverty. We would like to examine from our ground level data the role of credit in the poverty alleviation. Here, the total income of household is compared with the poverty level income. The poverty line of India for the year 2004-05 estimated from the Report of Expert Group on Estimation of Proportion and Number of Poors, Planning Commission (2004-05) is Rs. 358.03 per month for India and Rs. 382.82 per month for West Bengal. Firstly we have estimated yearly (Rs. 358.03×12 for India and Rs. 382.82×12 for WB) poverty line of a particular member. After that we estimate the poverty line of a particular class/group by the method of multiplying total number of members of the households with yearly poverty line. In Table 7.4A and 7.4B we have found a comparable picture of per holding surplus or deficit of total income from the poverty line for West Bengal and India.

In Tables 7.5A and 7.5B shows the role of institutional, non-institutional and total credit (institutional plus non-institutional) in poverty alleviation. In the combined region when we add the institutional credit with surplus/deficit from poverty line it failed

Table 7.5B: Acreage Group-wise per Holding Credit Plus Surplus/Deficit from Poverty Line

Group	*Per hhs D/S*	*IC Plus S/D*	*NI Plus S/D*	*AC Plus S/D*	*Per hhs D/S*	*IC Plus S/D*	*NI Plus S/D*	*AC Plus S/D*
All regions								
0.00	–5137.01	–80688.12	59886.88	102486.88	–3556.40	42600.00	183175.00	225775.00
0.01 to 2.5	–3344.89	231070.16	650200.16	1352900.16	–1860.61	702700.00	1121830.00	1824530.00
2.5 to 5	31629.39	1105002.33	1110392.33	1298142.33	33436.33	187750.00	193140.00	380890.00
5 to 10	18640.85	145845.12	131545.12	165545.12	21694.91	34000.00	19700.00	53700.00
Total	2170.90	1401229.49	1952024.49	2919074.49	3760.62	967050.00	1517845.00	2484895.00
Advanced regions								
0.00	–6339.78	–68077.36	–59902.36	–51902.36	–4893.12	8000.00	16175.00	24175.00
0.01 to 2.5	6342.76	834751.20	798134.20	1239634.20	7742.75	441500.00	404883.00	846383.00
2.5 to 5	41865.49	1056925.31	1010115.31	1187865.31	43641.29	177750.00	130940.00	308690.00
5 to 10	19751.70	126758.52	113458.52	141458.52	22773.62	28000.00	14700.00	42700.00
Total	11933.81	1848630.67	1760078.67	2415328.67	13499.41	655250.00	566698.00	1221948.00
Backward regions								
0.00	–3934.23	–12610.76	119789.24	154389.24	–2219.67	34600.00	167000.00	201600.00
0.01 to 2.5	–9660.18	–501954.04	–46207.04	214992.96	–8109.75	261200.00	716947.00	978147.00
2.5 to 5	4759.63	48077.02	100277.02	110277.02	6648.32	10000.00	62200.00	72200.00
5 to 10	13086.60	19086.60	18086.60	24086.60	16301.40	6000.00	5000.00	11000.00
Total	–7592.01	–447401.18	191945.82	503745.82	–5978.18	311800.00	951147.00	1262947.00

Note: IC = Institutional Credit. NI = Non-institutional Credit. AC = All Credit. S = Surplus. D = Deficit

to lift the three deficit ridden classes say, landless, poor peasant and small peasants though their respective deficit declined. This is true for the poverty estimation of West Bengal as well as India. Adding up non-institutional credit with the institutional one makes to cover deficit of all the classes/size group. However this is not healthy tendency as it implies the possibility of the peasant to be tied up with money lenders.

6. Summary and Conclusions

We have found that the common thread of story between the NSSO survey and our study is that during the post-liberalization there is retrogression in the institutionalization of the rural credit, the commercial bank is not sufferer to that process, though its share declined to about 4 per cent in our field survey against 28.5 per cent. NSSO data in 2003. During the post-liberalization, we have also seen that the share of institutional credit has increased from 33 per cent in 1971 to 82 per cent in 1991 and thereafter it declined to 58 per cent in 2003 in rural West Bengal. On the other hand, the share of non-institutional credit is just opposite scenarios because both shares are 100 per cent.

We have found that there is high concentration among the different markets in rural West Bengal. The labour hiring classes (only 22.5 % households) have control over different markets such as assets (44%), land (49%), input (44%), output (50%), product marketed (60%) and credit market (46%). On the other hand, exploited classes (33% households) holds only 24 per cent in assets, 15 per cent in owned land, and 7 per cent in product marketed, etc., the landless labourers and poor peasant together can be referred exploited as they are basically dependent on the earnings of others, from the sale of their labour to others. The value of Gini-Coefficient of these markets are 0.286 (Assets), 0.410 (Owned Land), 0.349 (Input), 0.427 (Output). This means that there is high existence of peasant class differentiation in rural West Bengal.

This chapter addresses the sustainable growth of agricultural with institutional credit after bank nationalization. The main objective of rural banking was agricultural growth and alleviation of rural poverty during post-bank nationalization period. The three economic classes like landless, poor and small peasant failed to lift above the poverty line by the institutional credit in the rural

West Bengal. According to labour exploitation criterion, these three classes are basically exploited classes. But when we add non-institutional credit with holding deficit or surplus then its value indicates positive. It implies that they success to lift above the poverty line. It is not healthy environment for poverty alleviation programmes. These classes again are going to arrest to money lender in the informal credit market. They could not come out from the vicious circle of poverty. So, the sustainable agriculture growth has been arrested by the insufficient of institutional credit in rural West Bengal. In the section 3.1 we have mentioned in the first paragraph the NSSO data showed that the percentage share of institutional credit declined during the post-liberalization period.

7. Policy Prescriptions

1. I suggest that anyhow to increase the share of institutional credit for productive purpose for farmers in rural economy so that they are able to increase their production.Because after financial liberalization the price of all factors of production goes up. To meet their requirement, without institutional credit it is not possible to come out from problem of sustainable development in agriculture.

2. New Government of West Bengal might be realized this matter and introduced the State interventionist new policy for getting the institutional credit. The Government of West Bengal has accepted the policy of Kisan Credit Card on 18th August, 2011 so that they enjoy the formal credit against the collateral (Kisan Credit Card) up to fifty thousand for each Kisan household in rural economy. The impact of this policy will be reviewed in future.

REFERENCES

Bell, C., 1990, 'Interactions between Institutional and Informal Credit Agencies in Rural India', *The World Bank Economic Review*, September, Vol. 4, No. 3, pp. 297-327.

Bhaduri, A., 1973, 'A Study in Agricultural Backwardness under semi-feudalism', *Economic Journal*, Vol. 83, No. 1, pp. 120-37.

Bhaduri, A., 1993, "Mathematical Appendix: A Model of Differentiation among Initially Indebted Peasants", in A. Bhaduri (ed.)

Unconventional Economic Essays, Delhi, Oxford University Press, pp. 254-261.

Bhattacharyya, S., 2005, 'Interest Rates, Collateral and (De-) interlinkage: A Micro-Study of Rural Credit in West Bengal', *Cambridge Journal of Economics*, Vol. 29, No. 3, pp. 439-462.

Chayanov, A.V., 1966, *Theory of Peasant Economy*, ed. By D. Thorner, R.E.F. Smith and B. Karblay, Homewood, Illinois, Irwin.

Chayanov, A.V., 1991, *The Theory of Peasant Co-operatives*, London: I.B. Tauris.

Patnaik, Utsa (1979) 'Neo-populism and Marxism: The Chayanovian View of the Agrarian Question and its Fundamental Fallacy', *Journal of Peasant Studies*, Vol. 6, No. 4.

Patnaik U., 1987, *Peasant Class Differentiation: A Study in Method with Reference to Haryana*, Delhi, Oxford University Press.

Patnaik, Utsa (1988) 'Ascertaining the Economic Characteristics of Peasant Classes-in-Themselves in Rural India', *Journal of Peasant Studies*, Vol. 15, No. 3.

Patnaik Utsa (1976) 'Class Differentiation within the Peasantry: An Approach to the Analysis of Indian Agriculture', *Economic and Political Weekly*, Vol. 11, No. 39.

Ramchandran, V.K. and M. Swaminathan, 2002, 'Rural Banking and Landless Labour Households: Institutional Reform and Rural Credit Markets in India' *Journal of Agrarian Change*, Vol. 2, No. 4, pp. 502-44.

Roemer, J. 1982, *A General Theory of Exploitation and Class*. Cambridge, Mass., Harvard University Press.

Sen, A. K., 1966, 'Peasants and Dualism with and without Surplus Labour', *Journal of Political Economy*, Vol. 74, No. 5, pp. 425-450.

Government of India, National Sample Survey Organisation of different rounds.

8
Self-Employment among Rural Women in India
A Focus on Family Helpers

Sharmistha Sinha

Introduction

Gender relations play an important role in the division of labour encompassing all countries and regions. As Ester Boserup puts in her book *Women's Role in Economic Development*:

> "Even at the most primitive stages of family autarky there is some division of labour within the family, the main criteria for the division being that of age and sex. Both in primitive and in more developed communities, the traditional division of labour within the family is usually considered 'natural' in the sense of being obviously and originally imposed by the sex difference itself.[1]"

There is an obvious gender based difference in the distribution of work, both economic activities and non-economic ones, with some economic activities designated as unpaid family work in the official statistics, however, these tend to be largely specific to women.

> The "subsistence activities usually omitted in the statistics of production and income are largely women's work."[2]

Out of the three billion people that were employed around

the world in 2008, 1.2 billion were women amounting to about 40.4 per cent (global employment trends for women, March 2009, ILO). But more than half of the female workers were vulnerable workers (unpaid family workers and own account workers) (GET March 2009, ILO); there are countries where the shares of women in 'vulnerable employment' were even above 65 per cent. About one-fourth of the women workers were unpaid contributing family workers, worldwide; twice the share of the men. In South Asia, more than 50 per cent of the female workers were family helpers in 2009, male counterparts comprising just 14.2 per cent (International Labour Office 2010)[3]. These family helpers are documented as self-employed workers; the concern, however, is to what extent they can be recognized as workers. The family helpers work in the household enterprises without any regular wages or salaries. They neither own the enterprises nor have the autonomy to run it on their own; they simply assisted in running the enterprise. A worker has the lowest economic independence if she is a family helper. They do not even receive any compensation for their work. In rural context, unpaid family work largely means assistance in the family farm without remuneration for their work.

To what extent is the high prevalence of contributors to family work among women, though counted as workers, a reflection of choice? This chapter attempts to explore this in the rural Indian context, which has a significant share of female self-employment. *Prima facie*, it looks encouraging that there has been an increase in female employment, however, the sudden spurt raises doubts as well and indicates us to explore the plight of these women, what drives such large proportion of the women self-employed workers to contribute to family enterprises amidst the growing economy.

With growing informalization, there has been a structural change in the production process with increasing self-employment, subcontracting, outsourcing and increase in home-based work. Expanding informal sector with increasing flexibility in the production process generally employs more women than men (Marilyn Carr, Martha Alter Chen, and Jane Tate, 2000). Home-based work has a distinct characteristic that there is no account of who performs this work and who gets the actual remuneration. There might be someone getting the contract for work; he or she earning, mostly on piece rate basis but other family members might be involved in executing the task. Largely female members of the family, wives, daughters, wives of married sons, help in the family farms and businesses, working full or part time but without any regular salary or wages.

Women often join the labour force to supplement family income. It is a common phenomenon that they release male members of the family to look for better job opportunities and engage themselves in the family farm at a very low productivity level or work as helpers in family enterprises. India's economy has undergone a substantial transformation since the country's independence; with agriculture now accounting only one-third of the gross domestic product (GDP), down from 59 per cent in 1950, with increasing non-farm employment and other support services. Nevertheless, agriculture continues to dominate employment, employing two-thirds of all workers. More than 80 per cent of the female workers are engaged in agriculture and allied activities. Among the rural women workers 56.3 per cent were self-employed in 2004-05. This chapter is an attempt to explore the extent and nature of female self-employed in rural India, focusing on the family helpers that comprise a significant proportion of the self-employed; the core factors behind taking up these activities and their implications.

Data

All calculations are based on the Unit Level Data of two rounds of the Employment-Unemployment Surveys, 61st Round (2004-05) and 50th Round (1993-94) conducted by the National Sample Survey Organisation (NSSO), Government of India. If not mentioned otherwise, all the tables and figures are computed from the NSS unit level data.

Defining the Unpaid Family Helpers—Their Extent and Distribution

As per the NSS 61st Round estimates of 2004-05, adjusted with Census of India projections of populations, usually employed female workers as a proportion of population are about 24 per cent in rural areas. However, during this period the share of self-employed among women workers increased significantly, particularly in the rural areas (Table 8.1). The self-employed are further categorized into own account workers, employers and helpers in family enterprises. Women contributors to family enterprises comprised 42 per cent of the total female workforce in rural India in 2004-2005, an increase by 5 percentage points since 1993-1994.

Table 8.1: Distribution of the Rural Workforce (Principal Status[4] only)

	Self employed			*Wage workers*	
	Unpaid family helpers	*Own account workers*	*Employers*	*Casual*	*Regular*
1993-94	37.3	12.9	0.8	45.3	3.4
2004-05	41.9	13.9	0.5	38.9	4.8

Table 8.1 reveals that with fall in casual work among women, unpaid family work has increased in rural India. The extent of women taking resort to unpaid family work[5] also needs to be considered. Distribution of the self-employed reveals that in rural India, the proportion of unpaid female family helpers is three times higher than their male counterparts (Table 8.2). Widespread stagnation in the Indian agricultural sector since the late 1990s has adversely affected the earnings of the farm households. Slowdown in growth of wage rates and farm incomes, along with rising prices has, in turn, pushed a large number of the rural households already living at subsistence levels to even worse levels of poverty. The members of these households, the non-workers, mainly women and elderly are then bound to increase their joint family labour supply at least to that level which will ensure a basic minimum subsistence income for the family. Women previously engaged in domestic work joined the family farms, mainly as unpaid family workers, replacing hired labour, as the farm incomes

Table 8.2: Distribution of the Self-employed

	Rural female		*Rural male*	
	93-94	*94-95*	*93-94*	*94-95*
Family helpers	73.2	74.3	28.1	26.8
Own account workers	25.2	24.7	67.7	71.0
Employers	1.5	0.9	4.2	2.2
Total	100	100	100	100

declined to subsistence level (Vinoj Abraham, 2009). In rural India, about 90 per cent of these women assist in farm activities; 78 per cent of them growing cereals, pulses and other crops like oilseeds, cotton and sugarcane, though the majority assisted in growing of foodgrain crops only. Others help out in varying activities like breeding of cattle, rearing of goats and sheep, production of dairy products, raising of silk worms, logging to produce rough wood like pit props, fuel wood, etc., and gathering of other forest materials. About three-quarters of the women are cultivators in family farms and some 5 per cent work in rented land. Women are often discouraged to work in rented land, they are allowed mostly if the land is leased in by her husband or any other male member of the family (Amit Kundu, 2006). They are mostly engaged in sowing, weeding, harvesting, etc.

Among non-farm activities, unpaid family assistance from women is sought in manufacturing of "*beedi*", weaving and manufacture of cotton and woollen fabrics, wearing apparels from leather and its substitutes, embroidery, manufacture of products made of bamboo, cane, palm leaf, vegetable fibres, etc., for basic household utilities and manufacture of earthenware goods. They are also employed in cutting, shaping and finishing of stones. In services sector, they help in retail trade in non-specialized stores—selling basic food items like cereals and pulses, tea, spices, flour, in small cafes and food-joints, provide services in non-scheduled passenger and freight land transport. Other services include washing and cleaning of textiles, draperies, etc. and also minor alterations and repair of the garments, assistance in some recreational shows and fairs, managing lotteries, etc.

Worldwide, many self-employed women, particularly in the rural areas, working mainly with agricultural and minor forest products are linked into global value chains. For example, women shelling Brazil nuts in Peru, collecting shea nuts and processing shea butter in West Africa, growing fruits and vegetables in several developing countries cater to the export market of the US and Europe. And "the 'weakest' links in global agricultural or forest product chains are often women who produce agricultural products, collect non-timber forest products, and process agricultural or non-timber forest products" (Carr, Chen and Tate, 2000).

Since the women in our study are mere helpers in the family

farms or businesses, it is important for us to know the principal occupations of their households. Table 8.3 reveals that in rural areas, there are agricultural households, who are mainly cultivators, or dairy farmers or livestock farmers. So the women folk in the family can easily assist in the land or help in operating and managing the dairy or poultry or fish farms, in taking care of the livestock. However, these women mostly work in enterprises owned and run by the male members in the family. Evidence suggests that female proprietary businesses often tend to be smaller with small investment and fewer market linkages (S.V. Sethuraman, 1998) and the female self-employed tend to earn less than men (Jacques Charmes, 1998)

Table 8.3: Principal Occupations of Households with Female Family Helpers and their Distribution, 2004-05

Principal occupations of households with female family helpers	*Distribution*
Cultivators	73.6
Agricultural labourers	3.1
Farmers, other than cultivators	2.6
Merchants & shopkeepers in wholesale & retail trade	2.8
Spinners, weavers, knitting, dyers	1.3
Bricklayers and other construction workers	1.3
Working proprietors, managers in mining, manufacturing	1.1
Rest	15.0
Total	100.0

Note: The Distribution indicates the share of the respective occupation among all principal occupations of households with female family helpers.

Along with working in the household enterprises for the majority of the year, about 28 per cent of the women in rural areas pursue different activities for a shorter duration of the year as a subsidiary worker. They are engaged as both paid workers and also self-employed. However, the extent of casual workers and helpers in subsidiary status in household enterprises is the maximum which means they are employed as helpers in a particular activity for majority of the year and along with that they pursue different activities as a casual labour or again a family helper for a shorter time period. Since a considerable section of the women are engaged in agriculture, which is seasonal in nature, therefore, along with helping in the family land, they also work as casual workers in growing foodgrain crops and other crops, their packaging, etc. Construction, maintenance and manufacture of bricks are other activities in which these women are engaged to supplement their family income (Table 8.4).

Table 8.4: Distribution of Female Workers who are working as Helpers principally and Casual Workers in subsidiary capacity in different activities, 2004-05

Growing of foodgrain crops (cereals and pulses)	77.9
Growing of oilseeds, peanuts, soyabeans	3.7
Growing of cotton and other vegetable textile fibres	8.2
Growing of tea or mate leaves including activities of tea factories associated with tea plantations	0.1
Harvesting, cleaning, trimming, drying, bulk packaging of crops, cotton picking	1.3
General construction, maintenance of residential buildings on own-account basis, fee or contract basis; manufacture of bricks	3.6
Other services	5.3
Total	100.0

Poverty and Vulnerability

Employment characteristics of the household members are highly related with the household income. In an economy with 39 per cent of the female workforce being engaged as helpers in family enterprises, it seems there is high congruence with poverty. In India, data on the consumer expenditure of household collected by the NSS are used as proxy for income of household and form the basis of estimates of poverty. Table 8.5 reveals that more than 80 per cent of these female helpers suffer from poverty and vulnerability. The classification of the income groups is based on the *Report on Conditions of Work and Promotion of Livelihoods in the Unorganised Sector* by the National Commission for Enterprises in the Unorganised Sector (NCEUS) in 2007. One plausible reason is that the increase in self-employment in the rural sector is mainly confined to the households with marginal landholdings with less than 0.4 hectare (Vinoj Abraham, 2009). The theory of U-shaped curve of the female labour force participation, as discussed by Ashok Mathur, 1994, and C. Goldin, 1995, suggests higher female labour force participation rates in traditional agricultural societies, where they participate mostly as unpaid family labour. With decline in agricultural yield and growth and widespread stagnation in real wages in the rural sector, there might have been a restructuring in the employment status among the poorest households. The casual workers earlier might have turned into being self-employed in their marginal landholdings. Joint family labour increases to ensure subsistence of the household members. Neither do these households have sufficient capital nor adequate skill to venture into a more remunerative enterprise. Apart from assistance in agriculture and allied activities, "beedi" rolling and small retail trade are the major occupations wherein they are engaged in rural India.

Table 8.5: Percentage Distribution of the Unpaid Female Helpers by Different Income Groups, 2004-05

Income group	
Poor and vulnerable	82.0
Middle income	16.9
High income	1.1
Total	100.0

Note: 1. Poor and vulnerable: < 2PL; middle: 2PL – 4PL; high: > 4PL
2. PL: Poverty Line as per Planning Commission estimates used by the NCEUS Report.

In rural India, the apparent rise in the share of self-employed workers in the recent period was mainly due to the increasing presence of unpaid family workers, putting in labour to the household's own farm. It becomes all the more evident in the case of distressed[6] regions, where the share of unpaid family workers is considerably higher than that of non-distressed regions. A comparison of regions suffering from agricultural distress and normal regions by Vinoj Abraham (2009) reveals that the share of unpaid family workers in the distressed regions is higher by 4.5 percentage points at 27.47 per cent, when compared to 23 per cent in non-distressed regions (Table 8.6).

In rural Punjab, Kerala and West Bengal, women family helpers in agriculture is relatively less (<60%) than those in other States. The options are limited to agriculture, manufacturing of food products, textiles, retail trade, etc. In Madhya Pradesh,

Table 8.6: Share of Unpaid Family Helpers among Self-employed in Each State (2004-05)

	Rural	
1. Jammu and Kashmir	74.8	(1.4)
2. Himachal Pradesh	60.4	(5.2)
3. Punjab	28.4	(2.7)
4. Uttaranchal	59.8	(5.5)
5. Haryana	43.6	(4.5)
6. Delhi	—	—
7. Rajasthan	76.0	(10.0)
8. Uttar Pradesh	71.8	(26.9)
9. Bihar	73.8	(19.6)
10 .Sikkim	84.9	(6.1)
11. Arunachal Pradesh	13.8	(3.2)
12. Nagaland	74.5	(0.0)
13. Manipur	54.6	(3.2)
14. Mizoram	76.9	(1.7)
15. Tripura	42.4	(5.2)
16. Meghalaya	77.2	(0.4)
17. Assam	88.2	(5.7)
18. West Bengal	33.2	(9.2)
19. Jharkhand	86.5	(26.9)
20. Orissa	77.4	(66.7)
21. Chhattisgarh	92.6	(34.4)
22. Madhya Pradesh	89.5	(35.0)
23. Gujarat	77.5	(8.8)
24. Maharashtra	86.3	(15.5)
25. Andhra Pradesh	74.6	(14.9)
26. Karnataka	76.9	(22.0)
27. Goa	55.8	(0.0)
28. Kerala	24.0	(0.9)
29. Tamil Nadu	62.6	(11.5)
All India	74.3	—

Note: Figures in parentheses indicate the share of female family helpers living below the poverty line in each State.

Maharashtra, Jharkhand, Rajasthan and also Gujarat—the States with high incidence of family helpers among women—more than 90 per cent of the female family helpers are engaged in agriculture. Also in these States a large number of women are engaged in manufacturing of tobacco, non-metallic minerals and fabricated metal products. In urban areas too, these industries determine a lot in terms of the presence of female family helpers.

Family Helpers across Social Groups

Participation of the female family workers is substantially high in every social group. In general, the share of self-employed among female workers has increased over the ten years period, irrespective of social classification or rural-urban division (Figure 8.1 and Table 8.6). In rural areas, the occurrence as well as increase in female self-employed is quite significant. Among rural Scheduled Tribes, Scheduled Castes and 'others[7]', self-employment has increased significantly, but the majority of them are family helpers. In fact, it seems that the increase in self-employment among 'others' is because of the rise in these unpaid family helpers.

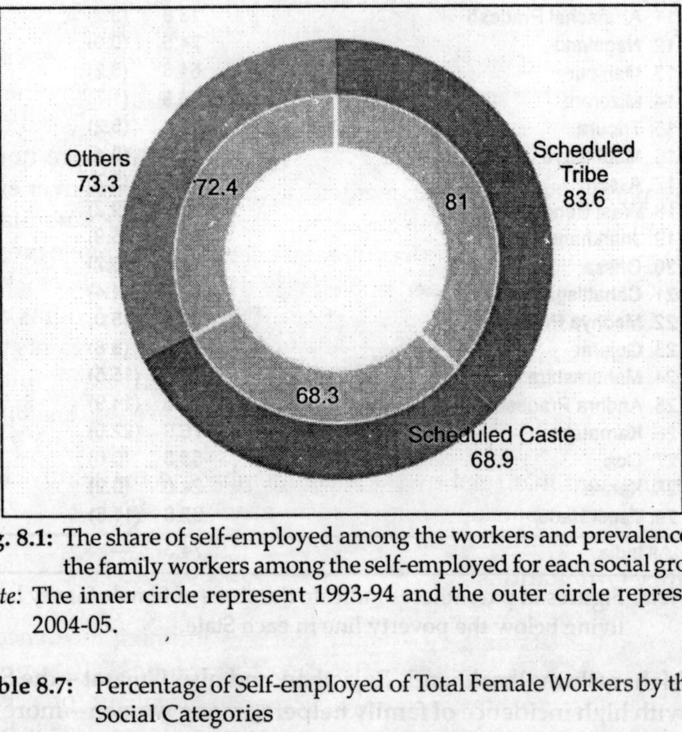

Fig. 8.1: The share of self-employed among the workers and prevalence of the family workers among the self-employed for each social group

Note: The inner circle represent 1993-94 and the outer circle represent 2004-05.

Table 8.7: Percentage of Self-employed of Total Female Workers by their Social Categories

	Scheduled Tribe	*Scheduled Caste*	*Others*
1993-94	51.2	28.1	58.8
2004-05	55.1	36.3	63.5

With increase in regular work by just 4 percentage points during the period, this is evident that lack of wage-paid work has pushed them to self-employment, which is primarily helping household members in running a family enterprise, without any compensation for their work done. The incidence of family helpers is particularly high for other backward class: 75 per cent of the self-employed women in rural areas are unpaid family helpers; in urban areas it is about 55 per cent. This indicates that there is a direct relation between this kind of exploitive, non-remunerative work and socio-economic deprivation.

The fact that about 40 per cent of the female workforce is merely family helpers is because they do not own the resources. In rural areas, most of the women are employed in agricultural activities, however, they do not own the land, so basically if they work in the land they will remain as helpers forever because it is never going to happen that they would be paid for sowing or weeding or harvesting in their family land, nor they would be accounted as own account workers as the land titles are not in their names. Not only that, women's access and control over even a small plot of land act as an important asset base for rural non-farm enterprises as well. More than three quarter of these women mostly work in enterprises owned and run by the male members in the family. Gender based discrimination in terms of land rights and other significant economic resources and cultural constraints that restrict women from accessing the market, all effectively imply that contracts are in the name of the male members of the family, shops are owned or managed by the men and thus, obviously, the earnings are managed by the male members in the family. This has a direct impact on women's socio-economic status.

Policy Orientations

The increase in number of family workers and high incidence of working poor among them, calls for policy responses to improve the insecure and inferior status of women in the labour force. First and foremost, massive employment generation is required in both rural and urban areas in all States. The Mahatma Gandhi National Rural Employment Guarantee Act promises 'not less than 100 days' of unskilled manual public work to all rural households at the statutory minimum wage, with the provision that at least one-third of the workers be women, work should be in the village, and promises child-care facilities at the worksite, thus providing ample scope for women's participation. Though there is a huge potential to empower women by providing them employment opportunities, studies reveal that full potential of this Act is far from being realized (Reetika Khera and Nandini Nayak, 2009). To ensure greater participation of women at all levels, it should go beyond household entitlement to individual entitlements to avoid negotiation at the household level.

In rural areas, since most women are dependent on land, effective and independent rights to land and other productive assets need to be ensured to empower them socially, economically and politically. Ensuring women's right to cultivable land as well as homestead plots that they have been using productively can bring a change in their employment status. Women's access and control over land can act as an important asset base to venture into non-farm enterprises as well.

Given that women play a key role in agricultural activities, improvement in post-harvest facilities, irrigation systems, portable water systems and other farm projects are required that will provide long-term advantages to a large section of women in agriculture, particularly those in vulnerable employment. Not only physical infrastructure building but other social initiatives directed towards improved education, training and healthcare facilities will enrich the status of women in the economy and would be a foundation for a sustainable growth in the economy.

Further there are no social security measures to ensure a decent living for them; they are neither organized by formal trade unions nor protected by labour legislation, thus being unable to bargain for increased access to credit, improved technologies and improved working condition. Unemployment benefits, facilities to take care of children and elderly so that women can come out for work; allowances specially meant for women should be introduced such that women can easily go out for work. Unemployment allowances would provide women time to seek new jobs and improve their skill level. Employment information services meant especially for women need to be strengthened so that genuine information regarding jobs can be relayed to women. This will raise their confidence level and help them to go out to work combating the social adversities. Investment in training women is another supportive measure.

Simply granting such women the status of worker does not end public responsibility. The very basic nature of their work is self-exploiting with no access to a regular stream of cash income and no fixed working hours. Though they are accounted as workers in the labour surveys, they are denied the basic rights of workers with no regular compensation for their work.

Not only is women's work never done, the definition keeps changing—Bill Copeland

These women are practically invisible as they work from home and not any designated "business place" as such and are not given any regular salary or wages. They do not have any employment security, social security or any income security with virtually no capacity to organize and bargain for an improved status. Herein arises the importance of right to land, access to resources and income to strengthen women's bargaining position in the households and, hence, in the economy. Employment and welfare policies should consider the gender specificities in the labour market and address the women workers' rights to ensure decent work.

NOTES

1. Unpaid contributing family workers as percentage of total female workers: Bangladesh (2005)—66 per cent, Indonesia Yogyakarta (2009)—68.4 per cent; Indonesia Banten (2009)—74.4 per cent; Nepal (2008)—69.8 per cent; Philippines—58.7 per cent; Mongolia—70.2 per cent
2. The activity status on which a person spent majority of the time during the reference period of one year preceding the date of survey is considered as the *usual principal activity status* of the person.
3. This unpaid family work is exclusive of the domestic duties and the other forms of activities that are not defined as work.
4. The Expert Group on Agricultural Indebtedness in India, under the Government of India has identified 100 distress affected districts in the country, which includes the 31 distressed districts where the Prime Minister's special rehabilitation package is being implemented (Vinoj Abraham, 2009).
5. 'Others' comprise 'Other backward class' and those who are out of the scheduled groups. The Constitution of India recognizes a list, or

schedule of Castes, The Constitution (Scheduled Castes) Order 1950 and Tribes, The Constitution (Scheduled Tribes) Order 1950, who are socially deprived, and provides a framework to improve their situation on the basis of protective arrangements, affirmative action and development.

REFERENCES

Abraham, Vinoj (2009). "Employment Growth in Rural India: Distress-Driven?" *Economic and Political Weekly*, 44(16): 97-104.

Berik, Rodgers and Seguino. (2009). "Feminist Economics of Inequality, Development and Growth." *Feminist Economics* 15(3): 1-33.

Carr, Marilyn, Martha Alter Chen, and Jane Tate. (2000). "Globalization and Home-Based Workers". *Feminist Economics* 6(3): 123-142.

Chandrasekhar, C.P. and Jayati Ghosh. (2006). *Working More for Less*.http://www.macroscan.org/fet/nov06/fet281106Working_More.htm. (accessed November 28).

Chandrasekhar, C.P. and Jayati Ghosh. (2007). *Self-employment as Opportunity or Challenge*. http://www.macroscan.org/fet/mar07/pdf/Self_employment.pdf. (accessed March 30).

Charmes, Jacques. (1998). Informal Sector, Poverty and Gender: A Review of Empirical Evidence. Washington, DC: World Bank.

Chen, Martha; Jennefer Sebstad; and Lesley O'Connell. (1999). "Counting the Invisible Workforce: The Case of Home-Based Workers." *World Development*, 27(3): 603-10.

Das, Maitreyi Bordia. (2003). "The Other Side of Self-Employment: Household Enterprises in India." Social Protection Discussion Paper Series, Social Protection Unit, Human Development Network. The World Bank.

Elson, Diane. (2006) *Macroeconomic Policy and Employment Generation: Gender Dimensions*, UN Department of Economic and Social Affairs, Development Forum on Productive Employment and Decent Work, May 8-9, New York.

House, William J.; Gerrishon K. Ikiara; and Dorothy McCormick. (1993). "Urban Self-Employment in Kenya: Panacea or Viable Strategy?" *World Development* 21(7): 1205-23.

Holmstrom, Nancy. (1981). "Women's Work, the Family and Capitalism." *Science & Society*, 45(2): 186-211.

International Labour Office. (2010). Women in Labour Markets: Measuring Progress and Identifying Challenges. March. International Labour Office. Geneva.

Khera, Reetika and Nandini Nayak. (2009). "Women Workers and

Perceptions of the National Rural Employment Guarantee Act." *Economic and Political Weekly*, 44(43): 49-57.

Kundu, Amit. (2006). "Wage-employment relationship in the Agricultural Labour Market of West Bengal." *Indian Journal of Labour Economics* 49(4):681-90.

Le, Anh T. (1999). "Empirical Studies of Self-Employment." *Journal of Economic Surveys*, 13(4): 381-416.

National Commission for Enterprises in the Unorganised Sector (NCEUS). (2007). *Report on Conditions of Work and Promotion of Livelihoods in the Unorganised Sector*. Government of India.

National Sample Survey Organisation (2006). *Employment and Unemployment Situation in India*, 2004-05. Report No. 515 (61/10/1). Ministry of Statistics & Programme Implementation. Government of India.

National Sample Survey Organisation (2006). *National Sample Survey Unit Level Data*. Government of India.

Planning Commission. (2007). *Poverty Estimates for 2004-05*. Press Information Bureau. Government of India. *http://planningcommission.nic.in/news/prmar07.pdf*

Sen, Amartya. (1987). "Gender and Cooperative Conflicts." Working Paper 18, World Institute for Development Economics Research, Helsinki.

Sethuraman, S.V. (1998). *Gender, Informality and Poverty: A Global Review*. Washington, DC: World Bank.

9

Employment Diversification in Ecologically Fragile Regions

The Case of Sundarbans in West Bengal

Jyotirmoy Sircar

1.0 Motivation

The ecology of a region has a direct impact on its economy and *vice versa*. In case of fragile ecosystems the impacts are more pronounced which more often than not experience a high level of underdevelopment. Many of these regions which have a unique history, nature and landscape are home to a significant population of humans who in turn have deep social, cultural and economic ties with the complex and fragile ecosystems. However, standard notions of poverty alleviation and interventionist development policies, often thrust down on these regions, may not bring the desired results due to the geographical and socio-cultural specificities of those regions.

The Sundarbans is remote and largely isolated. Although it is globally renowned as a unique ecosystem, it is ironically one of the most backward regions of India. The Sundarbans has a population of nearly four million people of whom 56 per cent are landless. Most of the villages still do not have access to electricity or safe drinking water and agricultural productivity is lower than the State average. Inadequate infrastructure, poor communication facilities, lack of access to health and education services and a fragile and limited natural resource base have contributed to a low level of development and high poverty incidence in the region. The productive and absorptive capacity of the agricultural sector is extremely low in the region. Moreover as the majority of the mangrove forests are protected accessing them for forestry and fishing activities is highly regulated and restricted. There is a dearth of employment opportunities in the traditional economic sectors of the region. On the other hand modern services such as tourism and brackish water shrimp farming have been gaining popularity since the late eighties. However, the absorptive capacity of these sectors in Sundarbans is quite limited. The standard models of rural development successfully executed elsewhere however have been quite unsuccessful in Sundarbans due to problems specific to this region with special geo-climatic characteristics.

In Sundarbans poverty seems to be highly correlated with lack of employment opportunities and diversification options. Hence, the issue of employment diversification in Sundarbans is quite a critical one to look into. An examination of employment diversification requires a nuanced view of the geographic, socio-economic and historical understanding of the region. Hence, the need for this study.

2.0 Livelihoods in Sundarbans

Vulnerabilities in the livelihoods of rural communities in the Bangladesh Sundarbans are increasing due to decline in agricultural production, income and natural sources of food (Swapan, 2006). This has led to employment diversification to the shrimp cultivation but ironically the net economic benefits from shrimp farming was even less and was actually contributing to augmentation of poverty. Kabir and Hussain (2007) argue that the Bangladesh Sundarbans suffers from the chronic problem of overexploitation of natural resources which in turn can be attributed as fallout of weak governance. They point out that more than half of the resource users are landless who suffer from off season vulnerability. Moreover the resource users came under the attack of wild animals for which the victim or victim's families do not get any compensation. The authors also focus on shrimp farming and shrimp fry collection which they point out is a serious threat to the mangrove and livelihood of the people. Chowdhury (2010) describes an example from Sonakhali in Sundarbans, Bangladesh, of a community in living in a balance with a surrounding mangrove forest, upon which it depends for subsistence and livelihoods. Their typical occupations are fisheries, farming, labour, trade and services, with half of the households depending mainly on the mangrove resources for their livelihoods, and the remaining ones to some extent. Rahman (2007) points out the need for several development initiatives in pursuit of sustainable resource utilization and an overruling need of poverty alleviation in order to assure a win-win situation rather than a development where both the mangrove forest and its communities stand to lose.

Since 1947, the Sundarbans mangroves are divided between India and Bangladesh as Sundarbans in Bangladesh and as Sundarban National Park in India, and the two parts differ considerably in the nature and extent of investigations, conservation and management (Rahman, 2007). Hence, studying the Sundarbans as a whole is extremely difficult. Singh *et al.*, (2010) are of the opinion that although the ecological significance of Sundarbans is a well-established fact, the economic significance and the dependency of this economic significance on the ecology of Sundarbans are less addressed due to which the mangroves are facing greater threats. The degradation of mangrove forests and encroachments in Sundarbans are shrinking the resources on which the local populaces are so heavily dependent. Bhattacharya *et al.*, (2005) found that people dependent on forests resources and non-forest resources switch to farming or agricultural activities during the off-season which shows that unless farming becomes more rewarding, it would be difficult to reduce pressure on forest and non-forest resources of Sundarbans. The results of their primary survey based study indicated that in areas with dense forests twenty three to fifty per cent people remain involved in jobs related to timbers from 9 to 12 months, the rest switching to other professions.

Though there are no human settlements within the mangrove forests, communities living in the fringe areas depend on the resources in the mangrove forests for their livelihoods. This livelihood dependence needs to be seen in the context of few livelihood options, poor access to even basic services, lack of opportunity to develop skill sets that could enable them to diversify their livelihoods in any sustainable way (Patel and Rajagopalan, 2009). They further point out that this region is concentrated mainly with backward classes, which accounts for more than 45 per cent of the total population as against the State figure of around 25 per cent, who are dependent of various types of forest and non-forest based NTFPs for their livelihood. This is mainly due to the aggrieved salinity of the soil, which prevents agricultural crops to grow (Singh *et al.*, 2010). Fishing is a major source of livelihood for communities living in the fringe area of the Reserve Forests and the Sundarban Tiger Reserve (STR). Around 2,069 sq km inside the Reserve Forest are considered ideal for riverine fishing using traditional methods (Nanda, K., in Mukherjee, 2007). Singh *et al.*, (2010) specifically propose that alternate livelihood options (both in the fishery and outside it) should be explored, based on proposals from fishing communities in the Sundarbans which would help in developing their skills and also in reducing pressure on natural resources in the longer term. Danda (2007) shows that employment opportunities in the Sundarbans exist primarily in agriculture, aquaculture, fishing and in tourism to a certain extent.

Guha and Ghosh (2007) examined the contribution of tourism towards improving the livelihoods of local people in a remote island village of the Indian Sundarbans. They found that although no village household subsists entirely on tourism-based income since such jobs are seasonal in nature, the households participating in tourism-related activity are better off than those who do not. There was, however, little evidence of any percolation of tourism related income to non-participating households through intra-village transactions. It must be mentioned that the tourism industry thrives only in particular pockets of the Sundarbans which are adjacent to the wildlife sanctuaries.

It is interesting to note that while there is a deluge of literature on the ecological aspects of the Sundarbans these studies hardly make any mention of the fact that there also exists a substantial human population in the Sundarbans. Barring a few ethnographic studies (Jalais, 2009 & Danda, 2007) and one historical study (Sarkar, 2010) there have been hardly any studies, in the last decade or so, on Sundarbans which focus exclusively on the people living there. A similar trend can also be seen in the preceding decades as well. The reason as to why it is equally important to focus on the human population residing in the Sundarbans for more than 150 years can be simply put as follows: It is a huge mistake to look at the ecosystem dynamics of the Sundarbans without taking into consideration the formidable impact the human society settled in the Sundarbans has on it (and *vice versa*) if the ultimate aim of all the research is to foster sustainable development. Just as it is wrong to ignore ecosystem dynamics while looking at issues of development it is equally wrong to just focus on the ecosystem dynamics and completely ignore the anthropogenic factors. While there have been a few studies regarding livelihoods of the people in Sundarbans there have been no academic inquiries regarding employment diversification in Sundarbans. If the various aspects of livelihoods of the people of Sundarbans are to be better understood it is imperative that the employment diversification of these people is analysed as well.

3.1 Diversification

The term "diversification" is defined as either an increasing multiplicity of activities (regardless of the sector), or as a shift away from traditional rural sectors such as agriculture to non-traditional activities in either rural or urban space, i.e., sectoral change (Start and Johnson, 2004). When it also involves moving the location of livelihood, or some other intrinsic economic quality, it is termed as adaptation. Rural diversification can be defined as economic development of non-agricultural activities or a livelihood which has multiple, part-time components. It can be associated with a booming or recessionary economy or with accumulating or immiserizing livelihood strategies (Start, 2001). In adjusting and unstable economies, which is most often the case in case of ecologically fragile regions, flexibility and adaptability are the order of the day because in these economies neither agriculture nor non-agriculture employment provide the scope for full employment. Hence, multiple livelihoods may be the only answer.

3.2 Rural Livelihood Diversification

Chambers and Conway (1992) proposed that a livelihood comprises of the capabilities, assets (stores, resources, claims and access) and activities required for a means of living. Livelihood is also considered as method of sustainability which can cope with and recover from stress and shocks, maintain or enhance its capabilities and assets, and provide sustainable livelihood opportunities for the next generation. Further, it contributes net benefits to other livelihoods at the local and global levels and in the short and long-term. Ian Scoones (1998) of IDS defined sustainable livelihood as one, which can cope with and recover from stresses and shocks, maintain or enhance its capabilities and assets, while not undermining the natural resource base. As an approach to understanding and facilitating rural development the 'sustainable livelihoods approach' captures the concern about food and nutrition security, income security, health and education security as well as security of shelter and water resources (Datta and Singh, 2011). This is in conformity with a shift in stress from a materialist perspective focused on food production to a social perspective which focuses on the enhancement of people's capabilities to secure their own livelihoods (Drinkwater and Rusinow, 1999).

Livelihood diversification is a pervasive and enduring characteristic of rural survival which reflects the continuing vulnerability of rural livelihoods. Barrett, Reardon and Webb (2001) posit that multiple motives prompt households and individuals to diversify assets, incomes, and activities: The first set comprises of "push factors" namely risk reduction, response to diminishing factor returns in any given use, reaction to crisis or liquidity constraints, high transactions costs that induce households to self-provision in several goods and services, etc. The second set comprises of "pull factors" like realization of strategic complementarities between activities, such as crop-livestock integration or milling and hog production, specialization according to comparative advantage accorded by superior technologies, skills or endowments, etc. The authors further point out that these micro level determinants have their aggregate counterparts at the macro level of the economy. In the case of "push factors" diversification is driven by limited risk-bearing capacity in the presence of incomplete or weak financial systems that create strong incentives to select a portfolio of activities in order to stabilize income flows and consumption, by constraints in labour and land markets, and by climatic uncertainty. Whereas for "pull factors" diversification occurs due to local engines of growth such as commercial agriculture or proximity to an urban area create opportunities for income diversification in production and expenditure-linkage activities. In the case of the economy of Sundarbans it is clearly the "push factors" which play a central role in livelihood diversification owing to the fact that it is situated within an ecologically fragile region.

Further, in the case of Sundarbans both individual and farm household diversification into non-farm activities emerges from *ex ante* risk management and *ex post* coping with adverse shocks (Webb *et al.*, 1992). The former relates to chiefly the various "pull factors" while the latter deals with factors like super cyclones, breaching of river embankments during the monsoon, etc.

If one were to put rural livelihood diversification in the Sundarbans within the context of a broad distinction between necessity and choice as motivations to diversify livelihoods away from reliance on farming one has to consider six main determinants namely seasonality, risk, labour markets, credit markets, asset strategies, and coping behaviour which in turn are mediated through social relations and institutions. Moreover, one has to look at the interplay of these determinants within the wider context of global and national socio-economic and political dynamics and the fragile ecology of the region. In the case of Sundarbans seasonality, risk and coping behaviour play important roles but primarily *via* the labour markets and that is why looking at employment diversification in the Sundarbans is of paramount importance if one has to understand livelihood diversification in terms of both individual and household.

3.3 Employment Diversification

Employment diversification means shifting of labour force from one sector to another for employment (Mukhopadhyay and Rajaraman, 2007). It must be noted further that employment diversification can have two units of analysis: the household and the individual, i.e., we can analyse employment diversification in terms of the household where each individual might very well be employed in only one sector but the household overall gets income from various sectors of employment or in terms of the individual who might be employed in single or multiple sectors. In India, agriculture is the single largest employment providing sector, which employs approximately 58 per cent of the total workforce. Over the years there has been considerable inter-sectoral movement of workforce, which has somewhat declined the importance of agriculture in providing employment to labour force (Chaddha and Sahu, 2002).

The farm sector is generally portrayed as the safe and secured arena for absorbing a large proportion of the rural working population but it does have its absorptive limitations as is evinced in the emergence of disguised unemployment and low productivity. Further, agricultural operations involve high degree of seasonality along with dependence on rainfall and natural munificence which is more so in the context of ecologically fragile regions. Accordingly, a need is felt for livelihood diversification which also helps in risk spreading, consumption and labour smoothing and ensuring resilience (Datta and Singh, 2011). Farm economies in ecologically fragile regions like the Sundarbans are typically characterized by increasing population pressures, an ever declining land-man ratio, small and fragmented holdings, highly skewed land distribution structures, lack of access to forest resources, distance from both urban and large scale rural markets, etc., as a result of which the traditional form of agriculture cannot obviously cater to the employment needs of the people of these regions and hence, diversification in rural employment has become a critical issue over time. This is so, because numerous rural households are faced with the increasing need of looking for alternative jobs to supplement their land-based livelihood (Chaddha, 1993). Unequal socio–economic attainments, differential access to assets and available diversification opportunities as a form of insurance to guard against uncertain income shocks influence differences in the level of diversification across households which in turn influence individual earnings (Datta and Singh, 2011).

The nature, extent and speed of rural employment diversification in India have been studied by several researchers over the past two decades and most of them have concluded that the share of non-farm sector was increasing over time and the capacity of the farm sector to absorb additional labour had almost reached its limit (Anjani Kumar, 2008). However, some studies (Basant and Kumar, 1989; Visaria, 1995) have shown that there are strong possibilities of enhancing labour absorption in the agricultural sector itself through introduction of appropriate technological, institutional and organizational innovations promoting agricultural diversification. However such a scenario in the Sundarbans does not seem at all feasible in the near future. The rural non-farm sector is being increasingly viewed as an important alternative for reducing rural poverty levels as well as providing employment by absorbing surplus labour from the agricultural sector (Nayyar and Sharma, 2004). But again in the context of Sundarbans the presence of an ecologically fragile ecosystem impedes not only the farm economy but the non-farm economy as well. Thus given such a context it becomes increasingly important to look at the trends and patterns of employment in the Sundarbans in general and employment diversification in particular.

The analysis starts with a review of the Block level information available on employment and employment diversification in Sundarbans. Then a case is made for the need for a primary survey and the survey results are analysed both at the inter-village level and the intra-village level.

4.1 Block Level Information

Till date there have been no studies whatsoever regarding employment diversification in the Sundarbans. Recently the Government of West Bengal came out with the District Human Development Reports 2010 for both North and South 24-Parganas. We can get some aggregate Block level information on employment diversification in the Sundarbans from these reports as the Sundarbans is spread across these two districts. These reports have relied mainly on the 2001 Census data. The Sundarbans comprises of 13 Blocks in the 24-South Parganas and 6 Blocks in the 24-North Parganas. At the overall level minimal participation of female population in economic activity is observed in the sense that percentage of total male workers is nearly three times that of total female workers. However, it is not surprising in the context of West Bengal because this State has one of the lowest recorded rates of female work participation in the country (District Human Development (DHD) Report: South 24-Parganas, 2010). If the two districts are disaggregated into Blocks and analysed the picture as shown in Table 9.1 emerges. From Table 9.1 it can be clearly seen that the proportion of total male workers is much higher across all Blocks. The DHD Reports further point out that in the case of the Blocks lying in South 24-Parganas there is a higher proportion of main workers for males and that of marginal workers for females. This in a way further provides evidence that there is "invisibility" of women's work to a large degree which in turn also contributes to the skewed distribution of total workers in the population across the categories of males and females.

Table 9.1: Block-wise Percentage of Total Workers by Gender in Sundarbans

Block	*% of total male workers*	*% of total female workers*
Canning I	51.14	12.64
Canning II	48.48	11.16
Basanti	50.73	12.35
Gosaba	56.04	20.4
Joynagar I	49.33	10.85
Joynagar II	49.25	14.4
Mathurapur I	48.44	5.6
Mathurapur II	52.84	10.92
Kultali	51.36	9.75
Patharpratima	54.99	29.6
Kakdwip	52.61	16.24
Namkhana	55.96	29.03
Sagar	52.72	27.66
24-South Parganas Sundarbans	51.84	16.20
Haroa	52.07	10.18
Minakhan	50.59	9.49
Sandeshkhali I	51.6	14.46
Sandeshkhali II	53.41	18.07
Hasnabad	54.31	18.84
Hingalganj	57.22	21.25
24-North Parganas	53.20	15.38
Sundarbans	52.27	15.94

Source: District Human Development Report: North and South 24-Parganas, 2010 and author's own calculations.

Next we look at the district-wise distribution of total workers by occupation for the Sundarbans in Table 9.2. Here, it is the category of "other workers" which comprises forty per cent of total workers for Sundarbans followed by cultivators and agricultural workers. These "other workers" chiefly comprise of daily wage workers in the unorganized and organized sectors and point to the casualisation of the workers in Sundarbans. Moreover it is important to identify whether such structural transformation is due to progressive labour saving technique of productive agriculture releasing labour which is absorbed in the modern industrial sector, or it is the distress in agriculture that is pushing workers out of it into a semi-saturated non-agricultural sector characterized by low return. The latter seems to be the case here. From Table 9.2 it can be seen that some Blocks like Canning-I, Joynagar-I, Mathurapur-I and Hasnabad have greater dependence on non-agricultural sector which is in sharp contrast to the Blocks like Canning-II, Basanti, Kultali, Gosaba, etc., where more than 70 per cent of the main workforce is engaged in agriculture even in 2001.

Table 9.2: Block-wise Distribution of Total Workers by Occupation in Sundarbans

Blocks	*Cultivators*	*Agricultural workers*	*Total workers in Agriculture*	*HH Industrial workers*	*Other workers*
Canning I	14.61	17.83	32.44	4.43	63.13
Canning II	26.55	45.74	72.29	1.43	26.28
Basanti	32.22	38.47	70.69	1.82	27.5
Gosaba	33.07	34.5	67.57	1.35	31.08
Joynagar I	12.51	17.95	30.46	5.61	63.93
Joynagar II	18.91	32.28	51.19	8.83	39.99
Mathurapur I	14.09	23.72	37.81	6.19	56
Mathurapur II	24.73	35.81	60.54	4.35	35.12
Kultali	34.53	36.06	70.59	1.57	27.84
Patharpratima	33.05	28.1	61.15	1.86	36.99
Kakdwip	20.92	28.17	49.09	2.87	50.04
Namkhana	31.39	20.26	51.65	1.74	46.6
Sagar	36.33	30.72	67.05	1.72	31.24
24-South Parganas Sundarbans	25.61	29.97	55.58	3.37	41.21
Haroa	22.58	30.11	52.69	3.78	43.52
Minakhan	21.21	34.76	55.97	1.92	42.11
Sandeshkhali I	18.64	34.74	53.38	2.22	44.41
Sandeshkhali II	25.41	41.66	67.07	1.91	31.02
Hasnabad	16.35	20.76	37.11	15.34	47.6
Hingalganj	30.82	27.28	58.1	8.69	33.21
24-North Parganas Sundarbans	22.50	31.55	54.05	5.64	40.31

Source: District Human Development Report: North and South 24-Parganas, 2010 and author's own calculations.

So although most of the Sundarbans is predominantly rural and backward in nature there is indeed heterogeneity in terms of employment across occupations which in turn points to heterogeneous development. Those Blocks which are nearer to Kolkata and away from the forests seem to have a lesser dependence on agriculture for their employment needs *vis-a-vis* those Blocks adjacent to the forest. The Blocks like Patharpratima and Namkhana which are in way in between the two types of Blocks just mentioned are also between them in terms of dependence on the agricultural sector for employment generation.

Table 9.3: Livelihood Patterns of Rural Households at Block Level in Sundarbans

Block \ Category	D/W Worker	Cultivator	Self Employed	Regular labour oriented worker in the unorganized sector	Others in the Organized Sector
Canning I	49.93	19.76	10.53	7.93	11.85
Canning II	61.56	24.81	5.1	3.63	4.89
Basanti	49.44	32.69	5.98	4.69	7.2
Gosaba	41.54	36.19	5.05	6.26	10.95
Joynagar I	53.51	14.57	10.24	9.24	12.46
Joynagar II	44.45	23.31	13.39	11.01	7.83
Mathurapur I	55.97	16.77	9.58	6.12	11.56
Mathurapur II	58.42	21.47	6.46	4	9.66
Kultali	47.75	36.67	5.76	4.92	5.19
Patharpratima	48.84	30.56	4.05	5.43	11.1
Kakdwip	54.93	20.39	4.72	8.8	11.16
Namkhana	58.54	23.64	5.42	3.87	8.52
24-South Parganas Sundarbans	52.30	25.41	6.93	6.16	9.23
Sagar	54.97	29.45	3.86	4.15	7.58
Haroa	47.71	24.78	9.01	7.85	10.63
Hasnabad	56.45	18.66	6.03	6.89	11.97
Hingalganj	49.8	34.46	3.17	4.3	8.27
Minakhan	47.69	27.58	5.5	7.09	12.15
Sandeshkhali I	43.81	27.1	6.34	11.06	11.69
Sandeshkhali II	56.04	28.97	3.42	4.74	6.83
24-South Parganas Sundarbans	50.25	26.93	5.58	6.99	10.26
Sundarbans	51.65	25.89	6.51	6.42	9.55

Source: District Human Development Report: North and South 24-Parganas, 2010 and author's own calculations.

Table 9.3 examines the livelihood patterns of rural households at Block level in Sundarbans.

The aggregate numbers for Sundarbans suggests greater casualisation of the workers. Moreover, although Sundarbans Blocks in both districts have more than 50 per cent of their workers employed in the agricultural sector only half of them derive their main source of income from cultivation which in a way points the low level of returns from agriculture and also the overall depressed socio-economic condition of the Blocks mainly dependent on agriculture. Again, a variation can be seen among Blocks far away from forests and nearer to Kolkata and those which are nearer or adjacent to forests in the Sundarbans. Areas like Canning-I, Haroa, Joynagar-I and II, Mathurapur-I have higher proportions of people deriving their major source of income from being self-employed as compared to Blocks like Gosaba, Kultali, Basanti Namkhana, etc. There is also a similar difference with regard to proportion of people deriving their major share of income from the organized sector. People in the Blocks adjacent to the forest have an overwhelming dependence on cultivation and daily wage work whereas Blocks nearer to Kolkata are more diversified in terms of income and employment generation.

Thus, we see that in terms of employment diversification the Blocks can be divided into three categories: Blocks adjacent to forests, Blocks near to Kolkata and Blocks lying between the two. This is in resonance with the discussions in chapter 2 where it was noted that Blocks adjacent to forest had lower levels of overall socio-economic development as compared to Blocks farther away from the forest. In nutshell it seems that the geographical location of the Blocks does play an important role in determining the socio-economic condition of the people residing in that Block in general and employment diversification in particular. Interestingly a similar notion has been discussed by Jalais (2010) in her ethnographic analysis of a village in Gosaba pointed out that there are "up" and "down" islands in the Sundarbans wherein the islands closer to Kolkata are "up" and those near to the forest are "down" and there is stark difference in their socio-economic conditions. The spatial characteristics of these "up" and "down" lands are very dissimilar in the sense that the "up" areas have agglomerate, compact settlements whereas the "down" areas have semi-nucleated dispersed settlements

(Banerjee, 1998 quoted in Jalais, 2010). There are stark differences in terms of infrastructure and communication facilities as well not to mention the overall socio-economic condition. She further pointed out that in the village of Garjontala; the site of her ethnographic exercise, the better off people lived in the centre of the island whereas those worse off were settled around the embankments and the periphery. Hence, it can be argued that the notion "up" and "down" land exists at both the inter-island and intra-island level in the Sundarbans. This ethnographic idea of "up" and "down" lands can be applied in economic analysis as well but with some necessary modifications.

While the notion of "up" and "down" lands at the intra-island level remains the same, the notion at the inter-island level changes a bit from what is envisaged by Jalais (2010). This slight change is in the sense that for her two adjacent islands near the forest might not be "down" islands because according to the people's perception one island which is a bit farther from the forest can very well be an "up" island. This kind of complexity, however, cannot be accommodated within economic analysis where some amount of generality is the order of the day. Hence, for economic analysis the islands can be divided into "up" and "down" categories depending upon their proximity to forests and their distance from Kolkata. However, if this is done at the Block level problems arise in the case of some Blocks like Patharpratima whose one part is nearer to Kolkata and the other is adjacent to the forest. Thus, it makes eminent sense to undertake this exercise at the village level. One more modification which is introduced is that forests are divided into those with tigers and those without tigers simply because these two types of forests offer different levels of access and hence different levels of economic returns to the people. The access to forests which are part of the tiger reserves for fishing is very limited while it is not so for forests which are not part of the tiger reserves. Hence, it is economically advantageous for a village to be situated adjacent to a forest which belongs to the latter category. Moreover, the risk involved is also quite less in case of jungles which are not inhabited by the man eating royal Bengal tigers. However, employment data at the village level is not available in the Sundarbans and, hence, the need arises for a primary survey.

4.2 Survey Methodology

The sampling procedure used in this survey can be termed as multi stage stratified random sampling. In the first stage all the villages of the 19 Blocks of Sundarbans were divided into three broad groups on the basis of a combination of three factors namely distance from the urban metropolis of Kolkata, distance from a forest with tigers and the same from a forest without tigers. Thus all villages were grouped into one of the following three groups:

1. The first group of villages was near to Kolkata (around 3 to 5 hours by road) and was far away from forests with or without tiger inhabitation.
2. The second group of villages was far away from Kolkata (8 to 12 hours by a variety of transports including both surface and water) and was adjacent to forests which were not inhabited by tigers.
3. The third group of villages was far away from Kolkata (8 to 12 hours by a variety of transports including both surface and water) and was adjacent to forests which were inhabited by tigers.

Then one village was selected from each of three groups *via* random sampling. The three villages thus obtained from the three groups were Ramganga, Herambogopalpur and Kumirmari respectively. Both Ramganga and Herambogopalpur belong to Patharpratima Block whereas Kumirmari belongs to Gosaba Block. This sampling was primarily for the inter-village analysis. But otherwise Ramganga is the "up" village whereas Herambogopalpur and Kumirmari are the "down" villages.

For the intra-village analysis, again a multi-stage stratified random sampling procedure was followed. A list of all the households in these three villages was generated from the household list obtained from the Block Development Offices (BDO) of Patharpratima and Gosaba. Then for each village all the households were first divided into four categories on the basis of cultivable land ownership. The four groups were landless, owners of upto 2 bighas of land, 2-5 bighas of land and more than 5 bighas of land. Next for each of these four groups a two sub-groups was created in the sense that each group was divided into two groups on the basis of the distance of the cultivable land from the river embankments. In the case of landless households the distance of the homestead from the river embankments was considered instead. Then a random sampling was done for each of these sub-groups so as to generate 70 households from each village in such a way that the population proportions for each sub-group were maintained in the sample sub-groups. The sample represents around twenty-five per cent of the actual population in all the villages.

A pilot survey was conducted in Ramganga and Herambogopalpur for a week from 22nd November, 2010 to 29th November, 2010 and a total of 30 houses were surveyed. Thereafter, necessary changes were incorporated into the questionnaire and a survey pretesting was done from 5th December, 2010 to 12th December, 2010 in 15 households in Kumirmari. The final questionnaire was further fine-tuned and finally the survey was conducted in three villages from 20th December, 2010 to 28th January, 2011 wherein 165 houses were enumerated of which 150 households have been used for analysis. The case studies were done during this same period after extensive focused discussions with the village elders, school-teachers and social workers so as to choose the correct subjects.

4.3 Village Level Analysis

The analysis of the three villages is divided into two sections: inter-village analysis and intra-village analysis. For the inter-village analysis we compare the trends and patterns in employment and employment diversification of the three villages and try to analyse and situate the differences, if any, within the context of the overall geographical location of the three villages. As far as the short section on intra-village analysis is concerned we will look at the differences in employment and employment diversification at the household level for each village and try to contextualize it with the help of the geographical location of their cultivable plots of land.

4.4 Inter-Village Analysis

This section is divided into three broad parts: first the socioeconomic summary of the data collected in the three villages is analysed and second the socioeconomic condition of the villages is reflected upon with reference to the colonial land reclamation process discussed in chapter 3. Finally the third section looks at the labour market participation of three villages and the resultant employment diversification.

4.4.1 Socio-economic Summary of the Three Villages

All the three villages namely Ramganga, Herambogopalpur and Kumirmari fall under the jurisdiction of 24-South Parganas. The first-two belong to Patharpratima Block while Kumirmari belongs to Gosaba Block. In terms of proximity to Kolkata, Ramganga is best off whereas Kumirmari and Herambogopalpur are worst off. It takes around three hours to reach Kolkata from Ramganga while it takes around eight to twelve hours to reach the same place from the other two villages. Moreover, the economy of Ramganga is much bigger and vibrant than that of the other two villages. The primary reason for this, being the fact, that it is the last village in Patharpratima which is connected directly by road to Kolkata. After Ramganga the network of rivers and estuaries start; and hence, communication and transport to the villages beyond Ramganga is both time consuming and strenuous. Hence, all the goods (essential and otherwise) which are to be sent to these villages are brought by road from Kolkata and other semi-urban areas nearby Ramganga by road. Thereafter, they are loaded on mechanized boats and shipped off to the remote villages. Thus, in a way Ramganga is a transport hub of all sorts in this area. Moreover, it also acts as a bus depot for all buses plying to and from Kolkata and other places on that route. The constant flow of traffic from and to Kolkata has resulted in the demand of various goods and services mostly by people coming over and staying overnight for work which in turn has resulted in the sprouting of two private guest houses and a few eateries alongwith numerous ubiquitous tea and pan stalls. Moreover, the area around the jetty has developed into a successful commercial centre with shops selling everything from grocery to fruits to apparels. In a nutshell although double cropping agriculture is the basis of the Ramganga economy there is a presence of retail and transport/storage sectors as well. The locational advantage which Ramganga has is also leveraged by quite a few NGOs which have their offices in and around the area adjacent to the jetty. The economic importance of the area can be gauged not only from the fact that the villages is nearly completely electrified but also most of the roads of this village are paved with bricks which is quite a rare phenomenon in any Sundarban village. Moreover the relative affluence of the people residing in this village can be gauged from the boisterous community celebration of numerous fairs and religious festivals. Finally the locational advantage also plays a role in minimizing the impact of cyclones as was seen during *Aila* when only half the village got submerged under saline water for two days and this being a commercial centre the district and Block administration saw to it that the river embankments were repaired very quickly.

In contrast both Herambogopalpur and Kumirmari are anything but rural commercial centres. The prohibitive distance from any urban/semi-urban markets coupled with virtually no protection from cyclones have resulted in a precarious economic situation for these two villages. There is hardly any area in these two villages which can be called a commercial centre. There is the ubiquitous village market but the scale of economic activity is very low compared to Ramganga. All the pecple go to the weekly village markets in the other islands "nearby" which sometimes means that one entire day of the week has to be devoted to buying of essential food items and other goods. The economy of these two villages is based on single cropping agriculture and there are simply no other industries here which can provide employment to the labour force. Another difference is the condition of roads in the sense that very few roads are paved with bricks and even those are in a terrible condition post-*Aila*. The geographical location of the villages is such that it offers no natural barriers to impediments like cyclonic storms and this was acutely felt during *Aila* in 2009 when both the villages got submerged under saline water for more than a week. Further, the socio-economic backwardness of the two villages ensured that the river embankments were repaired quite late which in turn resulted in very high salinity of the agricultural plots resulting in virtually zero agricultural production in 2009. There is, however, one essential difference between Herambogopalpur and Kumirmari. The former is adjacent to forests which are not part of the tiger reserves while the latter is adjacent to a tiger reserve. This locational specification translates into very limited access to the mangrove forests and its estuaries and creeks for Kumirmari and hence the fishermen of this village are at a distinct disadvantage as compared to their compatriots in Herambogopalpur. Moreover, there is much less threat to human life in Herambogopalpur as there are no tigers in the adjacent forests. This in a nutshell is a broad outline of the idea of "up" and "down" villages discussed by Jalais (2010). Thus given the socio-economic context Ramganga can be very well termed as an "up" village while Herambogopalpur and Kumirmari are "down" villages. Table 9.4 helps us to understand this better.

Table 9.4: Socio-economic Condition of the Three Villages (%)

Village / *Category*	*Ramganga*	*Herambogopalpur*	*Kumirmari*
Tomato Farming	8	4	0
Betel Leaf Farming	6	0	0
Cropping Nature	Double	Single	Single
Landless	28	46	32
Land Mortgaged Out	12	14	18
Electrification	Yes	No	No

Source: Primary Survey, 2010.

That Ramganga has diversified into commercial vegetable farming while the other villages have not. Ramganga has a vegetable wholesale market just one kilometre away by road on the way to Kolkata and hence, even small cultivators can diversify into farming of vegetables. On the other hand both Herambogopalpur and Kumirmari are so remote that it would take a minimum of six to eight hours for the farmers here to reach the wholesale markets. Hence, as far as commercial farming of vegetables and betel leaf is concerned it can be seen that Ramganga scores over the other two villages. Given the distance and time required it obviously translates into a significantly high transport costs which again can be overcome only by large scale farming of vegetables which in turn is constrained by the fragile ecology of the region in general and the salinity of the soil in particular. The percentage of households which have mortgaged out land is higher for the two "down" villages. However, the proportion of landless households is much higher in Herambogopalpur compared to the other two villages. This has to be seen in the light of the disturbing fact that nearly seventy per cent of the Muslim households are landless.

4.4.2 Demography and Educational Status of the Three Villages

Table 9.5 compares some socio-economic parameters of the three villages. The sex economically active population (EAP) as percentage of total population does not show much variation across the three villages. The sex ratio is skewed towards males in Kumirmari (0.77) as compared to Herambogopalpur (1.06) and Ramganga (0.98). However, when it comes to illiteracy rates of both EAP and principal labour force (PLF) there are big variations.

Table 9. 5: Socio-economic Parameters (%)

Parameters / *Village*	*Ramganga*	*Herambogopalpur*	*Kumirmari*
Male Female Ratio	0.98	1.06	0.77
EAP as % of total population	63.40	61.35	62.71
Illiteracy Rate (EAP)	5.88	19.15	17.12
Illiteracy Rate (PLF)	4.94	15.91	8.64
HDI (Block)	0.56	0.54	0.54

Source: Primary Survey, 2010.

Ramganga (5.88%) has the lowest illiteracy rate followed by Kumirmari (17.12%) and Herambogopalpur (17.12%) for the EAP. As far as PLF is concerned the ranking is maintained but with lower illiteracy rates for all the three villages. The rates are much lower because the majority of the females in EAP are not part of the PLF. The Human Development Index (HDI) for the Blocks to which the three villages belong does not show much difference which once again highlights the need for a village level study.

As far as demographic profile is concerned the majority of the population in the three villages (males, females and combined) is concentrated in the first-three age groups as can be seen from Table 9.6: around 80 per cent for both Ramganga and Herambogopalpur and around 75 per cent for Kumirmari. While the first-two villages have 8.68 per cent and 6.38 per cent of people aged sixty years and above Kumirmari has a much higher share at 13.14 per cent. It is interesting to note that the proportion of females for both

Table 9.6: Demographic Profile (%)

Age Group \ Village	Ramganga M	Ramganga F	Ramganga T	Herambogopalpur M	Herambogopalpur F	Herambogopalpur T	Kumirmari M	Kumirmari F	Kumirmari T
0-14	12.08	15.85	27.92	12.77	19.15	31.91	16.53	7.63	24.15
15-29	13.96	14.34	28.30	15.25	15.96	31.21	14.41	13.98	28.39
30-44	12.08	10.94	23.02	9.22	8.87	18.09	11.44	10.59	22.03
45-59	7.17	4.91	12.08	7.09	5.32	12.41	8.05	4.24	12.29
60 and above	5.28	3.40	8.68	4.26	2.13	6.38	5.93	7.20	13.14
Total	50.57	49.43	100.00	48.58	51.42	100.00	56.36	43.64	100.00

Source: Primary Survey, 2010.

Ramganga (15.85%) and Herambogopalpur (19.15%) in the age group 0-14 years is much higher than that of males (12.08% and 12.77%). This will go a long way in ensuring that the sex ratio is not skewed towards males in these two villages at least in the near future. Moreover for the age group 60 years and above Kumirmari has a higher proportion of females (7.20%) than males (5.93%). Further Ramganga (63.40%) has the highest share of EAP followed by Kumirmari (62.71%) and Herambogopalpur (61.71%). The male share of EAP is highest for Kumirmari (33.9%) followed by Ramganga (33.21%) and Herambogopalpur (31.56%). For females Ramganga (30.19%) has the highest share of EAP followed by Herambogopalpur (30.15%) and Kumirmari (28.81%). Ramganga and Kumirmari have the highest share of its population (28.30%

Table 9.7: Educational Qualification of Economically Active Population (EAP) in per cent

Status	Ramganga M	Ramganga F	Ramganga T	Herambogopalpur M	Herambogopalpur F	Herambogopalpur T	Kumirmari M	Kumirmari F	Kumirmari T
Illiterate	1.79	4.76	6.55	6.36	14.45	20.81	3.38	11.49	14.86
Literate	1.79	1.19	2.98	0.58	1.73	2.31	5.41	2.70	8.11
KG-Class IV	9.52	9.52	19.05	10.40	12.72	23.12	12.16	7.43	19.59
Class V–Class X	32.74	27.98	60.71	27.75	16.18	43.93	23.65	16.89	40.54
Matriculation	2.38	3.57	5.95	4.05	1.73	5.78	4.05	4.73	8.78
HS	1.19	0.00	1.19	0.00	0.58	0.58	0.68	2.03	2.70
Graduation	1.79	0.60	2.38	1.73	1.16	2.89	2.70	0.68	3.38
Post Graduation	1.19	0.00	1.19	0.58	0.00	0.58	2.03	0.00	2.03
Total	52.39	47.62	100	51.45	48.55	100	54.06	45.94	100

Source: Primary Survey, 2010.

and 28.39% respectively) in the 15-29 years age group while the 0-14 years age group accounts the highest share (19.15%) for Herambogopalpur which in way point towards the fact the general profile of the population in all the three villages is quite young which makes the issue of employment diversification quite critical. But before venturing into the issue of employment diversification one needs to have a look at another critical social characteristic, i.e., education.

It can be seen from Table 9.7 that the two remote villages of Herambogopalpur and Kumirmari have much higher rates of male and female illiteracy as compared to Ramganga. The disaggregated information shows that most of the literate economically active population has educational qualification in two categories: KG Class IV and Class V-Class X. It can be argued that these two groups also represent two successive generations of people in these villages. It was observed from the field survey that even the most destitute families now attach a premium to the education of their kids and are willing to go to any lengths to educate their children at least up to the matriculate level. This realization of the importance of education stems from their own experiences of being educated mostly till class IV which was a distinct disadvantage as they could not fulfil the minimum educational qualifications for most of the Government jobs. Thus these households have realized the importance of having a minimum education level (read class X) as it heavily influences the quality of employment diversification options. Further with the mushrooming of NGO activities all over Sundarbans local educated youths can aspire for the jobs generated by these agencies and they too require a minimum level of higher education. The extremely high rate of illiteracy in Herambogopalpur has to be seen in the light of the fact that 30.95 per cent of its Muslim economically active population is illiterate.

Another interesting aspect is the fact that in terms of higher education Kumirmari has the highest proportion of its economically active population (16.89%) followed by Ramganga (10.71%) and Herambogopalpur (9.83%). This again has to be interpreted in the light of existence of employment opportunities in the three villages. Ramganga being the closest of the three villages to Kolkata and being a commercial centre has much more employment opportunities for youths who have studied up to class X as compared to the other two villages. Kumirmari, on the other hand, suffers from lack of any such employment opportunities whatsoever and hence those families who can afford to educate their children tend to get them as much educated as possible so that they can compete in the urban formal job markets of Kolkata. Going by this logic Herambogopalpur should also have had a higher rate of higher education than Ramganga. Hence, this logic does not hold much water and this pattern may be attributed to another factor: in all the three villages the economically active females have higher rates of higher education and it is plausible that most of them are not in the principal work force. This aspect will be dealt with in detail later.

4.4.3 Social Composition of the Three Villages

From Table 9.8 it can be clearly seen that both Ramganga and Kumirmari have a complete majority of Hindu families (96% and 100% respectively) while Herambogopalpur has a sizeable proportion (26%) of Muslim families as well. If one were to disaggregate the Hindu families further it can be seen that Ramganga is dominated by general caste Hindus (80%) while scheduled caste Hindus (98%) hold sway in Kumirmari. As far as Herambogopalpur is concerned it is also dominated by general caste Hindus but its proportion (74%) is much less and it is the most heterogeneous village in terms of social composition. If one were to disaggregate the various castes a very interesting pattern emerges.

Table 9.9 gives the caste of all the Hindu households of the three villages at the disaggregated level. Ramganga is dominated by the Mahishya caste (80%) which is the cultivating caste and is

Table 9.8: Social Composition of the Three Villages (%)

Village / Religion	Ramganga	Herambogopalpur	Kumirmari
Muslims	4	26	0
Hindus	96	74	100
Social Group	Ramganga	Herambogopalpur	Kumirmari
General Caste	80	60	0
Scheduled Castes	14	12	98
Scheduled Tribes	0	0	2
OBC	2	2	0

Source: Primary Survey, 2010.

Table 9.9: Caste at the Disaggregated Level (%)

Category \ Village	Ramganga	Herambogopalpur	Kumirmari
Mahishya	80	60	0
Bagdhi	4	1	0
Kumbhokar	4	0	0
Namasudra	0	12	0
Paundra Kshatriya	8	0	98

Source: Primary Survey, 2010.

generally considered to be among the lower general castes. Herambogopalpur also is dominated by the Mahishya caste (60%) but it also has a significant proportion of Namasudras (12%) while Kumirmari is totally dominated by the Paundra Kshatriyas (98%). Both the Namasudras and the Paundra Kshatriyas belong to the Scheduled Castes category and are considered to be at the absolute bottom of the Hindu caste hierarchy (Risley, 1891). This pattern of social composition of the three villages finds resonance with the colonial land reclamation and conservation history of Sundarbans. It must be noted that the Namasudras and the Paundra Kshatriyas are considered to be the original settlers of Sundarbans. As they cleared one lot of "waste" forest they were forced or lured to clear the subsequent lot and this process continued till Forest Conservation Act came into being and suddenly these people could not clear the "valuable" forests. They had no option but to settle on the cleared islands on the fringes of the protected and reserved forests. As far as the lots which had been cleared initially were concerned they started getting filled up by the people of the general caste especially by the cultivating caste namely the Mahishyas (Chattopadhyaya, 1998). And interestingly the higher proportion of presence these two "lower castes" seems to correspond to the lower socio-economic well-being of the villages.

Thus, the colonial land reclamation policies for nearly a century and the colonial forest conservation policies thereafter resulted in the creation of a pattern of human settlement in the Sundarbans wherein most of the original settlers ended up at the fringes of the forest while the second and third generation of settlers occupied the initially cleared lands which were much closer to Kolkata and other urban and semi-urban centres. So, in a way the worst off socio-economically in the Sundarbans ended up settling in the locationally worst off regions in the Sundarbans. This is turn has affected the socio-economic conditions of future generations as well. A concrete example of this can be seen in the inter-village analysis done so far. Add to this, the fact the skewed land ownership patterns persisting due to a less successful implementation of land reforms it becomes quite clear that the history of the landscape changes of Sundarbans has had a major role to play in influencing the socio-economic conditions of the people settled here. Hence, the issue of employment diversification in the three villages needs to be understood within this specific historical and resultant geographical context.

4.4.4 Labour Market Participation in the Three Villages

Table 9.10 gives the Labour Force Participation Rates (LFPRs) of various age groups in the three villages. The age group 45-59 has the highest share of the labour force participation in all the three villages: 62.07 per cent for Kumirmari followed by 56.25 per cent for Ramganga and 51.43 per cent for Herambogopalpur. Next is the age group 30-44 which accounts for 52.46 per cent of labour force participation in Ramganga followed by Herambogopalpur (50.98%) and Kumirmari (46.15%). For the age group 15-29 Ramganga (33.33%) has the lowest share of labour force participation as compared to Herambogopalpur (40.91%) and Kumirmari (38.96%). From these patterns it can be gauged that there might not be too many barriers as far as entry into the labour market is concerned. However, while disaggregating in terms of gender it is noticed that there is hardly any female labour force participation except in Herambogopalpur for the age groups 15-29

Table 9.10: Age-wise LFPR (%)

Village	*Ramganga*			*Herambogopalpur*			*Kumirmari*		
	M	*F*	*T*	*M*	*F*	*T*	*M*	*F*	T
15-29	67.57	0.00	33.33	72.09	11.11	40.91	73.53	15.15	38.96
30-44	100.00	0.00	52.46	96.15	4.00	50.98	88.89	0.00	46.15
45-59	94.74	0.00	56.25	90.00	0.00	51.43	94.74	0.00	62.07
60 and above	42.86	0.00	26.09	58.33	16.67	44.44	57.14	0.00	25.81

Source: Primary Survey, 2010.

(11.11% of the total females in this age group) and 60 and above (16.67%). Similarly, Kumirmari has some presence in the age group 15-29 (15.15% of the total females in this age group). As noticed in Table 9.10 either there is a definite gender barrier in the labour market of these three villages or there is large scale invisibility of women's work.

It is interesting to note that quite a few people outside EAP seem to be actively participating in the labour market especially in Herambogopalpur where the age group 60 and above has higher participation (44.44%) than the age group 15-29 (40.91%). There is also labour market participation of this age group in the other two villages as well: Ramganga (26.09%) and Kumirmari (25.81%). This pattern in a way brings out the economic condition of the three villages. Ramganga being an "up" village has lower rates of LFPR for this age as most of the persons belonging to this group probably do not need to work while the most of the people in the same group has to work in Herambogopalpur which is socio-economically a "down" village. Going by this logic Kumirmari should also have had a higher rate of participation for this group. This is answered if one looks into gender-wise breakup of the LFPR for this age group. For both Ramganga and Kumirmari the labour force in this age group comprises entirely of males while Herambogopalpur has a few females as well. Comparing at the male LFPR for this specific

Table 9.11: Age-wise WPR and Unemployment Rates (%)

	Age Group \ Village	Ramganga			Herambogopalpur			Kumirmari		
		M	F	T	M	F	T	M	F	T
WPR in %	15-29	51.35	0.00	25.33	48.84	8.89	28.41	55.88	15.15	31.17
	30-44	96.88	0.00	50.82	53.85	4.00	29.41	37.04	0.00	19.23
	45-59	84.21	0.00	50.00	35.00	0.00	20.00	68.42	0.00	44.83
	60 and above	42.86	0.00	26.09	58.33	16.67	44.44	14.29	0.00	6.45
		Ramganga			Herambogopalpur			Kumirmari		
		M	F	T	M	F	T	M	F	T
Unemployment (UPS) rate in %	15-29	16.22	0.00	8.00	23.26	2.22	12.50	17.65	0.00	7.79
	30-44	3.13	0.00	1.64	42.31	0.00	21.57	51.85	0.00	26.92
	45-59	10.53	0.00	6.25	55.00	0.00	31.43	26.32	0.00	17.24
	60 and above	0.00	0.00	0.00	0.00	0.00	0.00	42.86	0.00	19.35

Source: Primary Survey, 2010.

age group it can be seen that in Herambogopalpur 58.33 per cent of the males are in the labour force while Kumirmari has a rate of 57.14 per cent. This is much higher than Ramganga's rate of 42.86 per cent. That overall all the three villages have male LFPRs of more than forty per cent reflects the overall poverty of Sundarbans. While it is seen that there is a definite gender bias to participation in the labour markets it is equally important to look whether those participating in the labour market are getting employed or not. This can be satisfactorily answered after looking at Table 9.11 which looks at Worker Population Ratios (WPRs) and unemployment rates for these different age groups across the three villages.

From Table 9.11 it can be seen that the WPRs of Ramganga is the highest for the age group 30-44 (50.82%) and 45-59 (50%). For the 30-44 age group Herambogopalpur (29.41%) comes second followed by Kumirmari (19.23%). In the case of 45-59 age group the order is reversed with Kumirmari (44.83%) coming second and Herambogopalpur (20%) third. For the age group of 15-29 Kumirmari has the highest WPR of 31.17 per cent followed by Herambogopalpur (28.41%) and Ramganga (25.33%). Thus for the age group 15-29 WPR is better in the two "down" villages as compared to that of the "up" village and in a way it can be argued that there are more employment opportunities for this age group in Herambogopalpur and Kumirmari than in Ramganga. Overall the 30-44 group has the highest sectoral share of Ramganga's workforce while it is the 60 and above group for Herambogopalpur and 15-29 group for Kumirmari. Given the extremely low female WPRs it makes no sense to concentrate on male WPRs for better interpretation of results as the trends and patterns remain more or less the same. There is one striking result though. The WPRs for the two age groups 30-44 and 45-59 are much higher for Ramganga (96.88% and 84.21%) as compared to Herambogopalpur (53.85% and 35%) and Kumirmari (37.04% and 68.42%) which again reflects the economic backwardness of the two "down" villages.

Next we look at unemployment rates (UPS) of the three villages. The unemployment rates of Ramganga for all age groups is much lower compared to the other two villages which once again reinforces the argument that Ramganga is socioeconomically much better off than Herambogopalpur and Kumirmari. For the age groups 15-29 and 45-59 Herambogopalpur has the highest male unemployment rate (23.26% and 55%) while Kumirmari has the same for the age groups 30-44 (51.85%) and 60 and above (42.86%).

The fact that none is unemployed in the last age group for both Ramganga and Herambogopalpur cannot be seen in the same light. In Ramganga the workforce belonging to this age group mainly run small retail shops and sometimes indulge in agriculture while in the case of Herambogopalpur the workforce of this age group are mainly into fishing and agriculture. Since the location of Kumirmari ensures that people over there have limited access to the estuaries and creeks hence the high unemployment rate for this age group.

As the participation of females in the principal labour force is minimal at best it is better to concentrate on the overall and male figures to understand the picture better. Overall the LFPR is highest for Kumirmari (33.90%) followed by Herambogopalpur (31.21%) and Ramganga (30.57%). However, the WPRs show that Ramganga leads (27.17%) followed by Kumirmari (20.76%) and Herambogopalpur (19.50%). Moreover in terms of unemployment Ramganga (11.11%) has the lowest followed by Herambogopalpur (37.50%) and Kumirmari (38.75%). As far as proportion unemployed is concerned Ramganga has the lowest (3.40%) followed by Kumirmari (13.13%) and Herambogopalpur (11.70%). In the case of male population the pattern remains the same in each case. In nutshell, looking at the aggregate figures in Table 9.12, it can be easily inferred that the "up" village of Ramganga is the best off village in terms of employment and unemployment than the two "down" villages of Herambogopalpur and Kumirmari.

4.4.5 Employment Diversification in the Three Villages

Table 9.13 looks at employment by industry for both Usual Principal Status (UPS) and Usual Principal Subsidiary Status (UPSS). Agriculture employs the highest proportion of the principal labour force in Ramganga (43.44%) as compared to Manufacturing in Herambogopalpur (23.64%) and Construction (42.86%) in Kumirmari. This can be easily explained by the fact that there are two cropping seasons in Ramganga as compared to one in the two "down" villages. Further the salinity of the soil is much higher in the two "down" villages as compared to the "up"

Table 9.12: Aggregate LFPR, WPR and Unemployment Rates (%)

Village	*Ramganga*			*Herambogopalpur*			*Kumirmari*		
	M	*F*	*T*	*M*	*F*	*T*	*M*	*F*	*T*
LFPR	30.57	0.00	30.57	28.72	2.48	31.21	31.78	4.85	33.90
WPR	27.17	0.00	27.17	17.38	2.13	19.50	18.64	4.85	20.76
Emp (UPS)	88.89	0.00	88.89	60.49	85.71	62.50	58.67	100.00	61.25
Unemp (UPS)	11.11	0.00	11.11	39.51	14.29	37.50	41.33	0.00	38.75
Prop Unemp	6.72	0.00	3.40	23.36	0.69	11.70	23.31	0.00	13.13

Source: Primary Survey, 2010.

Note: Emp is employment; Unemp is unemployment and Prop means proportion.

village of Ramganga courtesy *Aila*. Fishing employs quite a significant proportion of the employed labour force in Herambogopalpur (12.73%) but not for Ramganga (4.17%) and Kumirmari (0%). This can be easily explained in terms of the geographical location of the three villages. Ramganga is located far from the forests and only has access to fish in the river beside the village. Both the "down" villages are adjacent to forests but there is an essential difference: Herambogopalpur is adjacent to the forest which are not inhabited by tigers, i.e., it is not adjacent to the tiger reserves and hence have access to rivulets and creeks of the forest which are conducive for catching fish and crab while Kumirmari is adjacent to the tiger reserve and hence has very limited access to these locations. Tea shops also employ nearly one-tenth of the employed labour force in Ramganga while it is much less in the other two villages.

This is again explained by the fact that commercially tea shops are more viable and profitable in Ramganga than in the other two villages. Going by the same logic retail should have had a higher proportion in Ramganga than in the other two villages. That it is not so (6.94% for Ramganga, 5.45% for Herambogopalpur and 14.29% for Kumirmari) suggests that there is a large scale migration of the principal labour force from the two "down" villages. This argument can be further supported by looking at the sectoral shares of employment of construction, transport/storage, manufacturing and private household employers from Table 9.11. This is because none of the mentioned sectors have any significant presence in the two "down" villages. There is hardly any presence of construction, transport/storage and manufacturing in Ramganga as well which suggests migration of labour from this village as well. Education is another sector which employs quite a few people in both the "down" villages but significantly less in the "up" village. One reason for this might be the fact that there are more educated unemployed youths in the two "down" villages who do tuitions to make a living. Surprisingly health and social sector employs more people in the two "down" villages rather than in the "up" village.

As far as the subsidiary labour force is concerned most of it is employed in agriculture (over 70% of subsidiary labour force in all villages) and fishing (around 14% for Ramganga and Herambogopalpur and around 10% for Kumirmari). Interestingly for Kumirmari 5.83 per cent of the subsidiary labour force is employed by the construction sector which points to two things. First it again provides evidence of large scale labour migration in Kumirmari and second that this section of labour force participates in migration for a period of 30-40 days because otherwise it would have been captured in the principal status. In a nutshell the employment diversification trends by industry seem to suggest that there is large scale migration of labour force. In order to examine whether this hunch is correct or not we look at employment by occupation.

Indeed Table 9.14 shows quite clearly that there is large scale migration of labour force in both the "down" villages and lesser amount of it in the "up" village. Around 50 and 30 per cent of the principal labour force of Kumirmari and Herambogopalpur comprises of daily wage migrant workers: migrant workers within West Bengal (MWB) and migrant workers outside West Bengal (MWOB). The rate is much lower at around 18 per cent for Ramganga. Also it must be noted that most of the tailors and all maid servants are migrant workers. Moreover, the reason as to why health and social sector employs more people in the two "down" villages rather than in the "up" village can be explained with the help of this table. It can be seen the NGOs employ 2.36 per cent of the PLF in Ramganga and 4.08 per cent of the PLF in Kumirmari. It is actually the government health service which gives employment to the labour force in the health and social work sector: 4.17 per cent for Ramganga, 3.64 per cent for Herambogopalpur and 4.08 per cent for Kumirmari. Moreover, sectoral share of education sector for Kumirmari is divided

Table 9.13: Employment by Industry in 2010 (%)

Industry	*Ramganga*		*Herambogopalpur*		*Kumirmari*	
	UPS	*USS*	*UPS*	*USS*	*UPS*	*USS*
Agriculture	43.44	73.00	14.55	79.84	6.12	81.55
Fishing	4.17	14.00	12.73	14.52	0.00	9.71
Manufacturing	8.33	2.00	23.64	1.61	4.08	0.00
Retail	6.94	2.00	5.45	0.00	14.29	0.00
Tea Shops	9.72	0.00	7.27	0.00	4.08	0.00
Transport/Storage	9.72	1.00	7.27	0.81	12.24	0.97
Education	4.17	2.00	7.27	0.00	8.16	1.94
Health & Social Work	2.39	1.00	3.64	0.00	4.08	0.00
Construction	11.11	5.00	14.55	1.61	42.86	5.83
HH Employers	0.00	0.00	3.64	1.61	4.08	0.00
Total	100	100	100	100	100	100

Source: Field Survey, 2010.

between tuition masters and NGOs. Also there is a higher sectoral share of tuition masters for the two "down" villages (7.27% and 4.08%) as compared to the "up" village (1.39%) which in a way indicates that there are probably more educated unemployed youths in the two "down" villages. One interesting fact observed from Table 9.13 is that the proportion of people employed by tea stalls was higher in Ramganga than in the "two" down villages. This can be explained by the fact in the two "down" villages quite a few people are employed in the mechanized/non-mechanized vans business wherein they own one or more vans which they rent out. Looking at the employed subsidiary labour force one can see that most are employed as unpaid family labour (over 50% for Ramganga and Herambogopalpur and around 45% for Kumirmari) which indicates that probably the employed female subsidiary labour force comprises the most in these sectors. The rest are chiefly employed as cultivators or forest and river workers. The fact there are hardly any local daily wage workers in either UPS or UPSS attest to the failure of the village economies to create jobs and hence create the "push" factors for employment.

Thus in a nutshell it can be surmised that employment diversification in these three villages has seen a sectoral shift from the agricultural and fishing sector to the construction, manufacturing and transport/storage sectors. This diversification of employment has occurred chiefly *via* the avenue of migration with intra-State migration holding centre stage. There is a trend of greater casualisation of labour force in all the three villages as well. However, the rates of both migration and casualisation of the labour force are much higher for Herambogopalpur and Kumirmari as compared to Ramganga. This has to be interpreted in the context of the geographical location of the three villages. Ramganga being located near to the urban metropolis of Kolkata has lower rates of unemployment, migration and casualisation of labour as compared to Herambogopalpur and Kumirmari which are far away from Kolkata and adjacent to the Sundarban jungles. Hence, it does seem that the geographical location of these villages does seem to have some impact on their employment diversification *via* migration. We examine this in detail next.

4.4.5.1 *Employment Diversification* via *Migration*

From the inter-village analysis it is quite clear that employment diversification in all the three villages has occurred *via* a shift from agriculture to other industries. This can be seen from the patterns emerging from the sectoral shares of employment in terms of both occupation and industry. In nutshell employment diversification

Table 9.14: Employment by Occupation in 2010 (%)

Occupation type	*Ramganga*		*Herambogopalpur*		*Kumirmari*	
	UPS	*USS*	*UPS*	*USS*	*UPS*	*USS*
Cultivator	43.06	19.00	12.73	20.16	6.12	31.07
Farm Labour	5.17	3.00	1.82	3.23	6.75	4.85
Tailor	2.65	0.00	5.78	0.00	0.00	0.00
Maid Servant	0.00	0.00	2.75	0.00	2.90	0.00
D/W Worker	2.78	5.00	3.64	2.42	0.00	0.00
Tuition Master	1.39	2.00	7.27	0.00	4.08	1.94
Small Businessman	16.67	1.00	20.00	0.00	22.45	0.00
Fishery Owner	0.00	1.00	1.82	0.00	0.00	0.00
Prawn Seedlings Catcher	1.39	4.00	0.00	0.81	0.00	5.83
Forest & River Worker	1.39	8.00	9.09	13.71	0.00	2.91
Government Service	4.17	0.00	3.64	0.00	4.08	0.00
NGO Services	2.36	0.00	0.00	0.00	4.08	0.00
D/W MWB	12.02	2.00	29.75	1.61	35.25	4.85
D/W MOB	5.56	0.00	1.82	2.42	14.29	3.88
Bidi Worker	1.39	2.00	0.00	0.00	0.00	0.00
Unpaid Family Labour	0.00	53.00	0.00	55.65	0.00	44.66
Total	100	100	100	100	100	100

Source: Primary Survey, 2010.

had resulted in a high degree of casualisation of the labour force especially in Herambogopalpur and Kumirmari and this has happened through the avenue of migration of the labour force. In this section we try to examine the trends and patterns of migration of labour force in the three Sundarban villages.

Trends of Migration in Sundarbans: One interesting aspect we must understand is the fact that migration of labour force in the Sundarbans is not a very new phenomenon and in fact has been going on for more nearly a decade now. This can be easily understood by looking at Table 9.15 below.

Table 9.15: Number of Workers Migrating for the first time both within and outside West Bengal

Year	*Ramganga*	*Herambogopalpur*	*Kumirmari*
1991-2000	6	8	9
2001-2010	26	37	55
2006-2010	22	32	53

Source: Primary Survey, 2010.

Table 9.15 shows that there has been a spurt in migration of workers in the last decade. The number of workers migrating for the first time either within or outside Bengal has increased from 6 to 22 for Ramganga, 8 to 32 for Herambogopalpur and 9 to 53 for Kumirmari during the last twenty years. This in a way reinforces the earlier argument regarding the socio-economic backwardness of Herambogopalpur and Kumirmari *vis-à-vis* Ramganga. More specifically it has been the last five years where migration of workers from these villages has become quite large.

Table 9.16 shows the trend of both intra-state and inter-state migrant workers of the three villages for the period 2007-2010. From the combined growth rates it can be easily seen that overall migration has come down over this period. In the case of Ramganga (–4%) the growth rate is actually negative in 2010. It is quite low for Herambogopalpur (2.5%) but quite high for Kumirmari (18.18%) which again reflects its socio-economic backwardness which transmits push factors in its village economy. This socio-economic inequality becomes starker given the fact that there was not much difference in the growth rates of all the three villages 2007. Further, the sharp increase in the rates for both Herambogopalpur and the sharp decline in Ramganga have to be

Table 9.16: Annual Growth Rate of Migrant Workers

Year	*Ramganga*			*Herambogopalpur*			*Kumirmari*		
	WB	*OB*	*Total*	*WB*	*OB*	*Total*	*WB*	*OB*	*Total*
2007	33.33	0.00	25	16.67	200.00	25	21.74	100.00	25
2008	6.25	50.00	15	7.14	50.00	10	28.57	300.00	46.66
2009	17.65	–16.67	8	23.33	0.00	21.21	36.11	–25.00	25
2010	5.00	–40.00	–4	–2.70	66.67	2.5	10.20	83.33	18.18

Source: Primary Survey, 2010.

interpreted within the context of the socio-economic impact of *Aila* in these villages. The remote village of Herambogopalpur was completely submerged by saline water for at least a week and since all the embankments broke salt water would keep entering the cultivable fields with every high tide. This basically rendered agriculture totally unviable at least for the year 2009. Hence, the acute rise in growth rates of migration. That Ramganga's rate declined from 15 per cent in 2008 to 8 per cent in 2009 attests to the fact that it was not as badly affected by *Aila*. However, there is indeed a catch here in the sense that the growth rate was much higher for Kumirmari in 2008 (46.66%) compared to 2009 (25%) and 2010 (18.18%). One has to look at disaggregate level in order to make sense of this anomaly.

If one were to disaggregate and look at intra-state and inter-state migrant workers some interesting patterns emerge. For Ramganga inter-State migrant workers have decreased progressively throughout the period 2007-2010. As far as intra-State workers are concerned it has also fallen steadily except in the year 2009 when it rose nearly three times which in turn reflects that Ramganga too was affected to a certain extent by *Aila*. Nearly half of the village was submerged under saline water for two to three days although the extent of damage done was much less as compared to the two remote villages. Interestingly the rate of inter-State migrant workers fell drastically for all three villages in 2009 and this again can be explained in the context of *Aila*. Post *Aila* the situation of most of the affected households was quite similar in all the three villages: the houses were severely damaged and in some cases swept away by the rivers and the lands were not viable for cultivation. So the people had to migrate for income as there was no other option left especially in the two remote villages. However, the fact that their families did not have proper shelter probably led them migrate within the State so that they could come back within short periods and start building their houses or a new shelter at least. Further there was this widespread fear that a similar event might occur and hence they wanted to stay as close to home as possible. For Herambogopalpur and Kumirmaṛi both the inter-State and intra-State growth rates have actually declined over time. Nonetheless the decline is much sharper for Ramganga and Herambogopalpur as compared to Kumirmari which once again reinforces the socioeconomic inequality of the three villages. If we consider the total number of workers who have been both inter-State and intra-State migrant workers in the same year the trends remain the same except in 2006 when Herambogopalpur had the highest. Moreover, there is an increasing trend in Kumirmari while it is declining in the other two villages.

From the above analysis on migration for the period 2006-2010 what comes out is the fact that the overall geographical location indeed has an effect on both inter- and intra-State migration to a considerable extent. It can be clearly seen that the adverse geographical location plays a significant part in exerting push factors *via* its socio-economy which in turn affects the trends of migration in the villages. The "down" geographical location of Herambogopalpur and Kumirmari results in the exertion of push factors in these economies at a far greater strength as compared to Ramganga whose geographical location can be termed as "up". Thus, we have greater number of migrant workers in the two "down" villages as compared to the "up" village. Next we examine migration in these villages in 2010 in detail and try to understand the movement of the migrant workforce in terms of location, industry and occupation.

4.4.5.2 Location and Duration of Migration in Sundarbans

Table 9.17 gives us an idea about the amount of days the migrant workers work outside the Sundarbans but within Bengal (WB) in 2010. In the case Ramganga it can be clearly seen that more than half of the migrant workers worked for a month or less outside, i.e., Ramganga experienced seasonal migration of its labour force. In the case of Herambogopalpur only 27.78 per cent of the migrant

Table 9.17: Number of Working Days for Migrant Workers in 2010 (WB)

Period (Days)	*Ramganga*	*Herambogopalpur*	*Kumirmari*
0-30	57.14	27.78	22.22
31-60	0.00	5.56	24.07
61-90	9.52	5.56	14.81
91-120	0.00	0.00	5.56
121-150	4.76	0.00	3.70
151-180	4.76	5.56	7.41
181-210	0.00	11.11	7.41
211-240	0.00	2.78	3.70
241-270	0.00	5.56	0.00
271-300	4.76	25.00	5.56
301-330	19.05	11.11	5.56

Source: Primary Survey, 2010.

workers worked for a month or less outside and for Kumirmari the percentage is even lower. Surprisingly, the percentage of the migrant workers working nearly for the entire year also follows the same pattern.

For Kumirmari nearly half of its migrant workers stayed outside between two to three months whereas for Herambogopalpur one-fourth of its migrant workforce worked outside for nine to ten months. Interestingly if one were to consider migrant workers staying outside for more than nine months Herambogopalpur (36.11%) comes ahead of Ramganga (23.81%) with Kumirmari (11.12%) coming last. One way of explaining these patterns is by arguing that Ramganga being a much better off village socioeconomically has the highest number of migrant workers who work for one month or less and Herambogopalpur and Kumirmari being socioeconomically worse off have lower numbers of such migrant workers. This also explains the fact that Herambogopalpur has more migrant workers staying outside for more than nine months than Ramganga but does not explain why Ramganga comes ahead of Kumirmari in this respect. Similarly if one were to consider the number of workers migrating between one to three months it accounts for more than sixty per cent of the migrant workers for both Ramganga and Kumirmari whereas for Herambogopalpur the number of workers migrating for five to nine months account for nearly sixty per cent of its migrant workers. If one were to consider the conventional wisdom that long term migration has high costs associated with it which not everyone can bear then the situation is explained partially in terms of Ramganga and Kumirmari which are the best and worst off village but the trends in Herambogopalpur cannot be explained. In a nutshell the distribution of number of workdays of migrant workers is skewed at the top and the bottom for Ramganga and Kumirmari and in the middle for Herambogopalpur and we need to look into the distribution of the migrant workers according to location, industry and occupation in order to derive more precise conclusions.

Table 9.18 gives us a very good idea about the locations of the migrant workers of the three villages in 2010. For Ramganga nearly half the migrant workers went to Varddhaman followed by Kolkata and Howrah which also drew nearly one-third of the migrant workers. Thus most of the migrant workers who worked for a month or less, it can be argued, went to Varddhaman which has a large cold storage industry. Most of these seasonal migrants go to work as daily wage workers in these cold storages in Varddhaman and Medinipur in West Bengal for a month from mid February to mid March every year. This is the loading season of cold storages which primarily store potatoes. Next comes the nearly twenty per cent of the migrant labour force which worked outside for nearly the entire year. This category of workers, in the case of Ramganga, worked primarily as daily wage workers in the construction and manufacturing sector in and around Kolkata and Howrah in West Bengal. Other than that there are also a few tailors who worked in places like Metiaburz. Migrant workers in the agricultural sector and also working in hotels went to Haldia and Hooghly.

Table 9.18: Migration Location within West Bengal

Location	*Ramganga*	*Herambogopalpur*	*Kumirmari*
Kolkata + Howrah	33.33	55.56	57.41
Varddhaman	47.62	27.78	11.11
Budge Budge	0.00	0.00	11.11
Medinipur	4.76	2.78	11.11
Haldia	4.76	0.00	0.00
Hooghly	4.76	0.00	5.56
Metiaburz	4.76	8.33	0.00
Murshidabad	0.00	2.78	0.00
Arambagn	0.00	2.78	0.00
Nadia-Murshidabad-Bankura	0.00	0.00	3.70

Source: Primary Survey, 2010.

For Herambogopalpur it is the construction and the manufacturing industries in and around Kolkata and Howrah (55.56%) which absorbed most of the migrant workers. Then come the cold storages in Varddhaman (27.88%) followed by Metiaburz (8.33%) which absorbs quite a few tailors from the Muslim families in this village. Migrant workers in the agricultural sector primarily went to Murshidabad while Arambagh and Medinipur drew workers into their construction sectors. As far as Kumirmari is concerned a much lower proportion of migrant workers went to Varddhaman (11.11%) while a much higher proportion went to Medinipur (11.11%), Budge Budge (11.11%) and Hooghly (5.56%). Of the three villages this village has the highest proportion of migrant workers going to Kolkata and Howrah (57.41%). All these trends just cannot be explained in terms of wage differentials. If it were so then most of the migrant should have gone to the cold storages which pay the most. It must be understood that these workers migrate in groups which are created *via* social and kinship networks.

Thus most of the times it is the decision of the group as a whole to migrate to a particular place for work and there seems to be a certain amount of path dependent and risk averse behaviour involved here. Over the last few years there has been a large scale proliferation of "*dalals*" or middlemen in these villages who recruit young men and take them to work in the construction and manufacturing sectors especially outside the State and more often than not dupe the workers of a significant proportion of their earnings. This has led to this emergence of "migrating clusters" of workers not only outside West Bengal but within the State as well. Further there is tendency by these clusters to stick to a particular sector in a particular location especially if they get their wages on time. Another important factor is that working in the cold storages in Varddhaman involves a huge amount of physical strength and it is indeed very difficult for even the fittest of these workers to carry on working there for more than one month. Thus the workers who migrate for a month or less tend to go to the cold storages where they get the highest wages but if the migration period is three months or more then they tend to prefer sectors like construction, manufacturing and lastly even agriculture.

For migrant workers outside the State the trend is obviously to stay and work for longer periods of time. Generally the workers

Table 9.19: Number of Working Days for Migrant Workers Outside West Bengal in 2010

Period (Days)	*Ramganga*	*Herambogopalpur*	*Kumirmari*
0-90	0.00	40.00	27.27
150-180	33.33	20.00	36.36
300-330	66.67	40.00	36.36

Source: Primary Survey, 2010.

come home after six months or one year. It must be understood that these workers generally come from large households and hence can afford to leave their wives, children and aged parents behind. Those who cannot afford that and still have no option but to migrate do so far around three months. Table 9.19 shows that in Ramganga more than two-thirds of the migrant workers worked outside for nearly the entire year and one-third worked for five to six months. Herambogopalpur again shows different picture with higher proportions of workers working up-to three and eleven months respectively (40% each). Higher proportions of Kumirmari workers stayed outside for five to six months and ten to eleven months (36.36% each). The general trend is that highest proportion of workers stay outside for nearly the entire year which is but logical as the objective of the workers is to earn and save as much as possible and then come back. Frequent travelling to home would eat into their savings and also the fact that they travel in clusters means that most of them go and return at around the same time unless there are medical emergencies.

Table 9.20 gives us a clear idea about the locations outside West Bengal where migrant workers went to earn a living in 2010. Most of the inter-State migration for Ramganga (100% and 0%)

Table 9.20: Migration Location Outside Bengal in 2010

Location	*Ramganga*	*Herambogopalpur*	*Kumirmari*
Andaman	0	0	9.09
Tamil Nadu	100	40	36.36
Kerala	0	0	36.36
Maharashtra	0	0	9.09
Punjab	0	20	0.00
New Delhi	0	40	0.00
Karnataka	0	0	9.09

Source: Primary Survey, 2010.

and Kumirmari (36% each) occurred in the two southern States of Kerala and Tamil Nadu which have a booming construction sector especially in Ernakulam and Chennai. Andaman and Nicobar Islands is only preferred by workers in Kumirmari (9.09%).

One reason for this being the fact it is the most remote of all migrating locations which means that travelling from West Bengal to Andamans and *vice versa* involves a lot of time and money which entails in the workers staying away from home for a minimum of one year and sometimes up-to two years. Thus, in a way workers migrate to Andamans when all other options have failed. So, the fact that nearly one-tenth of the inter-State migrating workforce goes to the Andamans reflects the socio-economic backwardness of Kumirmari *via-à-vis* that of Ramganga and Herambogopalpur. A certain section of the inter-State migrating workforce of Kumirmari also went to Karnataka and Maharashtra (9.09% each) where the workers work in the fishery and manufacturing sectors respectively. The inter-State migrating workforce of Herambogopalpur went to three locations: the construction sector in Tamil Nadu (40%), the manufacturing sector in Punjab (hosiery industries in Ludhiana) and private household employers in New Delhi (40%).

One interesting aspect is the fact that hardly any women migrated for work either within or outside the State. There are quite a few reasons for this like the fact the women stay back to look after the kids and the aged in-laws and other relatives. Economically speaking, the fact that most of these households have some amount cultivable land means that the lady assumes the role of the cultivator in the absence of her husband. This is equally important for the household as the cultivation ensures foodgrains for most of the households for at least half a year and hence, it is a complement to the income from migration. Further, village customs seem to look down upon women migrating for work (at least outside the State) and it is generally accepted that women migrating for work is the last employment diversification option of these households.

4.4.5.3 Industrial and Occupational Structure of Migration in Sundarbans

From Table 9.21, it can be seen that as far as inter-State migration is concerned it is the construction sector which accounted for most of the workers in all the three villages in 2010: 100 per cent for Ramganga, 60 per cent for Herambogopalpur and 72.23 per cent for Kumirmari. For both Kumirmari (20%) and Herambogopalpur (18.18%) manufacturing sector comes second. It primarily comprises of hosiery industries in Ludhiana and some industries in and around New Delhi as well as the idol making industry in Maharashtra.

Private household employers (20%) in Delhi and the fishery sector (20%) in Karnataka come third for Herambogopalpur and Kumirmari respectively. As far as intra-State migration is concerned transport/storage industry (potato cold storages in Varddhaman and Medinipur) absorbed the highest amount of workers for Ramganga (52.38%) and Herambogopalpur (30.56%). However, for Kumirmari it is the construction sector (51.85%) in Kolkata and Howrah which tops the list and it is followed by the transport/storage sector (22.22%) and agricultural sector (16.67%) in places like Budge Budge, Hooghly, etc. respectively. After the transport/storage sector workers from Ramganga were absorbed by construction (28.57%), manufacturing (9.52%) and agriculture (4.76%) respectively. For Herambogopalpur manufacturing (33.33%) comes second followed by construction (25%) and household employers (5.56%).

Thus diversification for the migrant workers within Bengal has occurred from agriculture in Sundarbans to the transport/storage sector in Varddhaman and Medinipur, construction and manufacturing in Kolkata and Howrah followed by agriculture in a few places like Hooghly, Budge Budge, etc. Ramganga workers have also diversified into hotel sector in Haldia whereas the other two villages have diversified into the private household employers sector in Kolkata. As far as inter-State migrant workers are concerned there has been no diversification in Ramganga with all the workers concentrated in the construction sector. Herambogopalpur has diversified into construction, manufacturing and private household employers sectors while for Kumirmari private household employers gets replaced by the fishery industry. Thus within Bengal all the three villages are more or less equally diversified but outside Bengal the two worse off villages are much more diversified. Partly it can be explained by the fact that the number of inter-State migrants is very small as

Table 9.21: Migration by Industry in 2010

Industry	*Ramganga*		*Herambogopalpur*		*Kumirmari*	
	WB	*OB*	*WB*	*OB*	*WB*	*OB*
Agriculture	4.76	0.00	2.78	0.00	16.67	0.00
Fishing	0.00	0.00	0.00	0.00	0.00	9.09
Manufacturing	9.52	0.00	33.33	20.00	0.00	18.18
Construction	28.57	100.00	25.00	60.00	51.85	72.73
Retail	0.00	0.00	0.00	0.00	3.70	0.00
HH Employer	0.00	0.00	5.56	20.00	5.56	0.00
Hotel	4.76	0.00	0.00	0.00	0.00	0.00
Transport/Storage	52.38	0.00	30.56	0.00	22.22	0.00
Health & Social Work	0.00	0.00	2.78	0.00	0.00	0.00
Total	100	100	100	100	100	100

Source: Primary Survey, 2010.

compared to the other two villages. Another reason is the emergence of migrant clusters as explained earlier.

If one were to look at the diversification trends in terms of "push factors" it can be argued that they operate with a far greater intensity in the two "down" villages as compared to the "up" village. This can be seen from the fact that the migrant workers from Ramganga migrate the least in terms of days. In order to maximize their returns from migration the majority of the migrant workers of Ramganga (52.38%) tend to go to the cold storages in Varddhaman where they can earn the most.[19] However, working in the cold storages for more than one or two months is physically extremely demanding. Hence, the migrant workers from the other two villages who go for a long period of time opt for manufacturing and construction sectors.

Finally looking at migrant workers in terms of occupation, from Table 9.22, helps us to reinforce the trends of migration from the three villages in 2010 and their possible reasons. As far inter-State migration from the three villages is concerned it has resulted in complete casualisation of the migrant workforce across industries and locations. For intra-State migration as well we have a very high degree of casualisation of the workforce.

From Table 9.22, it is evident that migration is highest for Kumirmari followed by Ramganga and Herambogopalpur respectively. As mentioned there are very female workers who migrate within the State. Those who do so go to Kolkata to work as maid servants. This has happened in the case of

Table 9.22: Migration by Occupation in 2010

Occupation	Ramganga		Herambogopalpur		Kumirmari	
	WB	OB	WB	OB	WB	OB
Daily Wage Worker	85.71	100.00	72.22	100.00	90.74	100.00
Maid Servant	0.00	0.00	5.56	0.00	5.56	0.00
Cook	4.76	0.00	0.00	0.00	0.00	0.00
Tailor	9.52	0.00	19.44	0.00	0.00	0.00
Honey Collector	0.00	0.00	0.00	0.00	3.70	0.00
Homeopathy Doctor	0.00	0.00	2.78	0.00	0.00	0.00
Total	100	100	100	100	100	100

Source: Primary Survey, 2010.

Herambogopalpur and Kumirmari. Kumirmari also has a few honey bee collectors who travel to a variety of locations throughout the year. Herambogopalpur seems to have a high proportion of tailors in the migrant workforce and these tailors come from the Muslim families in the village. These families have relatives in Metiaburz who run their own tailoring shops. When the young males of these Muslim households in Herambogopalpur finish schooling (upto 10 or 12) they are sent to Metiaburz where they work as apprentices in these shops and slowly learn the tricks of the trade. During this period they do not earn anything but do not have to pay for their food and accommodation. Once they acquire the requisite tailoring skills they become employees in that shop itself and earn a regular salary. This is a very good example of how social and kinship networks influence employment diversification in the Sundarban villages. There are also quite a few tailors from Ramganga as well. Other than that Ramganga provides cooks for hotels in Haldia while Herambogopalpur provides a few homoeopathy doctors who work in and around Kolkata and Kumirmari has honey bee collectors.

To surmise the migration story it can be seen that it is the primary avenue *via* which employment diversification occurs in the three villages of Ramganga, Herambogopalpur and Kumirmari in the Sundarbans. The geographical location of these three villages plays a significant role not only in influencing employment diversification but also in influencing the rate of migration among the labour force with the two "down" villages having much higher rates of migration as compared to the "up" village. But otherwise the geographical location of the villages plays an important role in creating the "push" factors for migration in these villages and ultimately have led to greater casualisation of the labour force in all the three villages.

4.4.5.4 Female Labour Force and Migration in Sundarbans

Table 9.10 and 9.11 have already shown that there is hardly any presence of females in either the principal work force or the principal labour force. The pattern remains quite similar as can be observed from Table 9.23. There are no female migrant workers outside West Bengal for all the three villages.

Table 9.23: Percentage of Females in Migrant Work Force

Category	*Ramganga*	*Herambogopalpur*	*Kumirmari*
MWB	0	9.76	6.15
MOB	0	0	0

Source: Primary Survey, 2010.

As far as migrant work within West Bengal are concerned less than one-tenth are females for Herambogopalpur (9.76%) and Kumirmari (6.15%). Ramganga has no females even within the West Bengal category. Moreover, as mentioned there seems to both gender barriers and invisibility of women's work in the three villages. The barriers to labour market entry for females are generally socio-cultural in nature rather than economic. It is widely perceived among the people in these villages that women should actively participate in the labour market if there are no other alternatives available. The general male consensus is that the women folk should concentrate on their domestic duties and leave earning activities to the "better" males. However, with the advent of National Rural Employment Guarantee Act (NREGA) programme some genders had been removed in the sense that many womenfolk actively participated in this employment generation programme. However, with serious issues like non-payment of wages cropping up there has been no NREGA work in 2010. As far as migration is concerned the socio-cultural barriers become all the stronger as migration of women is generally not seen in "good light". Only in exceptional cases of there being no

Table 9.24: Occupational Distribution of Total Females (%).

Category	*Ramganga*	*Herambo-gopalpur*	*Kumirmari*
In PLF	0	4.84	4.85
Studying	33.59	30.34	24.27
Household (hh) work/ hh work plus collection of goods	53.44	53.79	53.41
Others	12.97	11.03	17.47
Total	100	100	100

Source: Primary Survey, 2010.

other economic alternatives that women migrate for work. However, it must be pointed that migrating to Kolkata and working as housemaids is strictly the premise of young unmarried women. Married women do not migrate and are normally expected to take care of her immediate and extended family in the absence of the male counterpart.

Table 9.24 looks at the occupational structure of the total female population across the three villages. It can be seen that more than half of the females are involved in household work alongwith collection of goods for all the three villages. Understanding the nature of activity of this part of the female population requires that their subsidiary status be looked at in detail.

Table 9.25: Occupation of Subsidiary Female Labour Force

Category	*Unpaid family labour*	*Casual Labour*	*Culti-vator*	*Salaried*	*Total*	*Total**
Ramganga	78.57	5.36	14.28	1.78	100	80
Herambogopalpur	85.48	0	14.52	0	100	79.49
Kumirmari	76.60	4.26	19.15	0	100	85.45

Source: Primary Survey, 2010.

Note: * Indicates as proportion of females whose UPS is Household (hh) work/hh work plus collection of goods.

From Table 9.25 it can be seen that nearly eighty per cent of the women in all three villages engaged in domestic duties throughout the year also double up as subsidiary workers. Most of them (more than three-fourths for all the three villages) are engaged as unpaid family labour which again is concentrated in the agricultural sector. Other than that quite a few women are cultivators as well. That Kumirmari has the highest proportion of cultivators in the female subsidiary labour force suggests that there is a correlation with migration among the male labour force. The fact that both Ramganga and Herambogopalpur have nearly equal proportions in this respect should be seen in the light of the fact that agriculture in Ramganga is double cropping in nature whereas it is single cropping in Herambogopalpur. Thus the same rate of female cultivators has different interpretations for the two villages. As seen from Table 9.16 Herambogopalpur also has a high migration rate among its male labour force while in the case of Ramganga it is primarily due to double cropping that more females are engaged in cultivation. Thus a pattern emerges wherein the women in the migrant households also work as cultivators especially if the migration is for a period of six months or more.

In a nutshell most of the women in the three villages are employed as subsidiary workers in the agricultural sector and return their principal status as attended domestic duties as a result of which there is such invisibility of females in the principal labour force of all the three villages in Sundarbans.

4.4.6 Variations in Wages and Income

As far as wages within the villages is concerned the prevailing wage rate is rupees one hundred for male daily wage workers while it is rupees eighty for female workers in the agricultural and fishery sector. This wage differential results in the landed gentry preferring to employ female workers as agricultural labourers during the harvesting season. However, given the increased salinity of the soil for the past two years there are hardly any employment opportunities in agriculture in either Herambogopalpur or Kumirmari. In Ramganga the situation is a little better as double cropping is practiced there. Tuition teachers charge from fifty to rupees one hundred and fifty depending upon the class in which the student is studying. Government school teachers are the best off in terms of salaries while NGO workers earn in the range of rupees two thousand and rupees four thousand.

Wages for migrant workers vary across industries and regions. The wages are around rupees one hundred and fifty per day for workers in the manufacturing and construction industry within

West Bengal whereas it ranges from rupees two hundred to three hundred per day outside West Bengal. The situation is completely different in cold storages where the payment depends entirely upon the number of sacks a worker is able to carry per day. Wages in migratory jobs in the agricultural sector range from rupees one hundred to one hundred fifty. Sometimes the wages are paid entirely in terms of the harvested grains. Also the wages in the agricultural sector are generally lesser if the migrant workers are given three meals a day by the employer. Housemaids in Kolkata earn around rupees five hundred a month while those outside the State earn in the range of rupees five hundred to one thousand.

Table 9.26: Variations in Average Annual Household (HH) Income in Rupees

Village	Ramganga	Herambo-gopalpur	Kumirmari
Average HH Income	40670	34330	30430
Average Migrant HH Income	41150	36954	31385
Average Non-Migrant HH Income	40350	29235	27900

Source: Primary Survey, 2010.

From Table 9.26, it can be seen the average annual household income is the highest for Ramganga (Rs. 40,670) followed by Herambogopalpur (Rs. 34,330) and Kumirmari (Rs. 30,430). The difference of around rupees ten thousand in average annual income between Ramganga and Kumirmari and around rupees four thousand between Ramganga and Herambogopalpur has to be seen, once again, in the context of Ramganga being a rural commercial centre. Moreover, double cropping is widely practiced in Ramganga as opposed to mono cropping in the other two villages. However, the difference in the average annual household income of the two "down" villages cannot be easily explained. One reason might be that the migrant workers from Herambogopalpur worker for longer periods of time than those of Kumirmari. Interestingly there is hardly any difference between the average annual incomes of migrant (Rs. 41,150) and non-migrant households (Rs. 40,350) in Ramganga. This can be attributed to the fact that Ramganga being a rural commercial centre has quite a few employment diversification options other

Table 9.27: Income Slab-wise Distribution of Households (%)

Income Slab	*Ramganga*	*Herambogopalpur*	*Kumirmari*
Upto Rs. 10000	2	8	16
Rs. 10001 – Rs. 20000	22	23	28
Rs. 20001 – Rs. 30000	26	28	26
Rs. 30001 – Rs. 40000	20	17	12
Rs. 40001 – Rs. 50000	8	10	6
Above Rs. 50000	22	10	12
Total	100	100	100

Source: Primary Survey, 2010.

than *via* migration available. Also the advantage of nearby access to wholesale markets has resulted in some households diversifying into tomato and betel leaf farming. On the other hand the absence of such local employment diversification options for the other two villages translates into a substantial income difference between migrant and non-migrant households.

Table 9.27 shows the income distribution of the three villages across six different income slabs. Once again the socio-economic hierarchy of the three villages is quite evident. For Ramganga more than half the households earn more than Rs. 30,000 on an average annually which by Sundarbans standards is a decent amount of money. In sharp contrast only thirty per cent of Kumirmari households and thirty seven per cent of Herambogopalpur households fall in the same category. Ramganga (2%) has the lowest share of households whose average annual income is less than rupees ten thousand followed by Herambogopalpur (8%) and Kumirmari (16%). The highest proportion of households in Ramganga (26%) and Herambogopalpur (28%) earn in the range of rupees twenty thousand to thirty thousand annually on an average. For Kumirmari twenty eight per cent of the households earn in the range of rupees ten thousand to twenty thousand. The sharp inequality further comes out if we consider household with an average annual income of rupees fifty thousand or more with Ramganga (22%) accounting for the highest share followed by Kumirmari (12%) and Herambogopalpur (10%). These figures in a way reveal the level of destitution in the two "down" villages of Herambogopalpur and Kumirmari and the relative affluence of the "up" village of Ramganga.

4.5 Employment Diversification and the Hysteresis of Land

As the agricultural and fishery sector in these villages cannot prove sufficient employment opportunities the need for employment diversification arises. The story of employment diversification in these three villages of Sundarbans ultimately boils down to the story of inter- and intra-State migration of labour from them. The fact that the "up" village of Ramganga is relatively better off than the other two villages gets reflected in its higher employment rates, lower migration rates and higher annual average income. One of the major reasons why the other two villages are lagging behind has to be interpreted in the context of the overall geographical location of these villages: Ramganga is situated much closer to the mainland and hence the urban and semi-urban markets whereas Herambogopalpur and Kumirmari are prohibitively remote to say the least. This overall geographical location of the three villages in turn has to be understood in the context of the colonial land reclamation and conservation policies of Sundarbans which resulted in the specific human settlement pattern that can be seen today. This settlement pattern contributes to higher rates of unemployment and migration and lower annual average income for the two "down" villages of Herambogopalpur and Kumirmari. Hence, it can be very well argued that there exists a hysteresis of the effects of colonial land tenure and forest conservation policies in the Sundarbans which manifests itself in the present *via* the overall geographical location of the people in the different regions of Sundarbans in terms of socioeconomic hierarchy especially caste and the skewed pattern of ownership of land. This in turn has an impact on the socioeconomic condition of Sundarbans in general and on employment diversification in the region in particular.

5.0 Conclusion

The villages of Ramganga and Herambogopalpur in Patharpratima Block and Kumirmari in Gosaba Block of Sundarbans are located in three different areas of Sundarbans. Ramganga which is a rural commercial centre is located adjacent to mainland and is well connected to the urban markets of Kolkata and other semi-urban markets. On the other hand the other two villages are located in the remotest areas of Sundarbans. Herambogopalpur is situated adjacent to forest which is not under the tiger reserve while Kumirmari is adjacent to forests under the tiger. They do not have access to any urban or semi-urban markets nearby. A comparison of the socio-economic profile of these villages reveals that Ramganga is much better off than the other two villages. Interestingly Ramganga also has the highest proportion of general caste Hindus. On the other hand Herambogopalpur has a significant share of scheduled castes and Muslims whereas Kumirmari is completely dominated by scheduled castes.

This pattern of social composition of villages has to be interpreted in the context of the colonial land reclamation policies for nearly a century and the colonial forest conservation policies thereafter which resulted in the creation of a certain pattern of human settlement in the Sundarbans. Most of the original settlers which included a majority of scheduled castes and few scheduled tribes ended up at the fringes of the forest while the second and third generation of settlers occupied the initially cleared lands which were much closer to Kolkata and other urban and semi-urban centres. Hence, the worst off, socio-economically, ended up settling in the locationally worst off regions in the Sundarbans. This in turn has affected the intergenerational socio-economic conditions of the people of the region. This gets easily portrayed *via* the detailed analysis done of the trends and patterns of employment diversification in the three villages. Moreover the skewed land ownership patterns persisting due to a less successful implementation of land reforms makes it quite clear that the history of the landscape changes of Sundarbans has had a major influence on the socioeconomic conditions of the people settled here.

All the three have experienced a sectoral shift from the agricultural and fishing sector to the construction, manufacturing and transport/storage sectors. This diversification of employment has occurred chiefly *via* the avenue of migration with intra-State migration holding centre stage *vis-à-vis* inter-State migration. There is a trend of greater casualisation of labour force in all the three villages as well. However, the rates of both migration and casualisation of the labour force are much higher for Herambogopalpur and Kumirmari as compared to Ramganga. Moreover Ramganga has higher employment rates and higher annual average household income as compared to Herambogopalpur and Kumirmari. Thus the geographical location of these three villages plays a significant role not only in influencing employment diversification but also in influencing the rate of migration among the labour force with the two "down" villages (Herambogopalpur and Kumirmari) having much higher rates of migration as compared to the "up" village (Ramganga). Put otherwise the geographical location of these villages plays an important role in creating the "push" factors for migration in these villages and ultimately has led to greater casualisation of the labour force in all the three villages.

REFERENCES

Bandyopadhyay, D. (2000): 'Can Sundarbans Be Saved?', *Economic and Political Weekly*, Vol. 35, No. 45, pp. 3925-3928.

Banerjee, Anuradha (1998): *'Environment, Population and Human Settlements of Sundarban Delta'*, Concept Publishing, Pvt. Ltd., New Delhi.

Basu, S. (1981): 'Socio-Cultural Profile' in Amal Kumar Das *et al.* (ed.), *A Focus on Sundarban,* Calcutta.

Batterbury, S. (2001): 'Landscapes of Diversity: A Local Political Ecology of Livelihood Diversification in South-Western Niger', *Ecumene,* Vol. 8, No. 4, pp. 437-464.

Bertocci, Peter (1997): 'Notes towards an Ethno-sociology of the Bengal Sundarbans', Paper presented at workshop on 'The Commons in South Asia: Societal Pressures and Environmental Integrity in the Sundarbans', Smithsonian Institution, Washington, DC, 20-21 November. Also published in John Seidensticker, Richard Kurin and Amy K. Townsend (eds), 'The Commons in South Asia: Societal Pressures and Environmental Integrity in the Sundarbans', Washington, DC: The International Center, Smithsonian, 1991.

Chattopadhyaya, Haraprasad (1999): *The Mystery of the Sundarbans,* A Mukherjee & Co., Calcutta.

Chaudhuri, Kalyan (1976): 'Poverty and Exploitation in Sundarbans', *Economic and Political Weekly,* Vol. 11, No. 50, pp. 1914-1915.

Chowdhury, T.A. (2010): 'Resource-dependent Livelihoods in the Sundarbans', CRBOM Small Publications Series No. 18, Center for River Basin Organizations and Management, January.

Coad, Lauren, Alison Campbell, Lera Miles and Katherine Humphries (2008): 'The Costs and Benefits of Forest Protected Areas for Local Livelihoods: A Review of the Current Literature' Working Paper.

Das, Amal Kumar, Sankrananda Mukherji and Manas Kamal Chowdhury (eds.) (1981): *A Focus on Sundarban,* Editions Indian, Calcutta.

Datta, S.K., and K. Singh (2011): 'Livelihood Diversification: Case Study of Some Backward Regions in India', *International Journal of Current Research*, Vol. 33, No, 2, pp. 139-151.

De, R. (1990): *The Sundarbans*, Oxford University Press, Culcutta.

Eaton, Richard M. (1990): 'Human Settlement and Colonization in the Sundarbans, 1200-1750', *Agriculture and Human Values*, Vol. 7, No. 2.

Guha, I. and Ghosh, S. (2007): 'Does Tourism Contribute to Local Livelihoods? A Case Study of Tourism, Poverty and Conservation in the Indian Sundarbans', SANDEE Working Paper No.26-07, *South Asian Network for Development and Environmental Economics*, October.

Guha, I. and Ghosh, S. (2009): 'A Glimpse of the Tiger: How Much Are the Indians Willing to Pay For It?', SANDEE Working Paper No. 39-09, *South Asian Network for Development and Environmental Economics*, February.

Haque, T. and G. Parthasarathy (1992): 'Land Reform and Rural Development: Highlights of a National Seminar', *Economic and Political Weekly*, Vol. 27, No. 8, pp. 395-397.

Hui, Katee (2006): 'Agriculture Under Strain in the Sundarbans', *Within Reach Magazine*, Vol. 5, Issue 2.

Jalais, Annu (2007): 'The Sundarbans: Whose World Heritage Site?', *Conservation and Society*, Vol. 5, No. 3, pp. 1-8.

Jalais, Annu (2010): *Forest of Tigers: People, Politics & Environment in the Sundarbans*, Routledge, New Delhi.

Kumar, A. (2009): 'Rural Employment Diversification in Eastern India: Trends and Determinants', *Agricultural Economics Research Review*, Vol. 22, No.1 , pp. 47-60.

Lanjouw, P, and A. Shariff (2004): 'Rural Non-Farm Employment in India: Access, Incomes and Poverty Impact', *Economic and Political Weekly*, Vol. 39, No. 40, pp. 4429-4446.

Mukherjee, K.N. (1983): 'History of Settlement in the Sundarbans of West Bengal', *Indian Journal of Landscape System and Ecological Studies*. Vol. 6, No. 1 & 2, pp. 16.

Mukherjee, S. (1981): 'Historical and Geographical Background', in Amal Kumar Das *et al.* (ed.), *A Focus on Sundarban*, Calcutta.

Pal, S., and J. Kynch (2000): 'Determinants of Occupational Change and Mobility in Rural India', *Applied Economics*, Vol. 32, No.12, pp. 1559-73.

Patel, V. and Rajagopalan, R. (Undated): 'Fishing Community Issues in the Sundarban Tiger Reserve (STR)', Report, International Collective in Support of Fishworker.

Rahman, L.M. (2000): 'The Sundarbans: A Unique Wilderness of the World', *USDA Forest Service Proceedings*, RMRS-P-15, Vol. 2, pp. 143-148.

Rahman, S. (undated): 'Ecology and Management of Sundarban: A Rich Biodiversity of the World's Largest Mangrove Ecosystem' *images.srmilan.multiply.com/./Sundarban%20Ecosystem.pdf?*

Richards, John F. and Elizabeth P. Flint (1990): 'Long-Term Transformations in the Sundarbans Wetlands Forests of Bengal', *Agriculture and Human Values,* Vol. 7, No. 2, pp. 17-33.

Rigg, J. (2006): 'Land, farming, livelihoods, and poverty: rethinking the links in the rural South.', *World Development,* Vol. 34, No. 1, pp. 180-202.

Samal, C. (2006): Remittances and Sustainable Livelihoods in Semi-Arid Areas', *Asia Pacific Development Journal,* Vol. 13, No. 2.

Samarakoon, Jayampathy (2004): 'Issues of Livelihood, Sustainable Development, and Governance: Bay of Bengal', *Ambio,* Vol. 33, No. 1-2.

SANDEE (2007): 'Can Tourism be a Vehicle for Conservation? An Investigation from the Mangrove Forests of the Indian Sundarbans', Policy Brief, *South Asian Network for Development and Environmental Economics,* No. 25-07, October.

Santhakumar, V., Enamul Haque, A.K., and Bhattacharya, R. (undated): 'An Economic Analysis of Mangroves in South Asia', http://citeseerx.ist.psu.edu/viewdoc/versions;jsessionid = F88D83F1982C0F4C14AB1405362CA891?doi = 10.1.1.122.7075

Sarkar, S.C. (2010): The Sundarbans: Folk Deities, Monsters and Mortals, Orient Blackswan, New Delhi.

Seidensticker, J., Kurin, R., Townsend, A.K. (eds.) (1991), 'The Commons in South Asia: Societal Pressures and Environmental Integrity in the Sundarbans of Bangladesh', *Proceedings from a Workshop held in November 20-21, 1987 in Washington, DC,* The International Center Smithsonian Institution.

Singh, A.; Bhattacharya, P.; Vyas, P.; and Roy, S. (2010): 'Contribution of NTFPs in the Livelihood of Mangrove Forest Dwellers of Sundarban', International Centre for Community Forestry, Indian Institute of Forest Management, *J Hum Ecol,* 29(3), pp. 191-200.

Start, D. (2001): 'Rural Diversification: What Hope for the Poor?', Background Paper, Overseas Development Institute.

Start, D. and C. Johnson. (2004): 'Livelihood Options? The Political Economy of Access, Opportunity and Diversification' Working Paper No. 233, Overseas Development Institute, London (UK).

Vasudevappa C. and Seenappa D., 2002. Literature Review of Shrimp Farming in India. Individual Partner Report for the Project: Policy Research for Sustainable Shrimp Farming in Asia. European Commission INCO-DEV Project PORESSFA No. IC4-2001-10042, CEMARE University of Portsmouth UK and FRS University of Agricultural Sciences, Bangalore – India, pp. 48 + Annexures.

10
Fiscal Decentralization under Left Regime in West Bengal

Manik Bhattacharya

Introduction

Fiscal decentralization is the fiscal empowerment of lower tiers of government which involves the devolution of taxing and spending powers along with the arrangements for rectifying mismatches in resources and responsibilities (Fukasaku and De Mello: 1999; Tanzi: 1996; and Oommen: 2004). Much before the 73rd Constitutional Amendment in 1993 (providing decentralization of authority to local governments in respect of development of rural India), an initiative towards the same was witnessed in West Bengal since 1978 with the introduction of effective Panchayati Raj in a democratic set-up through three-tier elections at five years interval. Based on the secondary sources of information and ground level reality this study wants to explore the experience of fiscal decentralization of West Bengal.

There has been a world-wide interest in decentralization of government in all parts of the world. Both developed and developing countries recuperate from Central Governments' monopoly of decision-making power through emphasizing decentralized system. Developing countries are turning to decentralization to escape from the traps of ineffective and inefficient governance, macro-economic instability, and inadequate economic growth (Bird and Vaillancourt, 1999). Throughout post-communist Central and Eastern Europe, decentralization of the state was the direct result of the transition from socialist system to market economy and democracy (Bird, Ebel, and Wallich, 1995). In Latin America, the origin of decentralization is the political pressure from the people for democratization (Rojas, 1999). In Africa, decentralization has served as a path to national unity (World Bank, 1999).

The performance of fiscal decentralization in India has not been satisfactory compared with the international standard (Oommen: 2006). Among the Indian States the experience of fiscal decentralization of the State of Kerala is remarkable where 35 per cent of plan expenditure had been devolved to *Panchayati Raj Institutions* (PRIs) in 1996-2001. The study of Oommen (2006) based on 15 Indian States including West Bengal reveals that the financial decentralization scenario is far from satisfactory. But, the per capita Own Source Revenue (OSR) of the *Gram Panchayat* and *Panchayat Samiti* has increased steadily during the Tenth Plan period. Based on the primary field survey this study focuses on interrelation between rural development and effectiveness of fiscal decentralization.

I. Methodological Issues

The sources of *Panchayat* finance in India are under following heads: (i) Own Sources of Revenue (OSR), i.e., tax and non-tax revenue such as fees and fines, user charges for services and rent from property; (ii) Shared taxes that are collected by the States with a share of the proceeds being disbursed among the local bodies of the State; (iii) grants from the State/Central Government (tied or untied). The progress towards fiscal decentralization of the *Panchayats* can be understood on the basis of the indicators Revenue Autonomy (RA) or Revenue Dependency (RD).

To understand the experience of fiscal decentralization of West Bengal we will go through the Panchayat finance data of West Bengal during the Tenth Plan period. On the basis of above indicators (per capita OSR, RA and RD) we will explore the scenario of fiscal decentralization of this State. To get ground level reality we have collected some field level data related to fiscal decentralization (three financial years from 2003-4) from two Panchayats of the district Bankura—one from Koalpara Gram Panchayat (in the advanced Block Kotulpur) and the other from Gopalpur Gram Panchayat (in the backward Block Hirbandh).

From the district Bankura we have identified two sample Blocks on the basis of some development variables (Kotulpur as the most advanced Block and Hirbandh as the most backward Block).

II. Fiscal Decentralization of Panchayati Raj Institutions (PRIs) in West Bengal

The key to effective functioning of the Panchayats lies in their ability to mobilize resources of their own. Requiring Panchayats to mobilize their own revenues strengthens the link between revenue and expenditure decisions, which is extremely important to promote both efficiency and accountability in the provision of services by them. In the State of West Bengal only the *Gram Panchayats* of the State have powers of taxation and the upper two tiers can collect non-tax revenue as per their bye-laws to be framed on the basis of the provisions of the State Panchayat Act. The most important sources of revenue of the Gram Panchayats are the property tax. Besides the tax revenue, non-tax revenue through mobilization of tolls, rates, fees, etc., has been proved to be a vital source of resource mobilization for Gram Panchayats, Panchayat Samiti and Zilla Parishads. The year-wise collection of Own Source Revenue (OSR) by the Panchayats of the State of West Bengal during the Tenth Plan period is shown in Table 10.1.

Table 10.1: Total Collection of OSR by the Panchayats During the Tenth Plan.

(Rs.in crores)

Year	Gram Panchayat			Panchayat Samiti	Zilla Parishad	All Tiers
	Tax	Non- Tax	Total			
2002-03	13.65	11.25	24.9	6.66	9.61	41.17
2003-04	15.61	17.98	33.59	8.25	10.07	51.91
2004-05	16.9	21.07	37.97	12.68	13.78	64.43
2005-06	20.2	25.42	45.62	15.44	13.03	74.09
2006-07	22.79	31.85	54.65	17.61	28.01	100.27

Source: State Institute of Panchayat and Rural Development, West Bengal.

Table 10.1 explores the fact that the OSR of all tiers of PRI bodies of the State was a little more than Rs. 41 crore only in 2002-03 and it has increased by around two and a half times in next four years. The OSR of the Gram Panchayat and Panchayat Samiti have been increased steadily during the Tenth Plan period.

Per capita OSR of all the three tiers in different districts during the Tenth Plan period is shown in Table 10.2. Information shows that there has been wide variation in per capita collection of revenue across the districts as well as within a particular district. In 2002-03 it ranges 2 in Purulia district to 13.48 in Hooghly, followed by Burdwan, 13.34. The same variation in 2006-07 was between 4.65 in Purulia to 32.42 in Burdwan. Due to continuous advocacy and introduction of the reward scheme there has been a general increase in awareness and drive for realizing higher revenue for their own development.

As a result collection of per capita OSR in West Bengal increases sharply and steadily from 7.13 in 2002-03 to 17.36 in 2006-07. All the districts also followed the same trend.

Table 10.2: Per Capita OSR of Different Districts during the Last Five Years

(in Rs.)

Districts	*2002-03*	*2003-04*	*2004-05*	*2005-06*	*2006-07*
Cooch Behar	4.74	6.09	8.44	11.13	12.45
Jalpaiguri	6.2	9.12	8.77	11.93	23.49
Darjeeling	4.84	6.06	10.17	14.46	18.26
Uttar Dinajpur	3.48	4.37	5.26	5.2	8.36
Dakshin Dinajpur	7.66	6.17	12.49	13.75	11.44
Malda	6.23	5.64	13.52	9.71	17.06
Murshidabad	5.2	4.67	6.52	8.11	7.63
Nadia	6.65	6.49	8.2	9.43	12.77
North 24-Parganas	7.23	6.59	9.78	12.06	16.91
South 24-Parganas	4.71	5.03	8.27	8.16	11.64
Howrah	10.29	12.02	13.57	17.9	28.22
Hooghly	13.48	16.96	21.83	22.18	25.85
East Medinipur	11.03	9.65	7.27	10.6	14.62
West Medinipur	4.89	6.38	11.43	14.35	24.64
Bankura	3.17	8.73	11.05	14.12	22.4
Purulia	2.00	1.54	6.07	1.91	4.65
Burdwan	13.34	19.34	23.25	26.84	32.42
Birbhum	7.67	10.62	13.25	14.08	18.46
West Bengal	7.13	8.4	11.11	12.61	17.36

Source: State Institute of Panchayat and Rural Development, West Bengal.

Though per capita own source revenue increases over the year, the dependency of the Panchayats on the higher level of governments' remains as earlier to meet their expenditure needs. This is not at all a healthy trend. In other words Revenue Autonomy (RA) of the Panchayats does not increase over the period of time (Table 10.3). In Table 10.3 the transfer of funds from State and Central Government sources as well as the own source revenue is displayed. It is revealed that the own source revenue increases from 41.17 crore in 2002-03 to 100.27 crore in 2006-07. However, it constitutes a tiny part of total revenue as measured in column 11 as revenue autonomy. The latter ranges from 3.55 per cent to 5.12 per cent and remains stagnant over the years. This is because the revenue from sources other than OSR increases steeply over the years. For example total funds from State budget increases from 464.13 crore in 2002-03 to 1233.95 crore in 2006-07. Also the Central's share about doubled during the period from 367.08 crore to 789.86 crore.

III. Ground Level Reality of Fiscal Decentralization

To realize the experience of fiscal decentralization we have collected some field level data related to fiscal decentralization from two Panchayats of the district Bankura—one from Koalpara Gram Panchayat (in the advanced Block Kotulpur) and the other from Gopalpur Gram Panchayat (in the backward Block Hirbandh).

The revenue autonomy and revenue dependency of the two Panchayats are depicted in the Table 10.4. Table 10.4 also furnishes some vital information of total revenue, per capita total revenue and per capita own source revenue for three successive years from 2003-04. It is observed that the per capita OSR of the Koalpara Gram Panchayat shows higher values than the State per capita OSR of the Panchayats in these three successive years. For example, the per capita OSR of the Panchayats of West Bengal in 2003-04 was Rs. 8.4, Rs. 11.11 in 2004-5 and Rs. 12.6 in 2005-06. The same values for the Koalpara Panchayat are Rs.12.48 in 2003-04, Rs. 27.74 in 2004-05 and Rs. 23.04 in 2005-06. But the Gopalpur Panchayat registers below the State average, the per capita OSR of the Gopalpur Panchayat for these three successive years are Rs. 1.86, Rs. 3.27 and Rs. 3.58.

Table 10.3: Transfer of Fund to the Panchayats, Total Revenue and Revenue Autonomy during Tenth Plan Period

(Rs. in Crore)

Year	Salary Grants by the State	Grants by the State including 2nd SFC Grant	State Share of Centrally Sponsored Schemes (CSS)	ACA and Central Finance Commission Grants	Total Fund (State Budget)	Central Share of CSS Direct to PRIs	Grand Total	OSR (All Tiers)	Total Revenue	RA
2002-03	147.84	94.38	144.59	77.32	464.13	367.08	831.21	41.17	872.38	4.72
2003-04	183.93	161.75	142.03	72.07	559.78	403.07	962.85	51.91	1014.76	5.12
2004-05	193.39	200.61	161.62	124.97	680.59	530.79	1211.38	64.43	1275.81	5.05
2005-06	192.43	425.23	273.77	174.79	1,066.22	948.99	2015.21	74.09	2089.30	3.55
2006-07	210.79	317.71	302.9	402.55	1233.95	789.86	2023.81	100.27	2124.08	4.72

Source: State Institute of Panchayat and Rural Development, West Bengal and Editor's Calculation.

However, the region-wise difference in value is not remarkable for per capita total revenue. For example, in the time period from 2003-04 to 2005-6, the per capita total revenue of the Koalpara Panchayat increased from Rs. 125.64 to Rs. 167.95 whereas, in Gopalpur Panchayat it increased from Rs. 139.19 to Rs. 151.51. Therefore, both the per capita OSR and per capita total revenue of these two Panchayats increased over time.

One of the most important indicators of fiscal decentralization is Revenue Autonomy (and the reverse is the Revenue Dependency). The RA of the Koalpara Panchayat is 9.33 in 2003-04, 20.32 in 2004-05 and 13.72 in 2005-06 and the same for the Gopalpur Panchayat is 1.34 in 2003-04, 2.29 in 2004-05 and 2.36 in 2005-06. Besides, the RA values of Koalpara Panchayat show the higher values than the State level RA. RA of West Bengal Panchayats is 5.12 in 2003-04, 5.05 in 2004-05 and 3.55 in 2005-06. Corroborating the low increasing trend of RA, the decrease of RD of Gopalpur Panchayat over the time period remained insignificant.

We now highlight the trend of another indicator, the Financial Autonomy (share of own fund in revenue expenditure). According to the Study of Oommen (2006), the FA of West Bengal has increased marginally from 16.89 per cent to 17.64 during the time period 1998-99 to 2002-03. However, in the time period 2003-04 to 2005-06 in the Koalpara Panchayat the same value increases from 11.53 per cent to 20 per cent. Though, in the same time period increase in the value of FA was much low in the Gopalpur Panchayat.

In this section we have already depicted that the RA of the Panchayats of the advanced Block is 7.43 times of the RA of the Panchayat of the backward Block in 2003-04. In 2004-5 and 2005-6 the RA of Koalpara Gram Panchayat is 8.89 times and 5.81 times more than the RA of Gopalpur Panchayat respectively. Similarly, the FA of Koalpara Gram Panchayat is 10 times that of FA of Gopalpur Panchayat.

Therefore, from the above information it can be said that there is a positive association between development and effectiveness of fiscal decentralization. Since the values of the RA and FA depend on the collection of the OSR, the higher the values of OSR the higher will be the values of RA and FA keeping constant of grants of the higher level of governments and expenditure of the Panchayats. In the advanced area the scope of the collection of OSR is high comparing to the backward region.

Table.10.4: Revenue Autonomy and Revenue Dependency of the Panchayats

Year	*Revenue from own sources*	*Grants*	*Total Income*	*Per Capita Own Revenue*	*Per Capita Total Revenue*	*Revenue Autonomy*	*Revenue Dependency*
Advanced Region (Koalpara Gram Panchayat)							
2003-04	249294.00	2261063.74	2510357.74	12.48	125.64	9.93	90.07
2004-05	560203.04	2197140.13	2757343.17	27.74	136.52	20.32	79.68
2005-06	467629.53	2941235.67	3408865.20	23.04	167.95	13.72	86.28
Backward Region (Gopalpur Gram Panchayat)							
2003-04	24633.16	1819597.50	1844230.66	1.86	139.19	1.34	98.66
2004-05	43544.66	1861974.00	1905518.66	3.27	142.95	2.29	97.71
2005-06	47798.16	1976881.00	2024679.16	3.58	151.51	2.36	97.64

Table 10.5: Financial Autonomy of the Panchayats

Year	*Own Revenue*	*Total Expenditure*	*Financial Autonomy*
Advanced Region (Kotulpur Gram Panchayat)			
2003-04	249294.00	2161332.50	11.53
2004-05	560203.04	2338240.00	23.96
2005-06	467629.53	2338240.00	20.00
Backward Region (Gopalpur Gram Panchayat)			
2003-04	24633.16	1710768.00	1.44
2004-05	43544.66	1706805.00	2.55
2005-06	47798.16	1843079.00	2.59

IV. Conclusion

From this study it can be concluded that the West Bengal rural local governance has raised per capita own source revenue to a significant extent, though the RA is not very significant precisely because of the fact that the tax structure in India is not at all decentralized, the need of the hour is to raise the tax base of Panchayats and to give more fiscal and financial autonomy to the Panchayats. It can also be said from this study that there is a positive association between development and effectiveness of fiscal decentralization. It can be recommended that the Panchayats can generate own source revenue through proper implementation of the different schemes. In this context, National Rural Employment Generation Scheme (NREGS) can play a vital role. This scheme will strengthen the process of rural development in two ways. Firstly, the rural unemployed persons will get jobs under this scheme and this will help to eradicate poverty in the rural areas. Secondly, Panchayats can use the manpower for plantation of banana trees and other fruits and selling these they can earn revenue. Panchayats can use this manpower in any other programmes.

REFERENCES

Bird, Richard M.; and Francois Vaillancourt. Fiscal Decentralization in Developing Countries: An Overview. In Richard M. Bird and Francois Vaillancourt, (eds.). Fiscal Decentralization in Developing Countries. Cambridge: Cambridge University Press, 1999.

Bird, Robert D. Ebel and Christine I. Wallich. (eds.) Decentralization of the Socialist State. Washington DC: World Bank, 1995.

Brennan, G., and J. Buchanan. The Power to Tax: Analytical Foundations of a Fiscal Constitution. Cambridge: Cambridge University Press, 1980.

Chitlangi, B.M. and Amarendra Kumar Tiwari (1998), July-Dec. "Financial Administration of Panchayati Raj Institutions in Rajasthan", *Prashasnika,* 25(2), 65-73.

Davoodi, Hamid, and Heng-fu Zou. Fiscal Decentralization and Economic Growth: A Cross-Country Study. *Journal of Urban Economics,* 43 (1998): 244-257.

Ehdaie, J. Fiscal Decentralization and the Size of Government: An Extension with Evidence from Cross-Country Data. Washington DC: World Bank, 1994. Policy Research Working Paper No. 1387.

Fukasaku, K., and L.R. deMello. Fiscal Decentralization and Macroeconomic Stability: The Experience of Large Developing and Transition Economies. In K. Fukasaku and R. Hausmann, (eds.) Democracy, Decentralization and Deficits in Latin America. Paris: OECD, 1998.

Oates, Wallace E. Fiscal Federalism. New York: Searching for Leviathan: An Empirical Study. *American Economic Review,* 75 (1985), 748-757.

Oommen, M.A. (1998), *"Devolution of Resources to Rural Local Bodies: A Comparative Study of Select State Finance Commission Reports"*, ISS Occasional Paper Series.

Oommen, M A (2004), 'Fiscal Decentralisation in Kerala' in Geeta Sethi (ed), *Fiscal Decentralisation to Rural Governments in India,* Oxford University Press.

Oommen, MA. (2006), "Fiscal Decentralization to the Sub-State Level Governments", *Economic and Political Weekly,* March 11, pp. 897-903.

Robert D. Ebel and Serdar Yilmaz (2002), "On the Measurement and Impact of Fiscal Decentralization", Policy Research Working Paper 2809, The World Bank, World Bank Institute Economic Policy and Poverty Reduction Division.

Singh, S.K. (1999), *Panchayati Raj Finances in Uttar Pradesh.* Occasional Paper, Hyderabad: NIRD.

Tarnzi, Vito (1996), Fiscal Federalism and Decentralization: A Review of Some Efficiency and Macroeconomic Aspects. Annual World Bank Conference on Development Economics, 1995. World Bank, Washington DC, 295-316.

Vithal, C.P. (1997), Aspects of Panchayat Finances: An Analysis of Panchayat Acts. *Journal of Rural Development,* 16(1), 123-134.

Vithal, C.P. and M. Sarumathi. (1996), Panchayati Raj Finances in Andhra Pradesh and Karnataka: An Analysis. *Journal of Rural Development,* 15(2), 215-248.

World Bank. World Development Report 1997: The State in a Changing World. New York: Oxford University Press, 1997.

_______World Development Report 1999/2000: Entering the 21st Century. New York: Oxford University Press, 2000.

Xie, Danyang, Heng-fu Zou, and Hamid Davoodi (1999), "Fiscal Decentralization and Economic Growth in the United States," *Journal of Urban Economics*, Vol. 45, pp. 228-239.

Zhang, Tao, and Heng-fu Zou. 1998. "Fiscal Decentralization, Public Spending and Economic Growth in China." *Journal of Public Economics* 67: 221-40.

11

Changing Patterns in Public Health Care Investments in Rural India

A Study of Kerala, Tamil Nadu and West Bengal

Indranil Mukhopadhyay

Introduction

Two main pillars of Economic Reforms, which are really fundamental to national and State level policy making in India are macro-economic stabilization policies championed by the IMF and Structural Adjustment Programme advocated by the World Bank. Both these sets of policies are derived from the same theoretical understanding that state interventions necessarily brings in inefficiency, whereas the market is the most efficient institution. However, *modus operandi* differs. IMF prescriptions mainly talk about macro-economic restructuring through curbs in fiscal deficits to restore Balance of Payment which essentially boils down to cutting public expenditure. SAPs are sector specific reforms intended to infuse market principles in areas where there is considerable presence of state, through various measures like user charges, contracting out of services, shifting from direct provisioning to insurance like mechanisms. State level policies are guided and often bound by the parameters set by neo-liberal reforms, and space for independent policy-making remains limited only within the set parameters. Here, we have attempted to study the impact of both these policy interventions on public policies and financing of health, especially in the rural areas.

States play a significant role in provisioning health services in India. As laid out in the Constitution, major responsibilities of creating, maintaining and managing health institutions rest with the States. The Centre's role remains limited to family planning, health policy making and research. Centre and States jointly provide public health services and take care of medical education. More than two-third of the responsibility in spending is done by the States and remaining one-third is carried out by the Centre. We have observed significant inter-State variations in the level of spending, even though the overall level is very low in the country.

Existing literature on public financing of health in India throw light on magnitude of public spending on health, priority accorded to health in overall budgets of governments. However, there are only few studies which have really looked at disaggregated patterns on spending. Studies done by Reddy and Selvaraju (1994)[1], Duggal (1989)[2] and Tulasidhar (1992)[3] were crucial in this regard. These studies threw light on quality of health financing in the country and provided insight for further improvement. Unfortunately, most of these studies have been carried out in early 1990s and do not capture the trends after the reforms were initiated. We have also reviewed some important studies, carried out later, which have looked at spending patterns on health during 1990s. Studies done by Mahendra Dev and Mooij (2002)[4] and others highlight the decline in priority on health during reforms period. The other set of studies, mainly by Mahal[5] and Berman[6] show the increasing role of private spending in financing and skewedness of public subsidy. However, most of these studies do not look at adequate details of spending pattern to show how decline in spending in 1990s has affected quality of service provisioning. National Health Accounts have provided a detailed picture of the overall magnitude of spending and share of various financing agents and some crucial disaggregation at the national level. However, the kind of depth that is required to make meaningful observations regarding quality of health service provisioning was beyond the scope. NHA also did not look at the time trends and limited the analysis to certain time points.

Here we focus on expenditure on health care incurred by three State governments: Kerala, Tamil Nadu and West Bengal. The three sample States are also quite diverse not only because of their diverse health outcomes but also due to their spending levels and priorities. For instance, Kerala has achieved health outcomes comparable to many developed countries. Tamil Nadu and West Bengal have achieved considerable progress in some health outcomes in last three decades but lags behind Kerala in many respects. The common thread that binds them is that in some period of history these States have shown considerable commitments in social sector spending including health.

International Comparisons

Public Spending on health in India is among the lowest in the world, when compared in terms of share in GDP and per capita spending. There were only seven countries in the world (Myanmar, Guiana, Lao PDR, Pakistan, Azerbaijan, Cote d'Ivore, Singapore) which spent lesser proportion of GDP on health in 2007[7]. Some developing countries like Brazil, Chile, Costa Rica, Cuba, Colombia, Thailand, Malaysia, South Africa, which have made significant efforts in recent history towards provisioning of

Table 11.1: International Comparison of Government Expenditure on Health (2000- 2007)

	*General govt. expenditure on health as % of GDP**		*General govt. expenditure on health as % of total expenditure on health*		*Per capita govt. expenditure on health (PPP int. $)*	
	2000	*2007*	*2000*	*2007*	*2000*	*2007*
Brazil	2.9	3.5	40.0	41.6	202	348
Chile	3.4	3.6	52.1	58.7	320	507
China	1.8	1.9	38.7	44.7	42	104
Colombia	5.5	5.1	80.9	84.2	314	435
Costa Rica	5.0	5.9	76.8	72.9	360	656
Cuba	6.1	9.9	90.9	95.5	341	875
India	1.1	1.1	24.5	26.2	16	29
Malaysia	1.7	2.0	52.4	44.4	159	268
South Africa	3.4	3.6	40.5	41.4	223	340
Sri Lanka	1.8	2.0	47.9	47.5	49	85
Thailand	1.9	2.7	56.1	73.2	89	209
South-East Asia Region	1.2	1.3	31.2	36.9	18	36
Low income	1.8	2.2	37.6	41.9	14	28
Lower middle income	1.6	1.8	37.0	42.4	35	76

Source: World Health Statistics, 2010.
*Derived from WHS.

universal access to health, spend much higher proportions of GDP on health. Governments in neighbouring countries like Sri Lanka, China, and Thailand could mobilise more resources towards health than what was done in India. Per capita public investment on health, is almost at the same level with the average of the low income countries (LICs) and much lower than the low middle income countries (LMICs).

The above discussion clearly points out towards the essentiality of public investment in ensuring universal health care and draws home the point that the current level of spending in India is clearly unacceptable. Countries like Brazil, Thailand, and South Africa which have recently attempted to universalize have stepped up public spending on health to 3-5 per cent of GDP. However, it should be noted here that the increase in investment has not been sudden in many cases and taken up gradually.

State Level Trends

Health expenditure as a share of Net State Domestic Product is a good measure of trend in spending. Let us consider the expenditure by the State governments, which include Grants in Aid (GiA) from the Centre[8]. All-State average spending has remained less than 1 per cent of Net State Domestic Product during the entire period under consideration (Figure 11.1). For instance,

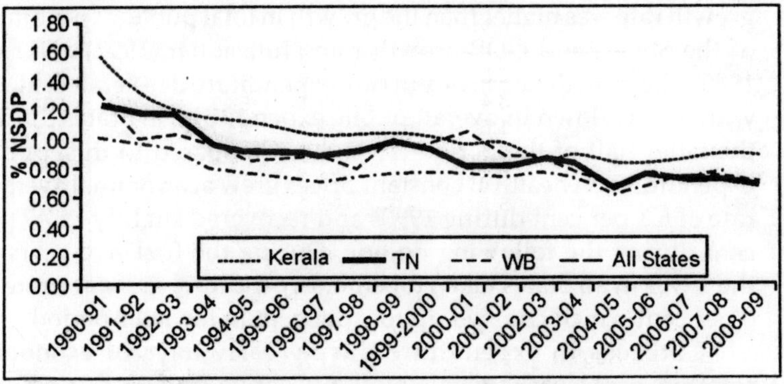

Source: Public Expenditure Data is from RBI (2010), "State Finances: A Study of Budgets". NSDP figures are from CSO.

Fig. 11.1: Public Expenditure on Health Services by States as per cent of NSDP

in Kerala, the share of public spending in GDP fell from 1.57 per cent in 1990-91 to 0.84 per cent in 2002-03 and remained almost at the same level for the remaining period. Similar kinds of decline could be observed in case of Tamil Nadu and West Bengal. The all India average level of spending was much lower than these States to start with, and fell down further by mid 1990s. The all India average spending remained almost at the same level for the remaining period of time. In case of Tamil Nadu and Kerala we observe continuous decline in share of health expenditure in NSDP. There was some sort of marginal reversal during the early 2000s in West Bengal, but since then there was a steep decline.

It must be noted here that the three States were spending significantly higher amount than the other States, which got reflected in their share of health spending in NSDP being higher. However, Tamil Nadu and West Bengal have gradually reached a lower level of spending compared to national average, whereas Kerala remains little ahead. Apart from all other things, what this convergence level of spending shows is that the limited independent policy space which was earlier available to States got further reduced in the reforms era.

Growth in Expenditure

During 1975-89, States' total expenditure on health care at constant prices grew at an impressive rate of 9.2 per cent per annum. This growth rate was higher than the growth in total public expenditure of the States, and GDP growth rate (Tulasidhar, 1992)[9]. During 1980s, the growth rate in health care expenditure decelerated, along with a slow down in overall public expenditure, in States during the latter half of the period (1982-89). Compared to this, public expenditure on health at constant prices grew at an annual average rate of 6.1 per cent during 1990s and recovered slightly to 7.7 per cent during the following decade. During the first five years of the 1990s in all States taken together expenditure grew at a rate of 6 per cent which climbed up to 7 per cent in the later period.

Cutbacks in expenditure during early days of economic reforms, was clearly visible by the negative growth during that period. However, there was a sudden jump in spending during latter half of the decade: a growth of 14.8 per cent was observed. This fell down to 3.8 per cent in early 2000s. As it is the case with the national trends, both in Kerala and Tamil Nadu growth rates were higher in 2000s, compared to 1990s. West Bengal however defies the trend as health expenditure grew at higher rate in the 1990s compared to 2000s. In fact, health expenditure almost stagnated in the 2000s in West Bengal. It would be important for our analysis to find out the causes of such stagnation.

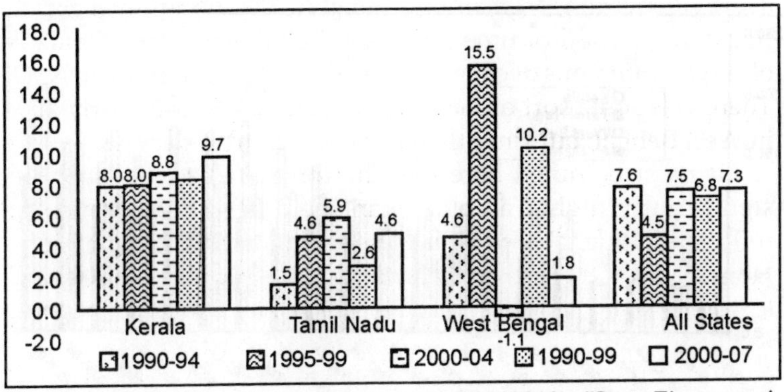

Source: Public expenditure data is from RBI (2010), "State Finances: A Study of Budgets".

Fig. 11.2: Growth Rate in Health Expenditure (at constant prices)

Per Capita Expenditure

With population growth the need for greater health care also increases. It is important that one takes out the impact of population growth from expenditure trends. It would be worthwhile here to look at trends in per capita expenditure. Per capita expenditure on health was Rs. 27 in 1974-75. By 1991-92 it went up to Rs. 62 at 1980-81 prices (Figure 11.3). It hovered around that level during entire first half of the 1990s and picked up during the later period. During 2006-07 per capita expenditure on health went up to Rs. 131. During the period of 1974-75 to 1989-90 per capita expenditure increased at a rate of 6.8 per cent per annum (Reddy, 1994).[10] Compared to this, between 1991-92 and 1999-2000, per capita expenditure increased only at a rate of 4.8 per cent. During the subsequent decade per capita expenditure grew at a rate of 5.9 per cent. Clearly the growth rate was higher during pre-reform days compared to the reform period.

All the States do not have similar levels of per capita

expenditure on health. From Figure 11.3, it can be observed that Kerala had high levels of per capita expenditure during the pre-reform decades. But by the early 1990s, per capita expenditure in Tamil Nadu was higher compared to other States under consideration. Similarly, West Bengal showed higher per capita expenditure during latter half of the 1990s.

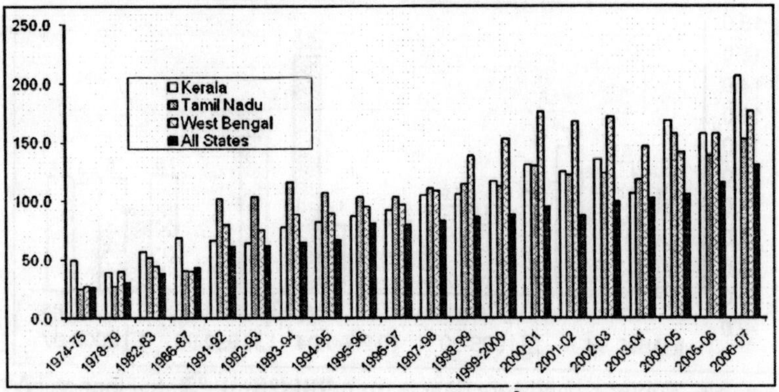

Source: Author's calculation based on Expenditure data from RBI, State Finances, Finance Accounts of States and Reddy (1994)

Fig. 11.3: Per Capita Expenditure on Health (at constant prices)

Revenue and Capital Expenditure

Within the health sector, government spends on different items. It pays salaries to health personnel, it may provide drugs to the patients, conduct immunisation programmes, it builds hospitals, buys equipments, privatizes some hospitals, etc. These expenditures can be demarcated into two distinct categories. In some of these activities governments asset position changes and in some it does not. For instance if the government builds a new hospital or health centre, it adds to the asset base of the government. Such items are called **'capital expenditure'.** Paying salaries or distributing drugs do not affect government's asset position. These items are classified as **'revenue expenditure'.** Revenue expenditures are generally meant for running the systems, like paying salaries, rents, maintenance charges, drugs and consumables. As government creates new assets through capital expenditure it needs support systems to maintain those assets and hence need to incur revenue expenditure. A proper balance between revenue and capital expenditure is crucial for the health sector to meet increasing need for health services. It has to be noted, however, that expenses in the nature of capital spending does always get reflected in case of Centrally Sponsored Schemes, which bypass State budgets. Any infrastructure built through CSS, is booked as revenue in Centre's account as the asset created is owned by the States.

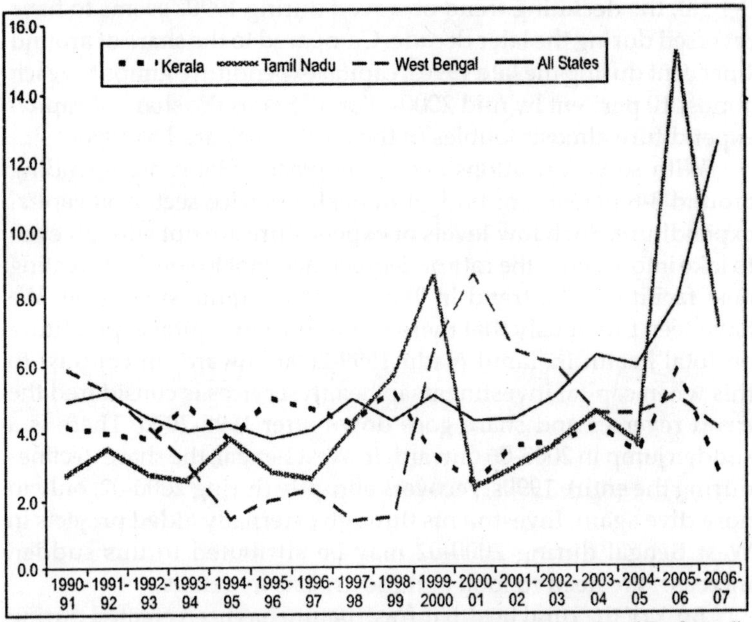

Source: Calculated from RBI (2010), "State Finances: A Study of Budgets".

Fig. 11.4: Share of Capital Expenditure in Health Budget (%) (Capital expenditure on MPH & FW as percentage of total expenditure)

It is also important to note that revenue expenditures are downward sticky, meaning that it is not easy to reduce revenue expenditures once they are made. For instance, salaries in government set-up in India cannot be easily reduced, because of the nature of employment and organized workers' movements. In contrast to this, capital expenditures are mostly one time in nature and decisions to raise capital expenditure are discretionary in nature, often resultant of conscious policy decisions.

The most important observation that we could make from Figure 11.4 is that in all the three study States, share of capital expenditure remained stagnant at less than 5 per cent of total health budget for the entire 1990s. The levels are less than half of what was prevailing at all the States. The share is found to increase in the later decade. In Kerala, we see the prevalence of low levels of capital expenditure in the entire period ot two decades. In West Bengal, the declining trend observed during 1990s seems to have reversed during the later decade. Compared to the share of around 1 per cent during the late 1990s, capital expenditure jumps to reach almost 10 per cent by mid 2000s. For all States the share of capital expenditure almost doubles in the 2000s compared to 1990s.

With some variations across the years, States are spending around 3-6 per cent of budget of health service sector on capital expenditure. Such low levels of expenditure are not enough even to take into account the rate of depreciation, not to speak of creating new facilities. The trend in Tamil Nadu is quite surprising. We have seen previously that there was a spurt in capital expenditure on total health in Tamil Nadu 1999-2000 onward. In contrast to this when capital investments in health services is considered the trend reverses and share goes down after 1999-2000. There is a sudden jump in 2005-06 onward. In West Bengal, the share declines during the entire 1990s, recovers abruptly during 2000-02, only to nose dive again. Investments through externally aided projects in West Bengal during 2000-02 may be attributed to this sudden increase. We need to look at these aspects in details.

Bulk of the rural health infrastructure has been created during 1980s. Since then we see a disturbing stagnation. Between Sixth and Seventh Plans there was a 60 per cent growth of Sub-Centres, PHCs and CHCs taken together. But since then number of PHCs, SCs and CHCs have grown by only 16.3 per cent. In Kerala, the corresponding growth rate was 145 per cent between Sixth and Seventh Plan, but for the rest of the period there is a decline in actual number. Similarly, for TN there was 60 per cent growth in 1980s but since then facilities have grown only by 1 per cent. In WB, number of facilities grew by 26 per cent during Sixth and Seventh Plan period and in the subsequent period also there is a growth of 26 per cent. However, most of this growth is during Tenth Plan and that too in a number of SCs. In fact during the last two decades, total number of PHCs and CHCs has gone down by

6 per cent in the State. This is in contrast to other States, which have converted many SCs into PHCs and PHCs into CHCs and thus number of PHCs and CHCs have increased (GoI, 2010).[11] It may well be the case that some of the CHCs have been upgraded to rural hospitals and sub-divisional hospitals. Figure 11.5 shows the trend in population served per government bed. Both in Kerala and Tamil Nadu, there is a sudden jump in population served per bed between 1994 and 2005. However, in case of West Bengal, there is a decline in the ratio. This is definitely a sign of improvement and may serve as an explanation why there is high dependence on government hospitals in cases of hospitalisation in the State. According to estimates by Health Information of India, nationally there is a gradual decline in number of beds per lakh population.

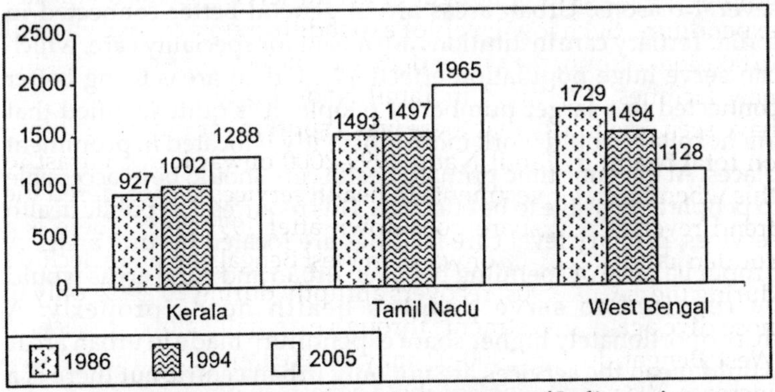

Source: Data on bed is from Health Information of India, various years, Population data is from Census population projection.

Fig. 11.5: Population Served per Government Bed

There are huge gaps in required health institutions and that are in position in government sector. However, both Kerala and TN has more PHCs and CHCs against the Indian Public Health Standard (IPHS). The gap is quite high in case of WB. There is a shortage of 1084 PHCs and 150 CHCs in WB. This gap can be fulfilled only through substantial jump in capital expenditure.

Rural-Urban Dichotomies in Spending: One of the dichotomies in the delivery of health services in the country is that most of the hospitals and institutions of health service delivery are located in urban areas whereas most of the people live in rural parts of the country. Even the doctors are mostly located in urban areas. Several authors have analysed the reasons of urban centric health service development in the country (Banerjee, 1985; Qadeer, 2001).[12,13] When India became a signatory to Alma Ata Declaration, the Union Government pledged to change the situation, lots of emphasis was given to set-up rural health infrastructure and gear up public health systems to cater to the needs of the rural people. Emphasis on water supply, sanitation, setting up of PHCs and sub-centres, etc., were steps in that direction. To know how much of it could be actually realized could be found out if, the total spending is disaggregated according to rural-urban differences.

It has to be kept in mind that the issue of rural-urban disaggregation of spending has certain issues about access and methodology. Firstly, let us look at the issue of access. Having a big hospital in a city makes quite some sense. This is because of several reasons. Urban areas are in general better connected in India. Tertiary care institutions are meant for speciality care, which can serve huge population effectively. Urban areas being better connected to a larger number of people, it is quite justified that big hospitals would work more efficiently if located in prominent places. At the same time primary health care should be as accessible to people as possible to be effective. This requires that public health services, primary level care facilities are located in rural areas. A proper balance of spending between urban and rural areas would be required to serve people's health needs properly. A disproportionately higher share expenditure made in urban areas would mean the services are not only urban centric but there is a negligence on public health and primary level care services.

Let us now look at the methodological limitations in this exercise. Certain items in the budget are clearly demarcated between rural and urban areas. For instance, rural family welfare services, programmes for tribal areas, are clearly meant for rural areas. Similarly, medical college hospitals, urban FW services, administrative services are located in urban areas. But not all of them are clearly distinguishable. For instance, family planning beneficiaries, public health services are the ones which are not clearly distinguishable. We have adopted different methodologies to derive the rural-urban break-ups of these non-distinguishable items. For the family planning beneficiaries, we have taken rural urban break-ups of beneficiaries of different family planning services. Similarly, for public health services and maternal health services we take the share of rural populations in the respective States. Here we essentially assume that the public health services are evenly distributed across rural and urban population, which is far from reality as most of these services would also be relatively urban centric. Due to unavailability of better data we would adopt this methodology.

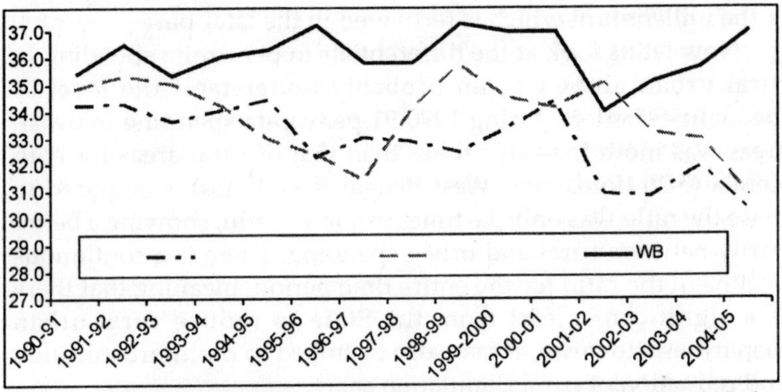

Source: Detailed Demand for Grants, State Budget, Kerala, Tamil Nadu and West Bengal, various years.

Fig. 11.6: Share of Expenditure on Rural Areas in Total Health Budget of States

Let us first take the share of expenditure in rural areas as a share of total expenditure derived by the above methodology. We consider the time period from 1990-91 to 2004-05. To start with, all the three States have almost similar shares in rural expenditure—a little more than one-third. If we look at the share of rural population in 1990-91, we find huge disparities in spending. In Kerala, although not strictly as germane as in the other States, almost three quarters of population (74%) lived in rural areas in 1990-91. In Tamil Nadu and West Bengal the shares are two-third and 72 per cent respectively. By the end of 2004-05, there is no significant decline in rural population share in Kerala, but expenditure on rural areas declines to 30 per cent. In Tamil Nadu, share in rural population declined to little more than half (52%), whereas share in spending goes down to 31 per cent. In case of West Bengal, there is marginal increase in share of rural expenditure (35%) when the population share of rural area remains the same. In Kerala, share in rural expenditure remains stable during early 1990s, but falls subsequently, recovers during late 1990s only to fall down during the later period. In Tamil Nadu, we could observe a continuous decline in the share of rural expenditure till 1997-98, since then it rises for two consecutive years but falls subsequently. In contrast to Tamil Nadu share of rural expenditure in West Bengal increases marginally during most part of the 1990s, however, there is a sudden fall during early years of the millennium which is recovered in the later part.

Now let us look at the differentials in per capita spending in rural urban areas we can probably understand the level of inequalities better. During 1990-91 per capita spending in urban areas was more than five times than that of rural areas for both Kerala (5.26 times) and West Bengal (5.17 times). Compared to these the ratio was only 3.6 times in Tamil Nadu, showing a better parity between rural and urban spending. There is a continuous decline in the ratio for the entire time period, meaning that there is a significant effort from the State to reduce rural-urban disparities. However, it may also be linked to rapid urbanization and reduction of rural population share.

Due to increasing urbanization population residing in rural areas has reduced in share. The other important pattern that has emerged is that the attention for family planning initiatives have also spread into rural areas compared to urban belts. These might contribute to decreasing rural-urban disparities in spending. One of the important proxy variables for health infrastructure can be

Table 11.2: Rural-Urban Disparities in Bed-Population Ratio

		Population served per bed			*Rural/Urban Ratio*
		Rural	*Urban*	*Total*	
Kerala	1981	956	223	591	4.3
	1991	566	236	414	2.4
	2001	317	354	325	0.9
Tamil Nadu	1981	8817	437	1204	20.2
	1991	8685	428	1145	20.3
	2001				
West Bengal	1981	4477	385	1174	11.6
	1991	6488	403	1261	16.1
	2001	12009	446	1456	26.9

Source: Data on beds is from Health Information of India, Population Data is from Census projections.

population served per bed. When we refer to Table 11.2 we find that there is a steep decline in population served per bed in Kerala since 1980s. Here the data is for both public and private sector. Both in TN and WB, the ratio is much higher than Kerala. In case of WB, there is in fact significant increase in population served per bed in rural areas. The same ratio is much less for urban areas. While in rural areas one bed serves more than 12,000 people, in urban areas the ratio is 446. Thus, there is significant disparity of health infrastructure between rural and urban areas. The disturbing aspect is that over the years this disparity has increased in WB. One bed in rural area serves 27 times more people than the population served per bed in urban areas. It has to be kept in mind that this disparity is clearly contributing to the growth of private hospitals, which are essentially located in large metros like Kolkata and its suburbs and other relatively affluent urban areas.

Fund Allocations under NRHM

National Rural Health Mission was introduced in 2005-06 to revitalize rural health infrastructure, especially in the backward States of the country[14]. It was pledged that public investment would be stepped up through this umbrella programme. However, there seems to be a semblance of order after initial momentum. Currently the dominant discourse is that States are not capable of spending funds that are being provided to them and hence, the increase in investment is futile. The present effort is an investigation on the financing of National Rural Health Mission (NRHM) to identify the implementation bottlenecks at the High Focus States which lead to underutilization of funds.

States like UP, MP, Bihar, Rajasthan, Orissa have very poor health outcomes. Recognizing the backwardness of these States the Government has categorised them as High Focus or Empowered Action Group (EAG) States. It is expected that focus on these States under NRHM would be reflected in the allocation and release of funds in these States, meaning that these States would get greater shares of funds than their shares in population. UP, Bihar and MP are among the most backward in terms of health indicators. Of the total NRHM funds in the period 2005-06 to 2008-09, UP received only 17 per cent of allocations—an amount less than half in proportion to maternal deaths and significantly smaller than its proportion of female population or live births. As much as 84 per cent maternal deaths takes place in EAG States and 57 per cent of live births takes place there[15]. However, the allocation of funds, seems to be based on their shares in rural population.

Table 11.3 : Allocation and Release of Funds *vis-à-vis* requirements up to 2008-09 (as % of total)

% Share	Maternal Deaths	Live Births	Rural Population	Allocations	Release	Expenditure
UP/Uttaranchal	39.9	23.0	18.6	17.1	19.2	17.8
MP/Chhattisgarh	12.4	9.4	8.2	8.6	8.8	9.3
Rajasthan	9.9	6.5	5.8	7.2	7.8	5.8
Assam	5.1	2.7	5.4	5.0	1.9	3.1
Orissa	3.7	3.1	3.9	3.8	3.7	4.2
Bihar/Jharkhand	14.8	12.1	10.9	9.0	8.5	12.8
High Focus States	83.9	56.8	50.6	48.8	50.1	48.3
Kerala	0.8	2.2	1.9	2.3	2.9	3.2
Maharashtra	4.2	8.2	5.8	6.1	7.1	7.5
Tamil Nadu	1.9	4.3	3.8	5.1	5.8	4.7
West Bengal	4	7.1	7.7	6.2	6.1	5.3

Source: Maternal Deaths are calculated from 'Population Projections for India and States 2001-2026', Census of India, GoI and SRS Bulletin on Maternal Mortality in India 2004-06, RGI.
Fund position, allocation and Expenditure data and rural population data are from MIS, NRHM

It is evident that the existing mechanism of fund allocation is enhancing the developmental deficit rather than eliminating it. The fact that the State with the highest population and huge developmental deficit is receiving a smaller share means that some better off States are actually receiving greater share, thus sharpening inequalities. Further, the situation has worsened for poorer States like UP, MP and Bihar under the current system of spending. Better-off States like Kerala, Tamil Nadu and Maharashtra receive greater share of funds compared to their shares in allocation. Since these States could spend funds more efficiently their shares in expenditure increase even further. These observations put the very nature of financial allocation under NRHM into question.

Financial allocation under NRHM is based on the Programme Implementation Plans prepared by States, subject to approval of the Centre. Though first-two instalments were released unconditionally, subsequent instalments are being released subject to expenditure up to at least 50-60 per cent.[16] States which fail to spend their previous instalments are not receiving subsequent instalments. When the new financial year starts, the unspent balance of the previous year is incorporated in the total envelop of allocation of a State, however, while releasing the instalments, this unspent amount is deducted. There are components within NRHM which are demand driven, i.e., if States demand, with proper utilization reporting, Centre would provide additional funds. States which have been able to spend their funds more efficiently have also got more funds in subsequent rounds. Thus, instead of financial allocations under NRHM being needs based, States ability to spend has become the criteria for flow of funds. In fact, after the introduction of NRHM, expenditure on health as a per cent of NSDP has not increased for the States, however, there is some increase in per capita spending.

Discussion

The level of public health service provisioning in India had never reached a level which could ensure universal and comprehensive health services. During late 1970s and early 1980s there was at least a process of building public health infrastructure in the countryside. Through the reforms phase the process of institution building was thoroughly reversed. The stated objectives of the reforms were to increase efficiency in spending through effective targeting, with greater emphasis on marginalised sections, poor and improved services in the under-served areas and more investments at primary and secondary level. What has been actually achieved is just the opposite-greater marginalisation of the deserving population, lesser emphasis on rural areas, higher burden of out-of-pocket spending, etc. Through chronic underinvestment, public health system today is pushed to a severely depleted state and the system is incapable of delivering quality health care. It has to be noted that though this is the case with major parts of the country, this may not be entirely true in case of Tamil Nadu and Kerala, where there is some standard of government health services could be maintained through sustained investment. The central point in the current exercise is to identify what kind of changes in the budgetary priorities happened during this period. It was also important to understand how the changing prioritization affected the quality of public health service delivery.

There are strong linkages with spending in rural areas and overall fiscal health of States. For instance, if we look at individual States, there are certain phases where share of spending in rural areas have gone down and these are also the phases where health spending as share of NSDP has gone down. This can be elaborated taking the case of Tamil Nadu and West Bengal. In case of TN, early 1990s saw some decline in the health spending to NSDP ratio. Similarly, share of rural areas in the spending goes down in that specific time period. Same holds true for WB during early 2000s. The explanation of this is the following. Among the different items of spending certain items are downward sticky, meaning that these cannot be cutback easily. Now, at a time, when there is overall squeeze in budget, these items cannot be reduced; the cut would fall on items which are flexible. Given the nature of health services, there is heavy reliance to salaries, which are very difficult to cut back. It is also the case that human resources are important elements of health service delivery and spending on salaries should not be cut back in real terms. It is only in relative terms that the share should go down and certain other essential elements should be prioritised, like for instance drugs, equipments, planning, monitoring, training, etc. Possibility of relative decline of share of salaries, even when the overall level is at least maintained, taking care of inflation, is only possible when spending on health is increasing at a very high rate and definitely not in contractionary scenario.

Now, the way health services are shaped in the country, most of the human resources are placed in urban areas, where big hospitals are located. Whereas in rural areas, services are in the nature of family planning interventions and preventive public health, with less emphasis on institutional care. At a contractionary situation, emphasis on primary and secondary health care, on preventive services would go down, because many of the softer interventions would be compromised. Thus, share of spending on rural areas goes down as services in rural areas are more of this nature.

Under-investment in rural areas is reflected in crumbling of systems to plan and effectively deliver on programmes, this again leads to under-utilisation in funds—thus a vicious circle is formed. Spending trends under NRHM is a reflection of this trend. Both Kerala and Tamil Nadu are highly urbanized States, which is not the case with West Bengal which remains pretty rural. However, all the three States spend almost similar proportion of funds for rural areas. In case of West Bengal the share should be much higher. Relatively higher spending in rural areas in Tamil Nadu and Kerala, in the context of overall higher per capita spending, leads to better utilization of funds. Thus these two States end up getting higher share of total funds—much more than the population or case load. Whereas in case of West Bengal, share in total utilization is lower than share of rural population.

NOTES

1. Reddy, K.N. and Selvaraju V. (1994), "*Health Care Expenditure by Government in India: 1974-75 to 1990-91*", Working paper, National Institute of Public Finance and Policy, New Delhi.
2. Duggal, R. and S. Amin (1989), *Cost of Health Care: A Household Level Survey in An Indian District, Bombay, Foundation for Research in Community Health.*
3. Tulasidhar, V.B. (1992), *States' Financing of Health Care in India: Some Recent Trends,* National Institute of Public Finance and Policy, New Delhi.
4. Mahendra Dev and Mooij (2002), "Social Sector Expenditures in the 1990s: Analysis of Central and State Budgets", *Economic and Political Weekly,* 37(9), pp. 853-866.
5. Mahal, *et al.* (2002), *Who Benefits from Public Sector Health Spending in India?,* New Delhi: National Council for Applied Economic Research.
6. Berman (1998), "Rethinking Health Care Systems: Private Health Care Provision in India", *World Development,* 26(8), pp. 1463-79.
7. WHO (2010): World Health Statistics. WHO, Geneva.
8. Process of GiA transfer has undergone significant changes since 2001. Earlier all the GiAs were transferred to States and the spending was reflected in State budgets. However, since 2001, GiAs are being transferred to autonomous bodies thus bypassing the budgets and legislative scrutiny of the States. This issue would be taken up later. Total health expenditure here include the spending on medical and public health, family welfare, water supply and sanitation and nutrition. It does not include spending by other departments on health.
9. Tulasidhar, V.B. (1992), *op. cit.*

10. Reddy, K.N. and Selvaraju V. (1994), *op. cit.*
11. Government of India (2010), *Rural Health Statistics 2010*, National Rural Health Mission, New Delhi.
12. Banerjee, D. (1985), *Health and Family Planning Services in India: An Epidemiological, Socio-cultural and Political Analysis and a Perspective*, Lokpaksh, New Delhi.
13. Qadeer, I. (edited) (2001), *Public Health and Poverty of Reforms: A South Asian Perspective*, Sage, New Delhi.
14. GoI (2005-06): NRHM, National Programme Implementation Plan.
15. Registrar General of India (2010).
16. GoI (2006-07): NPIP, NRHM, MoHFW.

Index